Narcissists in Divorce

From Love-Locked to Leaving

Also from Dr Supriya McKenna

Narcissists in Divorce: From Leaving to Liberty

The Narcissist Trap: The Mind-Bending Pull of the Great Pretenders

and

Divorcing a Narcissist: The Lure, the Loss and the Law

Narcissism and Family Law: A Practitioner's Guide

(with British law contributions from Karin Walker)

Narcissists in Divorce

From Love-Locked to Leaving

Dr Supriya McKenna

All rights reserved.
No part of this book may be reproduced
in any form on or by electronic or mechanical means,
including information storage and retrieval systems,
without permission in writing from the copyright
owner, except for the use of quotations in a
book review.

Copyright © 2024 Supriya McKenna

First Paperback Edition January 2024

ISBN 978-1-7394936-3-9 (Paperback)
ISBN 978-1-7394936-4-6 (eBook)
ISBN 978-1-7394936-5-3 (Audiobook)

Published by Tavistock Publishing
www.tavistockpublishing.com

Parts of this work have been fictionalized.
Names, characters, places, and incidents
either are the product of the author's imagination
or are used fictitiously. Any resemblance to actual persons,
living or dead, events, or locales
is entirely coincidental.

The author makes no guarantee and assumes no
responsibility for the correctness and recommendations
contained within the contents of this book.

Dedication

For my clients

The insights I have gained from you have not only been humbling, but have been the making of this book series; they have breathed life into it, and your experiences will help many.

Contents

Preface	1
Introduction	9
Chapter 1: The crux of the matter	15
Do you secretly feel as though you are a bit special?	22
The false persona	24
Narcissistic supply – the most important thing in this book	25
Why do narcissists behave so awfully in divorce?	27
What is Narcissistic Personality Disorder?	29
The four different types of narcissist	42
Chapter 2: Let's meet our narcissists	44
The Exhibitionist Narcissist	44
The Closet Narcissist	53
The Devaluing Narcissist	62
The Communal Narcissist	75
Chapter 3: A deeper dive into NPD	84
A textbook diagnosis	85
The shortcomings of being a narcissist	89

The things that narcissists are abnormally good at	99
Do narcissists know that they are narcissists?	129
Summary table of narcissistic traits and behaviors	130
Chapter 4: Let's talk about you	**132**
Why you?	134
It's easy for anyone to fall into the narcissist trap	141
Why did you put up with their behaviors for so long?	145
Chapter 5: The narcissist tests	**153**
Is your partner a narcissist?	153
The spectrum of narcissism	163
Am I a narcissist?	166
Chapter 6: Now what?	**170**
How do you 'get' NPD?	173
Can NPD be cured?	183
Should I try and get my partner diagnosed?	186
Should I tell my partner that I think they are a narcissist?	187
How about couples therapy or counseling?	189
Chapter 7: What about the children?	**192**
Becoming a narcissist's enabler	200
How do narcissists behave towards their children?	200
The long-term effects of narcissistic parenting	209

Protecting your children from narcissistic parenting	210
How the narcissist uses their children as weapons	212
The realities of co-parenting with a narcissist	217
When your child favors the narcissistic parent	219
Chapter 8: Deciding whether to leave	**221**
Why is this so emotionally difficult?	221
The realities of leaving a narcissist	227
Common behaviors in divorce and separation	236
Further considerations regarding leaving	243
Choosing to stay in the long term	249
Chapter 9: Becoming strong	**253**
Depression, anxiety, complex PTSD and addictions	254
Building resilience	258
Coping with being 'triggered'	271
Some final thoughts	277
Glossary	**281**
About the author	**295**

ACKNOWLEDGEMENTS

Thanks to Dr Geoffrey Harvey for his unfailing enthusiasm and encouragement for this project, and for his tireless editing. I am delighted to have joined a number of literary giants, by way of this editorial association, and will be dining out on that fact for as long as anyone will listen…

Preface

In 2020, I wrote my first books about how narcissism plays out in the divorce process. In those days, the word 'narcissist' was only just becoming known to the general public, and although many people had vaguely heard the term, they weren't really aware of its meaning.

But it wasn't just the general public who were in the dark about narcissism (more correctly known as Narcissistic Personality Disorder, or NPD). I had discovered that family lawyers weren't receiving any training in personality disorders, and worse, most family justice professionals were blind to the psychological effect on families of these high conflict divorces.

With this in mind, I was inspired to write *Narcissism and Family Law: A Practitioner's Guide* (with legal perspectives from UK solicitor Karin Walker). I wanted to enlighten lawyers about these cases, which were being mishandled through a lack of understanding of the drivers at play. I wanted to show them that 'real' narcissists actually behave in very predictable ways in divorce, and that the lies and manipulations that they employ could be foreseen, and so prevented to some degree.

I wanted them to understand that 'victims' don't always fall into preconceived stereotypes. I wanted to slay the harmful gender-based narratives about narcissism, which play into the hands of so many female narcissists in particular, with terrible long-lasting consequences for the children. I wanted to prevent lawyers, and the legal system itself, from becoming hapless tools of narcissistic abuse. I knew these were lofty ideals – but, perhaps in my zeal, I hadn't realized just *how* lofty they were. You can lead a horse to water, as they say, but you cannot make it drink.

As far as I am aware, that book currently remains the only book for family lawyers on the subject of Narcissistic Personality Disorder. And whilst many UK lawyers (in particular solicitors, who deal with the day-to-day managing of cases) have read it – many have not.

Disappointingly, of the UK lawyers who advocate for clients in court, the barristers, most do not yet understand the relevance of NPD to the function they perform. And what of judges, you may wonder? Again we have a serious problem – the majority still dismiss narcissism as not being 'real'. But depressing though that might sound, this book was definitely successful in sowing the seeds of change. Now those seeds just need to grow.

And what about the people who were struggling through their separations and divorces at the hands of their narcissistic partners? What could be done for them, other than through trying to educate their lawyers? This was the reason behind *Divorcing a Narcissist: The Lure the Loss and the Law* – a desperately needed emotional and practical survival guide for the spouses or partners of narcissists (with sections on UK divorce law written by Karin Walker). Now this book really *did* hit the mark with the target readership, and I was particularly stunned when the audiobook version became a long-term Amazon number one bestseller in the USA.

Much has changed since 2020, and the writing of those books. COVID lockdowns forced couples in narcissistic relationships to stay indoors together, with no outlets or means of escape. Domestic abuse (of all types) escalated – and divorce rates soared. The family courts, which (in the UK) were in crisis anyway, became even more overloaded, and the delays (even for urgent cases) now extend to years. This is a nightmare for anyone divorcing a narcissist, as those delays play beautifully into the narcissist's hands. In this regard, things are much worse now than they were in 2020.

But one of the biggest changes to occur since the release of *Divorcing a Narcissist: The Lure, the Loss and the Law* is the fact that by 2022 the word 'narcissist' had become a buzzword. You might be tempted to think of this as a good thing – but unfortunately, it has turned out not to be. These days, as any family lawyer will tell you, pretty much *everyone* in the divorce or separation process accuses their spouse of 'being a narcissist'. Today people use the word to describe anyone who is mean, vain or selfish. And because society has misappropriated the term in this way, the *true* victims of narcissistic abuse are not being identified by their lawyers until it is far too late, if at all.

And, because of this 'buzzword factor', many divorce lawyers, judges and social workers are actually *even more* dismissive of the 'narcissist word' than they were back in 2020. For starters, they often believe that the person who brings up the term is the real problem (which *is* occasionally true, by the way).

Over the last four years, due to the sheer volume of COVID-related divorces, I have been privileged to work with hundreds of clients, who have shared with me with their terrible stories. We have navigated their delay-ridden divorces together, over years filled with fear, trauma and despair. We have gathered evidence to present to the court. We have fought battles together, that should never have needed to be fought. We have tried to protect their children. We have stood side-by-side, in real time, as their narcissistic ex tries to annihilate them, emotionally, financially and spiritually. I have written their communications to their narcissistic ex for them, and worked with their lawyers (if they have been willing to listen). I have explained their ex's behaviors, over and over again, until they have finally believed that the abuse they suffered was never about them (and was never their fault).

And, thanks to the worldwide reach of my various books (including my book for the general public, *The Narcissist Trap: The Mind-Bending Pull of the Great Pretenders*) and their related podcast (Narcissists in Divorce: The Narcissist Trap), I have connected with thousands of people across the world on various platforms, and heard their awful stories too – stories which are exactly the same as those of my clients, here in the UK.

What I have learned over the last four years is this: Unless you are incredibly fortunate, neither lawyers, family court, nor the police, will deliver justice or fairness when it comes to divorcing a narcissist. And worse, these systems will be haplessly enlisted to become weapons of the narcissist's abuse *against you*.

Regardless of where in the world you live, and how the law is applied in your country, the legal system you hoped would protect you and your children is unlikely to be your salvation – it's surprisingly unfit for purpose where narcissists are concerned – and is likely to remain that way for at least a decade to come. It's completely unacceptable – but this is where we find ourselves.

Those with narcissistic personality disorder will ramp up their abuse tactics during divorce and separation, to levels which you may never have previously seen. They are wired to be manipulative, and to run rings around your legal team. To play the victim, with aplomb. To lie, utterly convincingly. To make serious false allegations against you, the person they claimed they once loved. To enjoy the drama and conflict of the court process. To use the children as weapons of financial, emotional and legal abuse. And to wish to continue this abuse for as long as they possibly can, even after the divorce is finalized, by trying to maintain contact with you under any pretense.

And that brings me to the major reason for this book, the first of a series. The fact is this – the true power you have lies with *you*. And you will be expected to deploy this power when you are at your most broken and weak, whilst under constant attack.

The purpose of this book series, *Narcissists in Divorce* is to walk with you, through every stage. In this book, *From Love-Locked to Leaving,* we begin with the debilitating confusion of working out whether your partner really is a narcissist – the very first challenge you will be faced with. If they are, you will learn what that means for you, for them and for your children. You will learn exactly what divorce and separation behaviors you are likely to encounter, and you will be walked through the considerations that might affect whether you choose to leave, and if so, at what stage. I also offer you strategies to strengthen you, regardless of your choice, so that you are better able to cope with what lies ahead.

The second part of the series, *Narcissists in Divorce: From Leaving to Liberty,* will be for those of you who do choose to leave. Whilst I can't promise you that your divorce or separation journey with me will be easy, I can promise you this: You will not be alone through your grief and your pain, and the hundreds of victims whose stories I have heard, will be with us throughout.

In *Leaving to Liberty* I will help to keep you and your children strong and safe, and give you tools to keep the narcissist at bay. I will predict what game-playing you can expect and offer strategies to protect yourself, including tips for your legal team. I will give you practical suggestions to help you to cope with your fear and your stress. And I will guide you to the other side, and once there, give you tips to help you construct your new life, free of your narcissistic ex.

But I have to tell you this: no matter what you choose to do, if you discover that your partner is a true narcissist, you will never be the same again – something will always remain lost, and the harsh realities of a world newly exposed will never be completely out of view. But even so, real happiness awaits you, with new opportunities for true connection – and the epic journey of self-evolution and growth that you will take will be a worthwhile one.

Introduction

So, here we are.

If you are reading this book, then I already know that you are not in a happy place. And, if you are in a relationship with a 'real' narcissist, that'll only be a small part of how you are feeling. You'll be confused. Wondering why the person you probably still love treats you the way they do (in private, at least). Why you constantly feel 'off-balance'. Uncherished. A diminished version of the person you used to be.

You'll have been used to taking the blame for everything that has gone wrong in your relationship. You'll have apologized, and fawned to try to make amends. You'll have tried to change, to do better – but you will always have fallen short. You will have been treated with cold contempt at times, especially if you showed your emotions (or heaven forbid, actually cried). Your feelings will have been deemed as being 'wrong', and invalidated time and time again. Perhaps they explained to you where you were going wrong, with a 'logical' air. Perhaps, with what superficially looked like humor. Or perhaps even with undisguised disdain or ridicule.

And when you tried so hard to talk to your partner – desperately trying to get them to understand, was it like trying to explain to an alien what normal human behavior looks like? Frustrated and hurt by their responses, did you ever raise your voice and stamp your feet? And if you did 'let yourself down' in this 'shameful' way, weren't they right when they told you that *you* were the unreasonable one?

Or, maybe, when you called them out on their behaviors, they played the victim instead, deflecting the blame and appealing to your empathy. Did they tearily tell you how hard they work, or how little you understand and appreciate them? Did they blame their terrible childhood, or tell you that they'd been bravely and silently struggling with depression, or physical illnesses, or pain? How many times did you forgive them? How many times, so far, have you berated *yourself* for not loving them enough to heal them of their pain? We all know that 'love conquers all'. Doesn't it?

And how many times did they trample over your boundaries, so that you gave into their demands? How many times were you called selfish, for simply trying to look after yourself, or meet your own needs, instead of putting theirs first? Can you even *remember* a time when you didn't put their needs first? When did 'love' start looking like possessiveness? And when did possessiveness start looking like control and jealousy? When did their unfounded accusations of infidelity start? And how did they react if you were ever suspicious of *them*?

When did you start to feel that you could never be enough for them? When did you start to think that perhaps they do deserve someone better than you, as they say? When did you stop being their soulmate? How many times did you jump through hoops to get back to those days of old? Those perfect days of perfect love, when you felt truly blessed that this incredible person had come into your life? And how many times did you nearly think you were back there, when things were lovely once again?

Have you got to the point of realizing that the good times never last? Or do you still harbor hopes of the future they promised you? Are you still flattered when they shine their light upon you? Or do you now wonder how they can flick that switch on and off, so very easily?

When did you first realize that they have never apologized to you and meant it? That they don't love the children equally? That their attractive public persona is nothing like the version of them that *you* see, behind closed doors? That they are prone to rages? That they have no real, long-term, deep friendships – and that somehow you have let go of many of yours?

How many times have you threatened to leave them, only to be pulled back in with desperate pleas, confessions of true love, and promises of change? How successfully did they guilt trip you into trying again? And how many times have you wondered what it even is that they see in you - because, if you think about it, *they don't really seem to see (or know) the real you at all?*

But what on earth gives *you* the right to label someone as a 'narcissist'? It's plain irresponsible. You're not a psychologist, with specialist training in this area. And, as everybody knows, *everyone is a bit narcissistic* – even you. Perhaps you should stop engaging in this trendy psychobabble, and get on with the morally worthwhile cause of forgiving your partner? Nobody's marriage or relationship is perfect, you know (although yours might appear that way to outsiders). And you'd be a fool for thinking that the grass is always greener on the other side.

And anyway (as many of your friends, work colleagues and family members may well say) your partner seems like a perfectly nice person – after all, they have never done anything remotely awful to *them,* so why should they believe what *you* say about them? Oh, and by the way, it takes two to tango – if there really is a problem, it's as much your fault as theirs.

And even if they are a narcissist, you were the idiot who was sucked into their trap. You did this. *You* let them sabotage you and steal your hopes and dreams. You let them violate the very core of you. You stayed with them. You are weak and pathetic.

Remember how, once upon a time, you were their biggest cheerleader? So, why the sudden change? *What makes you so sure that you are not the narcissist in this dynamic?*

Well, like I said. It's confusing. No matter how high your IQ, or how excellent your problem-solving abilities, there are sound psychological reasons why identifying that you have been in a narcissistic relationship is monumentally difficult. And why consistently *believing* your assessment of the situation, without flip-flopping from one extreme to the other, is even harder (especially when your inner critic makes an appearance).

But does it even matter to know for sure if your other half is a narcissist? It absolutely does, for lots of reasons. Not least, because you will need to understand their limitations – you cannot change them, or teach them how to behave 'normally'. And you certainly can't love them better. If you have children with them, you'll have to understand how they can be affected by narcissistic parenting, and how you can protect them from it. And if you are thinking of leaving them (whether you are married or not), they will behave in breathtakingly terrible ways, which you will need to be prepared for, if you are not to be traumatized further.

But perhaps most of all, it matters to know because then you can understand that *this is not your fault* (no matter what your couples counselor might have told you). You didn't deserve this, and actually, this isn't personal. The narcissist in your life would have been just the same with *any* partner, for reasons you'll come to understand. And if you discover from this book that your partner is *not* a true narcissist, then that's an even better result. So. Come on then. Let's try and sort this mess out.

1

The crux of the matter

First let's bust a few myths. It might be that you are still with your significant other, but have been drawn to this book because you need to know, for sure, one way or another, whether they are a narcissist, and what that would mean for the future of your relationship. Maybe a concerned friend, therapist, or suspicious family member alerted you to the possibility, and that's how you found yourself here, or maybe you stumbled upon it by chance, as you secretly researched your partner's odd or difficult behaviors.

Some of you will already be in a divorce or separation process, and will probably have arrived at these pages shell-shocked and reeling from the unrelenting behaviors of your ex. It may even be that your *lawyer* finally mentioned the 'narcissist' word to you, upon realizing that they were completely out of their depth. Or are you one of the unfortunates who left your partner years ago, expecting freedom, but found that they never let you go? Was it the havoc and chaos, that they caused at every turn, that finally set your narcissist alarm bells ringing?

Regardless of how you got here, it's likely that you will be wondering whether you are even in the right place. You will be questioning yourself, and your motives for being here. You will be wondering if you are simply trying to make your partner's, or ex's, behaviors fit in with a stereotype, just because you are upset with them. You might be overwhelmed by the conflicting information you are receiving. You are likely to be judging *yourself* harshly for being so judgmental of *them*. You may oscillate between guilt (at even daring to *contemplate* that they might be a narcissist) and outrage or self-pity that this is where you have ended up.

And, to add yet more uncertainty to the mix, if you have talked your suspicions through with *other people*, you will inevitably have been shamed or invalidated at times, and subjected to one or more of the following four myths. And all of this whilst you are upset – very upset, in fact – because the person you loved so, so much (whether a narcissist or not) turned out to be a heart-wrenching disappointment of monumental proportions.

I suggest we start by knocking these myths on the head, for once and for all, not so that you can justify yourself to others, but for your *own* clarity and peace of mind. (You will discover the futility of trying to explain narcissism to other people later). So, let's begin.

Myth #1: Narcissism isn't real

You already know that narcissism is a buzzword. You'll have heard it being thrown about with abandon, to mean anyone who is disagreeable in some way. How many weeks have gone by when you haven't chanced upon the word in a news or magazine article? Not many, I'll wager. And how many people have jumped on the narcissism social media bandwagon in the last few years? It's astonishing to see how much content (note that I didn't call it 'information') is available on the internet on the subject today.

It's mostly geared to appeal to our newly shortened attention spans, and often put together to play to algorithms which maximize visibility. Punchy video shorts about narcissism have made their way onto every social media platform you can think of. You know the ones – "The top 10 things that narcissists don't want you to know", "5 ways to annihilate a narcissist", "Why narcissists are pure evil" and the like. Online forums, such as Quora, are flooded with stories and opinions about narcissists.

Even self-professed narcissists *themselves* are telling us what they are really thinking, how they are really feeling, and how we should really deal with them. Hurt victims are publicly ranting about their experiences, in real time, in anger and frustration. And now professional platforms, like LinkedIn, are also becoming swamped with narcissism 'recovery' content (which, ironically, usually features filtered photos of the creator, pouting and posing in something tight and flattering).

It's all a bit much. Because an awful lot of this stuff is at best unhelpful, and at worst, just plain *wrong*. True narcissism is actually not complicated, once you get to grips with the basics. And the first, and most important point I want to make here is this – when I use the word narcissism, I am referring to a specific, real diagnosable personality disorder. And when I use the word 'narcissist', I am talking about someone who would qualify for a diagnosis of that disorder, *Narcissistic Personality Disorder* (or 'NPD').

So to be clear – there is narcissism the *adjective* (used by the man in the street to mean anyone mean, vain or selfish), and narcissism *the diagnosable personality disorder* (NPD). And this book is dedicated to helping you identify and manage the latter, with all the information you need in just one place. Narcissism, in the way that I mean it, is definitely 'real', let me tell you.

Myth #2: You shouldn't label someone as a narcissist unless you are qualified to diagnose NPD

If the world were perfect, then I would be agreeing with this statement wholeheartedly. I trained as a medical doctor, and know only too well the dangers of layperson diagnoses – they are not something I have ever routinely recommended. But here we have a bit of a problem. The fact is this – even though NPD can be diagnosed, most psychologists and psychiatrists in the world are *not* taught how to diagnose it, and are often not trained in it at all. I remember my own psychiatric training, and how the features of NPD were completely left out. Sadly, this remains a glaring omission in medical training throughout the world today. So although it is *possible* to get NPD diagnosed (and courts do occasionally order for such specialist assessments to be made), it's pretty rare in reality.

This lack of professional understanding of NPD is compounded by another issue. The criteria for diagnosing NPD are laid out in the American Psychiatric Association's manual, The Diagnostic and Statistical Manual of Mental Disorders (5th edition), or DSM-5. But not all countries in the world use this manual, and many mostly use the International Classification of Disease, 11th edition (ICD-11) instead. And in ICD-11, although there is a personality disorder category, into which NPD does fit, its specific features are not given in detail.

You might be forgiven for thinking that psychiatrists and psychologists in the USA would be streets ahead of the rest of the world when it comes to diagnosing NPD because of this, but I am reliably informed that, in spite of them having the 'right' manual, they are not much better trained there than anywhere else.

And you might wonder *why* no one is being trained in NPD. Well, the answer seems to be mostly because NPD is very difficult (if not nearly impossible) to treat. So, what is the point of diagnosing something you can't do anything with? It'll become pretty obvious as you go through this book, why *I* think there are extremely good reasons for professionals becoming aware of NPD, regardless of its largely untreatable nature.

But where does that leave the millions of people who have found themselves trapped in relationships with narcissists, who may even be experiencing abuse at their hands? Should they just stick their fingers in their ears and pretend that, as there is no piece of paper with a diagnosis written on it, they should ignore the possibility altogether? I think not. I'm not asking anyone at all to 'make a diagnosis' per se – but I am saying that it is perfectly possible for everyday people to recognize the features and behaviors of NPD in others, if they know what to look for. And by the end of this book, you will have achieved exactly this.

Myth #3: It's better to call people 'difficult' or 'toxic', rather than 'narcissists'

I hear this one all the time, from lawyers, mediators, divorce coaches, social workers, domestic abuse workers, and anyone else who feels uncomfortable with the idea of calling someone a narcissist. They will, most likely, tell you that using the narcissist word is 'judgmental'. They will assert that it's better to just focus on the person's abusive behaviors, rather than looking for reasons for them. They may even try to tell you that, in labelling someone, you are giving them an *excuse* for their behaviors, which lets them off the hook (given that NPD is a psychiatric condition).

Wrong, on all counts. In fact, labelling a true narcissist as being difficult or toxic (or worse) is actually far more judgmental than correctly labelling them as a narcissist, as you will discover later.

The reason why it's useful to know whether you are dealing with an actual narcissist, is because narcissists are driven to behave in the ways that they do by certain, very specific things. Understanding what these drivers are actually gives *you* the power, as you will find out later. And because narcissists behave in such specific ways, if you know that you are dealing with a narcissist, you can *predict* their divorce behaviors (and their post-divorce behaviors) in a way that you couldn't possibly with a non-narcissist.

So, in labelling a narcissist as just 'difficult' or 'toxic', not only are you are labelling them *incorrectly*, but you are *judging* them and giving them a label which has absolutely *no predictive value* when it comes to their behaviors. To my mind, if you are going to label someone, you may as well give them the *right* label.

Now I am not saying that you should use the narcissist word in court, without careful consideration, because, as things stand, judges are even less well versed in NPD than doctors and psychologists, which I'll tackle further in the second book of this series, *Narcissists in Divorce: From Leaving to Liberty*.

So, finally, on this last myth, is having a personality disorder an excuse for bad, and even abusive, behavior? Should we just 'let narcissists off', and continue to put ourselves in harm's way because they 'can't help it'? By the same token, should we let off psychopaths who have committed murder, and allow them to live in the community? After all – it's not their *fault* that their brains are wired in the way they are (as demonstrated by brain scan studies). It's a slightly extreme comparison, but I'm sure you get where I am coming from. This is not about *excusing* a narcissist's bad behavior – it's about really understanding it, so that you can protect yourself and your family from it.

Myth #4: Only men can be narcissists
It really is high time this myth was busted, because it's incredibly harmful. The truth is that no one really knows the real proportion of male to female narcissists – and the reason for this is because narcissists often present in different ways depending on gender.

We will look at the different outward presentations later, but the type that most people think of when thinking about narcissists is the so-called 'Exhibitionist Narcissist'. You know the type – the chest thumping braggart, who is loud, arrogant and superior. It is true that this type is mostly represented by men (around three-quarters) because, from a social perspective, it's more acceptable for men to behave in this way.

But there are three other types of narcissist, which are much harder to spot, and it's thought that woman often present in these ways instead. The lack of awareness around this means that female narcissists can wreak even more havoc in the legal process than their male counterparts. It's incredibly common for their false allegations of abuse, against their male partners, to be *believed* by the people who hold the power – the police, the social workers and the judges.

To recap, it's so important to be able to identify when you are dealing with a 'real' narcissist, especially if you are considering leaving them because:

- A narcissist's behaviors in divorce and separation are highly predictable. Being able to pre-empt these could mean that you

are able to prevent them from happening, or stop yourself from reacting to them in the way the narcissist wants. This could reduce your stress, and save you thousands on legal bills.
- A narcissist's post-divorce or post-separation behaviors are also highly predictable. With these in mind, you will need to construct a financial settlement and family set-up that minimizes the potential for further abuse.
- You will suffer psychologically much more in a narcissistic breakup than in a 'normal' break-up. You will need to be ready for this, and cut yourself some slack for it. You will also need some heavy-duty coping strategies.
- You have more power over the situation than you might realize, due to the drivers that lead a narcissist to behave as they do, but again, you will need to use specific strategies to leverage that power.
- You will have a lot of healing to do when this is over, and may want to work on yourself so that you are not attractive to (and attracted to) another narcissist in the future. Note that this is *not* blaming you for what happened in any way, as you will discover later on; this is not a victim-blaming book.

So now let's get stuck into the facts about Narcissistic Personality Disorder, starting with the most important one of all. Let's talk about feelings of 'specialness'.

Do you secretly feel as though you are a bit special?

Over the last few years, I have found myself asking that question to many audiences that I have spoken to about NPD. I usually 'innocently' ask for a show of hands from all those that do secretly feel as though they are a bit special. Of course, hardly anyone puts their hand up, but the reaction I get is always interesting, and ranges from an awkward silence to uncomfortable sniggering. You may be feeling the heat rising in your own face, if you are now considering this question yourself.

So let me put you out of your misery. Because it's actually *normal* to secretly feel as though you are a bit special – and even better than that, it is actually *good* for you. You will have better physical and mental health, and your relationships will be stronger, if you view yourself through these slightly rose-colored spectacles. This is known as the 'better than average effect'.

But crucially, narcissists do *not* secretly feel as though they are special. I know that might seem hard to believe, especially if you know one who puffs themselves up with pride and constantly tells people how brilliant they are, but I can assure you that underneath the bravado and swagger (if that is their particular brand of narcissism) lie deep feelings of shame, worthlessness and inadequacy. And actually, if your other half is a 'real' narcissist, you will probably have noticed this about them at various times – even if only in brief flashes. I've not had a single client who hasn't recognized this in their narcissistic partner once they've really got to know them.

But why is this so important to understand? Because it is this underlying low self-esteem that drives a narcissist to behave in pretty much *all* of the ways that they do. Let me explain.

You see, narcissists cannot bear to feel their true feelings of low self-worth and shame; of defectiveness and unworthiness. Let's face it, no one, narcissistic or not, likes to feel this way. But to a narcissist, these feelings are like an existential crisis – all consuming, huge, and awful. They spend their whole lives trying to avoid these feelings, and *this* is what results in the majority of their behaviors.

The false persona

So what narcissists do is construct an image, a false persona, to hold up to the outside world, which they hide behind. This false persona is like an armor, or a shield, and it prevents them from having to feel their *own* true feelings about themselves. We are all familiar with the classic false persona of narcissism – that of the extroverted, charismatic, super-confident or arrogant braggart – but as I've already alluded to, this is actually only one of four major types of false persona, as you'll discover very soon.

However, regardless of which *type* of false persona a narcissist is hiding behind, there is an important intrinsic problem: *The shield can only survive in the presence of other people's attention or emotional reactions.* Narcissists need constant attention (positive or negative) *from other people* to keep the shield of their false persona whole and strong.

Essentially, narcissists need *other people* to believe in their false persona, *so that they can believe in it themselves.* Because if they can believe in it themselves, they don't have to face (or feel) how they really feel about themselves.

This is the most important thing you need to grasp about narcissism, and, frustratingly, it's the very thing that most people (including mental health professionals) *don't* know about it. You see, a narcissist's narcissism is actually a *defense* against them feeling their true feelings. And right about now is where most partners of narcissists feel their empathy for the narcissist kicking in. I get it, honestly I do. It's an incredibly sad situation. But know this: You cannot love a narcissist better (even if they tell you that you can). Lord knows, you've probably tried, over and over again. There are going to be a lot of harsh truths in this book – and for that I'm really sorry.

But perhaps you are now thinking that *you* sometimes feign confidence or project a more polished image of yourself than is reflective of the true you. Perhaps at a party where you don't know anyone, or when presenting at an important meeting. You might be back to wondering whether *you* are the true narcissist in your relationship, after all.

"True 'narcissism' is actually Narcissistic Personality Disorder, a real, diagnosable condition."

So before we continue, I need to stress the fact that unhealthy, or pathological narcissism (NPD) is present where *normal traits* have become exaggerated to an unhealthy degree. Once again, a healthy amount of self-enhancement (such as through wearing nice clothes or caring about your appearance) is actually good for you. We'll talk more about this later on, so try not to dwell on such thoughts for now, if you can. Because at this point, I have to tell you about the absolutely crucial concept of 'narcissistic supply'– after which you might find that things start making an awful lot more sense.

Narcissistic supply – the most important thing in this book

You now know that a narcissist's false persona, the shield that protects them from feeling their own true feelings of defectiveness, only survives in the presence of *attention* or *other people's emotional reactions*.

You also know that a narcissist needs a constant supply of these if their shield is to stay intact. This is what is known as 'narcissistic supply' – it's basically the fuel a narcissist needs to keep feeling emotionally safe.

A narcissist gets their narcissistic supply from others through:

- adoration
- drama
- conflict
- instilling fear into others or
- any other emotional reaction

Every single person that a narcissist knows is a source of narcissistic supply – but their partner is usually their biggest, most reliable source. Let's now imagine that each narcissist stores their narcissistic supply in a bucket, but that that bucket has a hole in it. This means that their narcissistic supply is constantly draining away. The problem is that the narcissist needs to keep the narcissistic supply in the bucket above a certain level, because if it drops to below that level, there will not be enough to keep the shield of their false persona whole and strong. This is the reason why a narcissist is constantly on the hunt for more supply.

So what happens if the narcissist's narcissistic supply does fall below the critical level? How do they react? Well, in one of two ways, depending on the narcissist themselves, and possibly on how low the levels have fallen. The most common thing you will see is what is known as 'narcissistic rage'.

Narcissistic rage is a classic feature of NPD. It goes well beyond anger. It can be physical and involve shouting and screaming, or it can be a chillingly quiet, menacing sort of rage. Many people describe this last type as appearing 'as if the mask has dropped'. It's not so much a mask that has dropped, but the false persona, and you do get a terrifying glimpse of what lies behind it; of the true person you've been sleeping soundly next to.

One thing is for sure – if you've ever witnessed narcissistic rage, you'll know about it. Narcissistic rage is an extremely effective way for the narcissist to quickly top up the levels of narcissistic supply in their bucket. It gets them attention, causes drama and conflict, and instills fear into their onlookers – all premium types of narcissistic supply.

And how does the narcissist behave, once their bucket is overflowing with supply, once again? Why, as if absolutely nothing happened – and they'll expect *you* to do the same. You'll be expected to go to the dinner party with them and be all smiles, or sit next to them and chuckle at the comedy show on TV, or chat normally to them, as if they didn't just punch through a wall, slash the sofa, or hiss terrifying threats at you. If you recognize this in your relationship, it's no wonder you might be feeling confused.

The other thing that can happen when a narcissist is very low on supply in their bucket, is they can suffer from a 'narcissistic collapse'. Here the narcissist presents as if they are profoundly depressed. They might stop eating, or take to their bed for a few days. They might be only barely able to speak, and weep continuously. The shield of their false persona has well and truly dissolved, and they are feeling the full force of their own low self-esteem and their inadequacy.

But, unlike with true depression, which can take months or longer to get better, if the narcissist's self-esteem can be bolstered with enough attention and adoration, their mood will come back up relatively quickly.

Why do narcissists behave so awfully in divorce?

I've already alluded to the fact that narcissists behave predictably terribly in divorce and separation, but it's really important for you to understand *why* they behave so badly – and once again it largely comes down to the bucket with a hole in it.

Now imagine, if you will, that all the people (and even animals) that a narcissist knows (you, the children, wider family members, pets, friends, work colleagues and even casual acquaintances) are their sources of supply, and they are all pouring varying amounts of narcissistic supply into the narcissist's bucket, at various speeds, and at various times.

But *you*, the partner, are their biggest source of supply – and the one that they have relied upon the most. You are their biggest watering can, pouring in supply at the fastest rate. When you leave a narcissist, or even when *they* leave *you*, you are no longer there, pouring into their bucket. Their most important source of supply has suddenly disappeared, and the level in their bucket plummets.

They urgently need to top this up, so they try to have contact with you. Amongst many other behaviors, they stalk you, and send you a million text messages, desperate for supply through your responses. They try to see you, so they can get supply from your emotional reactions to them. They threaten you, to cause you fear – a superb source of supply. They play the victim to try to rope you back into the relationship, so that they can continue to procure their fuel from you. They withhold the children from you, causing conflict. They make false allegations about you to cause drama and prolong your divorce, because they need to keep you in play, as a source of narcissistic supply, for as long as possible.

You might be tempted to think that they have taken your leaving so badly because they love you so much. Again, I have to tell you something that I do not relish having to, that I simply cannot sugarcoat. If you are in a relationship with a narcissist, it was never about love, no matter how perfect your soulmate connection once seemed to be. You were, and are, just a fuel source.

And this has absolutely no bearing on how lovable and worthy you are as a person. None whatsoever. In fact, it is quite the reverse, as you will see when we look into the sorts of people that narcissists target to be their victims. But I have to tell you the following, and I am so, so sorry. Narcissists cannot love – not in the healthy way that you can, anyway. I'll explain all of this further.

But for now, please understand that if you really are or have been in a relationship with a narcissist, none of this is your fault. That I promise you.

What is Narcissistic Personality Disorder?

I've mentioned that the DSM-5 lists the diagnostic criteria for NPD, and we'll be looking at these a little later, but for now I want to give you a more general picture of what NPD is, which we can build upon, to make it a little less overwhelming.
So at its most basic, NPD is a condition where the person has:

- Low empathy
- A sense of entitlement
- A need to exploit others and
- An inability to see people as a blend of good and bad traits

Let's take each one of these in turn.

Low empathy

By empathy, I am talking about the ability to step into someone else's shoes and actually feel their pain, or joy (or any other emotion). Having a decreased ability to do that is a fundamental feature of narcissism – but here is where it can get get slightly confusing – because narcissists are often able to *appear* as if they do have empathy. This is because there are actually two types of empathy – emotional empathy, which is the 'feeling' type of empathy I just described, and 'cognitive' empathy; the 'thinking' type of empathy that many narcissists do have.

So, for example, if someone has recently been bereaved, a narcissist will know, from life experience, that the correct social response to this will be to look sad and express their condolences. However, unlike most people, they will not actually be experiencing any sadness on the bereaved person's behalf at all.

Quite often this will betray itself fairly quickly – the narcissist might very quickly become inappropriately jolly, for example, and perhaps suggest that the bereaved person join a dating app, now that their partner is no more. Very often the narcissist will misjudge the situation in the opposite direction, and express their supposed empathy in an inappropriately over-the-top way, perhaps by visiting the bereaved person every day, even if they don't really know them, and trying to get involved with the funeral arrangements.

Narcissists will very often make a big deal of telling others how empathic they are, with absolutely no idea that they are anything but. I recall a narcissistic work colleague who would constantly drop into conversations how she was supporting various people emotionally. The friend whose

> *"Narcissists have low empathy – one of the most important features of narcissism."*

daughter was getting divorced. Her secretary, who was in a toxic relationship, but finding it difficult to let go. Her own son, who was struggling at work. Despite the soft voice she reserved for telling you about her kind endeavors, it became painfully obvious over time that, in fact, she was deeply unempathic. This woman turned out to be cruelly dismissive of other people's pain, difficult situations or illnesses, but she was entirely unaware of this, and genuinely believed this part of her false persona.

I always remember the story of a narcissistic man, who donated a kidney to a stranger, after reading about the man's plight in the newspaper. His entire family were stunned by this gesture, as he had never shown them any empathy at all – and they found it terribly confusing. Of course, this was not about being empathic – it was about securing narcissistic supply. The man dined out on the story for decades, and once divorced, used it to lure many an innocent female into having unsatisfactory relationships with him.

Often a good way to tell if your partner has empathy is to look at how they treat you when you are ill, and they don't have an audience to impress. When you're shaking with a fever, in the middle of the night, do they get up and bring you water and medicine, or do they roll over and ignore your request for help? How do they treat the children in similar circumstances? Do they roll their eyes and blame them for their asthma attack, or do they make sure they take their inhaler, and sit up with them, through the night?

This lack of empathy will become very obvious indeed in the divorce process, if you are unfortunate enough to be divorcing a narcissist. It will be absolutely staggering how unrelenting their behaviors will be towards a person they once claimed to love, who may also be the parent of their children. Once again, remember this – they would not have been able to treat any other partner any better. This is entirely about *their* limitations, not yours.

A sense of entitlement

The classic example that people tend to give of this feature of NPD, is how narcissists treat the wait staff when eating out. Do they demand their favorite table in the restaurant, and complain if they are kept waiting? Do they expect to be given a free drink if they find fault with something? This certainly can be a presentation of a sense of entitlement, but many narcissists are a lot more subtle than this. For example, some might be extra nice to the waiter, and tip so generously that they know that they will always get the best table on subsequent visits, and be fawned over.

But narcissists are definitely entitled – entitled to have certain things and be treated a certain way, and also entitled to *not* have to do anything they don't want to do. Many partners of narcissists find themselves run ragged complying with the demands of their narcissist, in all sorts of different realms. At home the narcissist will expect you to do their share of the chores. If you also happen to work with them, they'll take credit for your work, and you might find yourself doing their taxes, taking care of their cars, walking the dog that they said they wanted, as well as doing their laundry and writing their thesis.

Another big area where entitlement rears its ugly head is in the violating of boundaries. Narcissists feel entitled to violate other people's boundaries, which can be personal or professional, or often to do with time – narcissists are very often late to things, because they feel *entitled* to keep people waiting.

Again, this trait is a damaging one when it comes to separation and divorce, because a narcissist will feel entitled to *all* the marital assets and to maintenance (alimony) from you, for the rest of their life. What's theirs is theirs – and what's yours will also be theirs (especially anything you are particularly attached to). They will feel entitled to have the children 100% of the time, or whenever they feel like it, regardless of what is best for them, and they'll feel entitled to use you as a continued source of narcissistic supply, forever, because they genuinely feel that they own you for life. You can see why being prepared for this, if you do find yourself divorcing a 'real' narcissist, will be so important.

A need to exploit others

This goes hand-in-hand with sense of entitlement, in many ways. Narcissists actually exploit everyone that they come into contact with in some way, but some people get off much more lightly than others. In my book, *The Narcissist Trap: The Mind-Bending Pull of the Great Pretenders,* I use a space metaphor to describe narcissism. Picture, if you will, that the narcissist is a sun, in their own solar system, and the planets orbiting them are the people in their lives. You, as their partner, will be in the closest orbit to them, which (if infidelity has been a feature of your relationship) you also might be sharing with another person. Your children might be in the next orbit out, and wider family members and the narcissist's friends, may be further out still. In the furthest orbit you will find the narcissist's casual acquaintances – the barman, or the builder who is working on the house, for example.

Anyone orbiting a narcissist will be being exploited, but say in the case of the barman, in the outer orbit, this might just be because he laughs at the narcissist's jokes (so providing narcissistic supply) or has the narcissist's drink ready for them, making them feel special – all very minor degrees of exploitation. But a work colleague might find that their work is being stolen by the narcissist, or that they are taking credit and payment for it – much more serious.

Your children might be exploited by having to be perfect for the narcissist, so that the narcissist can take credit for their achievements, and brag about them to everyone they know, and you might be exploited for all sorts of things. Perhaps for your tendency to forgive bad behaviors repeatedly, or because you cave in and do menial tasks for the narcissist, or maybe for your income, your social standing, or even for your good looks (because you are good to be seen with).

Have a think about this – do you ever feel as if you are being taken advantage of? Do you secretly harbor a sense of resentment towards your partner, because of everything that is expected of you? If your partner is a true narcissist, this will definitely ring true to you.

An inability to see people as a blend of good and bad traits

Narcissists need other people to be perfect (and they also need to believe that they themselves are perfect, because the only alternative to being perfect is feeling worthless and defective). Narcissists simply cannot see people in shades of grey – you are either 'all good' or 'all bad'.

This is actually a psychological phenomenon known as a lack of 'whole object relations', which narcissists never develop. If you've ever upset a narcissist, even in just a small way, you're likely to have felt as though they are suddenly unable to view you positively at all, as result of your misdemeanor. They are very much like toddlers in this regard (who also haven't yet developed whole object relations). Who hasn't seen a small child howling at their mother, who they hate in that moment, because she didn't let them have an ice cream before dinner?

Does this resonate with you? Do you find yourself going from 'hero' to 'zero' in your partner's eyes for any minor imperfection? Do you find yourself trying to jump through hoops to please them – to try to be as perfect as possible for them, as a result?

This lack of whole object relations also has an important role to play in relationship break-ups with narcissists. If you have permanently fallen off your pedestal, expect to be vilified forever. You will be viewed as 'all bad' and all your positive attributes will be wiped out of the narcissist's mind. And because you are so bad, you will deserve to be punished relentlessly.

I really hope by now that you are beginning to get to grips with why it is so important to know if you are in a relationship with a true narcissist, if you are considering leaving them. And I sincerely hope that at least some of you are beginning to realize that you might not be.

Love addiction, and the narcissistic abuse cycle

So, do all narcissists abuse others? Well, the answer is, yes they do, to some extent. But how obviously abusive a narcissist will be will depend on a number of factors. So if you are a very compliant partner, who showers them with adoration and does everything they want, then the narcissist will be getting lots of narcissistic supply from you in a positive way. They won't need to obviously abuse you, because the shield of their false persona will be whole and strong, and will be defending them adequately from their own true feelings of low self-worth. Most people recognize this from the beginning of their relationship with a narcissist.

But there will be times when you are not perfect, or you have needs of your own. Perhaps they have lost narcissistic supply in another way, perhaps with something going wrong at work. Or perhaps, as time goes on, they have just started to see you as the imperfect being that all of us really are. And this is where the narcissistic abuse cycle comes in – which is also known as the cycle of idealization and devaluation.

You also need to know that narcissists are completely dependent on other people for their narcissistic supply. They need to keep them trapped in their orbits so that they can feed off them. The narcissistic abuse cycle is a method that narcissists use to weaken people, so that they cannot leave their orbits. It destabilizes their victims, and worse, if you are in a close orbit to a narcissist, it actually makes you addicted to the narcissist. You may be tempted to scoff at this assertion, but I will explain exactly how this neurochemical addiction to narcissists occurs, in just a minute.

But here's the thing. If you are in a relationship with a true narcissist, you *are* likely to have felt an attraction to them of gravitational proportions. This may feel like an inability to be able to go on living without them in your life, or you may actually recognize it as an addiction to them. At the very least you are likely to have felt a 'soulmate' connection to your narcissistic partner, who you are closely orbiting (to return to our space metaphor). And of course, just like with real solar systems, the closer a planet is to the sun, the greater its gravitational pull on them. The partners of narcissists find it incredibly difficult to overcome these forces, with good reason, and this is why they don't just 'leave' – they *escape*. So, if this resonates with you, and anyone has had the gall to tell you that 'if it was that bad you would have just left them', you have my sympathy.

But let's now take a look at this cycle, which makes escaping so very hard to do.

Love bombing

Think back to the very beginning of your relationship. Were you showered with affection and attention? If you're the sort of person who likes receiving gifts, were you inundated with them? If you show your love to others by helping them out in practical ways, did the suspected narcissist in your life mirror this, painting your shed, cooking you delicious meals or digging over your vegetable patch for you? If you're physically very demonstrative when it comes to affection, did you notice that your partner was particularly attentive in this regard?

Narcissists are excellent at reflecting back their victims' *own* adoration, during the initial love bombing stage of the relationship. This is why they appear to be the perfect person for their target – they are merely holding up a mirror to them. It's absolutely heartbreaking, this, but the soulmate that you thought you had found, your 'twin flame', and the person that had felt 'too good to be true' was, sadly, exactly that.

These relationships also progress really quickly, because the victim is completely sucked in, and has no reason not to believe that they have found the love of their life. Did you move in with your partner after a matter of weeks? Were you inseparable, practically from the beginning? Looking back, did you even decide to start a family within a scarily short period of time? These are all huge red flags for narcissistic relationships – but even though the young people of today have heard of love bombing, and seem to understand its significance, until just a few years ago, far from just being unrecognized, it was actually hailed as a sign of true romance.

If you recognize that you were love bombed in the early stages of your relationship, it's easy to be angry with yourself, for being such a fool, and for being sucked in. Those Disney movies have a lot to answer for, when it comes to how certain generations learned to romanticize potentially unhealthy relationships. I'll be saying this a lot throughout this book, because it is true. No matter how foolish you feel, you cannot denigrate yourself for what you didn't know at the time. This simply was not your fault. Honestly it wasn't. Self-compassion is going to be a big part of this process for you.

Narcissistic relationships start with love bombing (also known as 'idealization') for a very good reason – because it's during this phase of the relationship that the brain is primed to become addicted to the narcissist.

During the love bombing phase, your brain will have been flooded with feel good neurotransmitters – dopamine, norepinephrine, serotonin, oxytocin and the like. You would have felt amazing, and the high levels of these brain chemicals would have made you blind to what was really going on. (When they say that 'love is blind', it can actually be taken literally, due to precisely this).

But it's what happens next that really kicks off the addictive process.

Devaluation

In this phase, the narcissist, often without a discernible reason, stops the love bombing, and starts to put their victim down. Devaluations often start small, perhaps with just a mild criticism, or a period where they inexplicably stop texting you. The victim experiences a sharp drop in brain chemicals when this happens, and they feel terrible. They don't know what they have done wrong, so they try to get back into the narcissist's good books by pandering to them.

Devaluations can be verbal or non-verbal, and the narcissist will ramp them up over time, slowly enough that the victim doesn't notice. Although the general trend of the devaluations will be that they get bigger, the narcissist will often randomly sprinkle little devaluations into the mix, to keep the victim off-balance. Perhaps just an impatient roll of the eyes, when you are speaking, will serve as a small devaluation, for example, as opposed to a three-day silent treatment – a much bigger devaluation.

Non-verbal devaluations can take many forms – from yawning and checking their phone when you are trying to have a deep conversation with them, to being three hours late for dinner without warning. From wincing as you sing along to the car radio, to looking at your new hairstyle with incredulity. From texting their new attractive secretary all evening in front of you, to pushing away the special meal you made for them, as if it is unpalatable.

Verbal devaluations can include actual put-downs, name calling, ridiculing and harsh criticisms, as well as third party devaluations ('My mother thinks you have put on weight – have you?'), and backhanded compliments ('Wow! You scrub up well! I'd never have recognized you!').

Even just refusing to do their share of the housework can be a devaluation, because it makes you feel as though you are less important than them. Physical abuse is also a form of devaluation.

So, upset, you ask the narcissist what you've done wrong, and start to jump through hoops to please them. You don't know it, but your brain is missing the high levels of neurochemicals that were present during the love bombing phase, and is trying to get them back. And suddenly, without warning, just as you are about to give up hope, the narcissist will go back into the love bombing mode, rewarding you with your neurochemical fix once again. You will feel a rush of relief that all is well, and will blame yourself for their previous bad behavior, or make an excuse for it, so that you can deny, minimize or justify it ('it wasn't that bad', 'you've got to take the rough with the smooth', 'they were probably just tired, stressed or hungry…')

But why is this addictive? Well, it's because these cycles repeat over and over throughout your relationship with the narcissist. Sometimes the narcissist plays at being 'nice narcissist' for ages – weeks or even months, before 'nasty narcissist' makes an appearance. But sometimes the cycles can be really short – hours even. Because the cycles vary so much in length, you tend not to recognize them as cycles at all, and the apparent randomness of the timings make the cycle particularly addictive.

Now add to that the fact that the love bombings, as well as the devaluations can be huge, tiny or any size in between, and you have another factor which increases the addictiveness of the cycles. This addiction is known as 'trauma bonding' in psychological circles.

Let's take a trip to Vegas, to explain further. Picture the scene. You are playing at the slot machines, and you have just had a semi-sizeable win. You are on top of the world, and your neurochemicals are sky high. So, you decide to keep on playing, because the jackpot could be just around the corner. So you sink more and more money into the slot machine, and as you do, you start to lose hope of winning again. Your neurochemicals are about to hit rock bottom, and you are thinking about giving up. But wait – just as you least expect it, you get a little win! Hurray you think, as your neurochemicals shoot up a bit – I'll play for a bit longer. Perhaps, after just a few minutes you win again – Yesss, you think – I'm on a roll. Your neurochemicals have gone up even more, but as you keep playing, and losing, your brain chemicals start to fall again.

You look around the machines and see that everyone is doing the same as you. Sinking money into those machines, with blank expressions, until they get a neurochemical releasing win. Why? Because the unpredictability of the wins and losses, together with the randomness of the sizes of the wins and losses are what makes gambling so addictive. It's known in scientific circles as intermittent positive reinforcement. Those machines were designed to use your brain chemistry against you, to fleece you – that is why they are profitable. You *think* you can win, but you can't really. Not overall. Very much like being in a relationship with a narcissist.

If you look back over your relationship, can you now see those cycles of 'nice narcissist'/'nasty narcissist'? Can you recognize devaluations, interspersed with love bombings? It is likely that you'll never experience love bombing to the extent that you first did, but you are likely to *hope,* in your heart of hearts, that one day, you'll return to those heady days of perfect love with your partner. This is often the case even if decades have passed since the first love bombing (and even if, these days, their devaluations include frank insults and name calling, or worse).

If your partner is a true narcissist, then I'm afraid I have yet another unenviable truth to convey. Those cycles won't ever stop.

They have to be 'nice narcissist' every now and then, to keep you hooked to them. If they were always just 'nasty narcissist' you'd eventually walk away. The 'good days' are as essential a part of the abuse cycle as the bad days.

And why does the narcissist want you to be addicted to them? So you can't leave your orbit, where they need you to remain, as a steady and reliable source of narcissistic supply. Once again, this is not about love (at least not for them), because you are simply a fuel source.

If this resonates with you, believe me, I feel your pain. And I know it won't help right now, but *this was never personal*. I've said it before, but I'll say it again: this was never about *you*, or how worthy you are of love. Hopefully you'll come to see this, as we continue our journey together.

The four different types of narcissist

So now you've had a look at the most basic features of NPD, and it's possible that things might be starting to fall into place for you.

However, narcissism is not an easy thing to spot, even if you know the suspected narcissist well, because of how differently narcissists can outwardly present. If you remember, there are four broad types of false persona, but these can overlap in a single narcissist, or different false personas can be employed at different times, depending on the circumstances. The four types are:

- The Exhibitionist Narcissist
- The Closet Narcissist
- The Devaluing Narcissist and
- The Communal Narcissist

In the next chapter, I will introduce you to the cast of characters, who will be accompanying us through this book, who hopefully will bring the different types of narcissist to life for you. You may well recognize some of them in the world that you inhabit. Let's see.

2

Let's meet our narcissists

THE EXHIBITIONIST NARCISSIST

Jonathan Delaney is 48 years old, and is the headmaster of an upmarket school in the South of England. He believes himself to be an exceptionally fine-looking man (even though he is a little rotund). Having said that, charisma does ooze from his every pore and, should you ever meet him, you would definitely find yourself chortling at his jokes, even if he does seem a little 'full of himself'.

His grand, oak-paneled office is the most salubrious room in the whole school, and it is filled with impressive leather-bound tomes of everything from literary classics to science books. Jonathan is a self-proclaimed 'polymath', and he'll tell you that he has read every single volume on those shelves. But Jonathan will be sure to inform you that he takes no credit for his extraordinary intelligence, and that it was inherited from his great grandfather, a renowned intellectual, whose stone bust takes pride of place by the fireplace.

A staunch traditionalist, Jonathan is rarely seen in anything other than his trademark three-piece pinstriped suits, which are custom tailored in London. If you are a prospective parent, viewing the school for your child, he will sweep grandiosely into the marble-floored waiting room, with a huge beam on his face, and call out your name in his unmistakable booming voice. And, if you happen to be extremely observant, you might glimpse Mollie, his new receptionist, swooning just perceptibly as he vigorously shakes your hand. You might also notice the two secretaries behind the glass partition to the office exchanging the tiniest of withering looks.

Jonathan will insist on giving you a personal guided tour of the school, chest puffed out as he struts like a peacock past the 'biggest swimming pool in the area', the 'finest squash courts' and the 'most well-equipped science labs'. Taking barely a breath between sentences as he leads you onwards, he will regale you with stories of his own school days, the well-known people he associated with whilst there, and the prominent alumni of this school. But, to his credit, he's good with the 'little people' too, as you'll discover when he regally waves at the school gardener, and bestows upon him a "Morning Phil! Excellent work, marvelous, marvelous! Do carry on!"

If you chance upon any pupils during your tour, he will be sure to make you aware that he knows their names. "Which lesson are you off to now, Harry?" "What about you Mimi? Very good, very good..."

And as you scurry after him (he's remarkably quick-footed for a man of his diminutive height), you may momentarily lose sight of him, as he unexpectedly bursts into classrooms where lessons are in progress. The sound of the scraping of chairs across the floor will guide you to him at such times, as pupils reflexively jump to their feet and stand to attention.

"Fourth Years!" he will boom with a flourish of his hand, looking terribly pleased at being greeted in this way, "Do sit."

You might feel a little flustered at suddenly having the eyes of twenty adolescents upon you, but Jonathan will be oblivious to this. Instead, he'll subject you to a display of lighthearted banter with the awkwardly smiling teacher, who is having to play along with the imposition. There can be absolutely no doubt that Jonathan Delaney loves an audience, and being the most important person in the school.

Jonathan doesn't really have many teaching duties these days, and so when he isn't striding around the school, chatting with staff, or having appointments with parents, he spends his time playing golf and hobnobbing with the wealthy locals at the golf club. He considers himself to be the highest authority on all things to do with education, and his ambition is to be interviewed on the TV or radio, like another local headteacher. At headteachers' conferences he genially slaps this particular chap on the back and ingratiates himself with him, but behind his back he tells others that he is just an attention seeker, who is actually jealous and in awe of *him*.

Jonathan very much thinks of himself as a 'man of the people'. He is a regular at the local village pub, where he is treated like a hero. Jonathan likes to think he can talk to anybody from any walk of life, and in the pub he greets people loudly. After some raucous banter, he will always make his way to the winged chair that seems to be reserved for him, lean back expansively in it and hold court. The locals love it, and they hang upon every word of this man of superior intellect, feeling flattered that he talks to them. After all, he's a local celebrity.

Brigitte Delaney is Jonathan's wife, and a French teacher at the school. They met at a mutual friend's wedding, and have been married for 23 years. She has not been happy for a very long time, but hasn't told a soul. After all, on the surface she has it all

– a successful, funny, clever husband, a meaningful job, a lovely house and a son. What right does she have to feel sad? When she burst into tears at her doctor's office a few years ago, she was prescribed antidepressants. Brigitte was shocked, but at the same time felt relieved – perhaps depression was to blame for her low mood, tearfulness and feelings of worthlessness after all.

She's been on the tablets ever since, but she's never really made it back to being the person she was when she met Jonathan all those years ago – the fun-loving, carefree optimist, surrounded by friends. No wonder Jonathan has a roving eye, and a penchant for flirting with the younger female members of staff – it is her fault, and she accepts it. But at least Brigitte can be reassured by Jonathan's high moral standards, and zero tolerance for those who fall short of them. She is pretty sure that this means that he himself would never actually stray.

And Jonathan still bows with exaggerated chivalry if he passes her in the crowded school corridors, and bellows "Ah there she is, the radiant Madame Delaney! Make way for her, children, make way!" Brigitte still feels momentarily flattered and relieved by Jonathan's public displays of affection. But these feelings never last long, and more and more she finds herself asking why these days he's only affectionate when they have an audience.

The truth is that Brigitte mostly feels like an accessory – someone who is expected, in public, to merrily laugh at his jokes, be a supportive, doting wife and to look good on his arm. And, in private, to play the role of uncomplaining domestic servant, sex kitten and private secretary. She doesn't want to admit it to herself, but Brigitte is feeling resentful – and if she ever shows it, Jonathan will coldly tell her to 'go and take a happy pill.' Her heart will sink at these times, but she knows better than to show her pain. Jonathan can be so careless with her emotions, and throw them back at her as ammunition when she least expects it.

"I am enough" is the positive affirmation she repeats over and over to herself in the bathroom mirror – but she doesn't feel that way. She's definitely not enough for Jonathan. But that's *her* fault, not his.

When Jonathan became headmaster, Brigitte was thrilled. Finally he had achieved the goal he had talked about incessantly for years, and at last they would be able to focus on other things. During the preceding school holiday she took on the refurbishment of his office for him, making sure she incorporated everything he asked for.

Despite the modest budget, she had managed to include the floor-to-ceiling antique books he had insisted on, which she had procured in bulk from an old manor house that was being turned into a nursing home. The Victorian stone bust of an anonymous gentleman Jonathan had wanted was another success – it took weeks of visiting architectural salvage yards to find.

The whole thing was a triumph, but when she had excitedly revealed the transformation to Jonathan, he looked like he was trying to put a brave face on his disappointment, and when pushed for a reaction, he simply said "I mean, it's not *terrible...*"

The headmaster job had come with a house on the school premises, but it wasn't at all to Jonathan's taste – far too poky and dark, with 'simply no architectural merit'. Jonathan was the first headmaster in the history of the school to opt to live out. Brigitte had known there would be no point arguing once his mind was made up, but did feel slight resentment that they would have to use the bulk of the money that she had inherited from her parents to fund buying a house in the village. After months of looking, whilst temporarily staying in the house on the school site, Jonathan had found a house which he considered to be worthy of his status, although it did need complete refurbishment. But rather than continuing to live in the headmaster's house at the school, he had insisted that the family move into their new home immediately, and live with the inconvenience of the renovations being done around them. Brigitte had felt she had little choice other than to agree.

For years Jonathan had been promising her the role of head of modern languages at the school, and rightly so, as Brigitte (a native French speaker and experienced teacher) was the natural choice. She was devastated when he promoted Fiona Jones to the job instead of her. Fiona had been teaching for ten years less than she had, but it seemed it was her turn to be in Jonathan's mutual fan club. At home it was all "Fiona said this" and "Fiona said that", and when Fiona wanted new equipment for the language lab it was instantly bought, even though Brigitte had been putting her case to him for it for years.

Brigitte was further flabbergasted when Jonathan asked Fiona to co-host the prize-giving ceremony with him at Sports Day instead of her, and could hardly bear it when she overheard a parent, who didn't know who she was, commenting to his wife on the 'chemistry' between the pair. Red-faced and fighting back the tears, Brigitte felt humiliated and wished the ground would swallow her up.

Of course, Jonathan denied any impropriety, and told Brigitte that good chemistry between staff members was essential to staff well-being, and she should be ashamed of herself for not prioritizing it as he did. It all sounded terribly convincing – and, as usual, Brigitte ended up apologizing for her churlishness and oversensitivity.

To make up for it, Brigitte spent the remaining money she had inherited from her parents on a surprise Easter week away for her and Jonathan, in the Caribbean. Jonathan was pleased, and for a while, all was forgotten. Brigitte loved these times, when things were almost as they used to be and they were getting on. He was the life and soul of the party when on holiday, and he would chat to wealthy holiday makers at the bar and by the pool, and make them laugh with his obtuse humor and his jokey demeanor. Brigitte felt proud to be with him at times like this, and as usual, hoped that things would stay like this forever.

Sadly, once back home, things took the inevitable nosedive. Brigitte went back to cleaning up around him, doing all the housework, cooking, sorting out the bills and doing all the shopping, whilst Jonathan relaxed for the remainder of the holiday, surfing the internet, playing golf, watching TV and visiting the local village pub. Once term restarted, she had all this to do and more – and she'd stay up late into the night marking her pupils' homework, whilst Jonathan concentrated on 'raising his public profile' on Twitter by commenting on education issues and the 'state of schooling today', in an erudite sounding tone. He was an important chap, after all, and had his mind in higher places than the mundane – but Brigitte still resented the fact that he had dropped all domestic duties as soon as they were married, leaving them entirely to her.

When her little car eventually gave up the ghost, Brigette would have been perfectly happy to replace it with a newer version of the same model, but Jonathan had other ideas. He insisted that she move with the times and buy a hybrid electric car 'for the sake of the environment', and that they sell his car too, and just have one car between them. He was so keen that he even did all the research and took her to various car showrooms to test drive the different options. The car he wanted was much bigger than Brigitte felt they needed, but Jonathan was adamant that it was the one for them, and reeled off various figures to do with 'carbon neutrality' and 'pollution indices' to convince her.

When the car arrived, it certainly did look quite impressive, but because it ran on electricity and switched to expensive petrol mode when it ran out of charge, Jonathan insisted that Brigitte drove it so it never ran out of electric charge. This meant she wasn't ever allowed to have the radio or the heating on, to preserve the electricity for as long as possible, even in bitterly cold winters. Worse, there was a setting which meant that Jonathan could check to see how economically the car had been driven in his absence, and he would regularly haul Brigitte over the coals, telling her that she was 'killing the planet'. Eventually she stopped driving it altogether, and just let him drive, and the rare times she went anywhere without him she would use public transport.

Why didn't she leave him? Because Brigitte was a fighter, and she was fiercely loyal. She wasn't going to give up on Jonathan like his mother had, when she left him as a teenager. He'd jumped through hoops for that woman, trying to be everything that she wanted him to be. Every success he had had (and there had been many of them) she had claimed as her own. And his father had hardly been any better. Jonathan becoming a headmaster was the ultimate disappointment to his father – even though it was far in excess of anything *he* had ever achieved.

Brigitte had promised Jonathan that she would never abandon him. And honestly, she felt sorry for him. She knew that under his bluster and bravado stood a sad, deserted child, with his toddler-style tantrums and episodes of deep dejection. What Jonathan needed was more love, because love can conquer all.

And when things were good, which they sometimes were, she felt that she was succeeding in helping him to heal from his upbringing. One day they would get back to the idyllic times of the past, she was sure. Poor, misunderstood Jonathan, so vulnerable and yet so brilliant. Her heart bled for him. Did she feel as though her whole life revolved around Jonathan, and that she was effectively orbiting him? Yes, she did. But what she didn't know was that she was sharing her orbit with the 31-year-old school receptionist, Mollie.

I do not expect you to be surprised to hear that Jonathan Delaney is a narcissist – he fits the commonly held stereotype perfectly. He's vain, extroverted, charismatic, self-important, attention seeking and a name dropper, just for starters. His has a profound lack of empathy for Brigitte, and does not care about how she is feeling, and he feels entitled to exploit her, when to comes to menial household tasks. Jonathan's needs and wants come before Brigitte's and his behaviors to do with their car indicate that he is definitely a bit of a control freak.

And how about the way he flaunts his friendship with Fiona Jones in front of her? This is triangulation, a tactic many narcissists use to keep their victims feeling off-balance and insecure, by openly bringing a third person into the dynamic. It is also clear that when Jonathan promoted Fiona instead of her, he was devaluing her – pushing her down a few notches in his hierarchy of importance, which he also did after she refurbished his office to his exact specifications, for no praise at all.

The 'Exhibitionist Narcissist' is by far and away the easiest type to spot. But you may well be surprised at how very differently our next type of narcissist shows up in the world.

THE CLOSET NARCISSIST

Lina is 42 years old, but her combination of South Asian skin and a rigorous skincare routine means that she could easily pass for a 32-year-old. These days she speaks the King's English in a soft, slightly breathy voice, which belies her working-class roots, and she looks up at people through her long eyelashes shyly, with her head tilted ever so slightly downwards. At first, it's endearing, how self-effacing and demurely she comes across, and her occasional childlike giggle is initially rather sweet. Lina has never been one to stand in the spotlight, and you can't help but be drawn to her quiet and easy manner when you first meet her.

When Lina brought Raj home to meet her parents, they were delighted – a handsome dentist, who was in the process of setting up his very own dental surgery! Lina's shopkeeper parents had worked hard all their lives, but they had always wanted so much more for Lina. But Lina had never been an academic girl, and university had never really been an option, so they were particularly thrilled at the thought of Raj as their son-in-law.

Things had been hard for Raj in recent years, as he had lost both parents to cancer. To make matters worse, when Raj met Lina, he had just come out of a six-year relationship with his dental school sweetheart. When his fiancée had broken off their engagement to take up a dentistry job in the USA, his heart had been shattered. He hadn't been ready for a new relationship, but he had agreed to meet Lina on a blind date anyway, expecting nothing to come of it.

Lina was the very first person that he had dated after his breakup, and he found himself opening up to her about his heartbreak. She listened intently, and consoled him for his losses. She was kind and caring, and she understood that he needed time to heal before he even thought about another relationship. But Raj was lonely, and he found himself spending almost every evening with Lina, just talking and walking arm-in-arm in the warm summer evenings.

Lina was an excellent cook, and Raj very definitely was not, so as the evenings drew in they would meet in the supermarket after work, buy ingredients and go back to Raj's flat, where Lina would cook delicious Indian food, as Raj caught up with paperwork. Gone were the instant noodles and the takeaway kebabs, replaced with fare that even Raj's mother would have been pleased with. Then they would talk, late into the night, about what they both wanted from life – and Raj was surprised and pleased at how similar their visions of the future were.

Things were easy with Lina, in contrast to with his former fiancée, who had been hotheaded and competitive. Here there was no competition. Lina had her role, and Raj had his. After just four months, now head over heels in love, Raj decided to ask Lina to move in with him, and they married a year later.

Lina, a Hindu, would tell him in the early days of their relationship that Parvati, the Goddess of love, would visit her in her dreams, and tell her that she had been sent to heal Raj of his pain. And to Raj, meeting this compassionate, shy person who couldn't do enough for him, did indeed feel like fate.

Two pregnancies and births quickly followed, and Lina outwardly relished her role of mother and housewife. By this time Raj's dental practice was up and running, and the money was coming in – and for the first time in her life, Lina told Raj, she felt that she was where she truly belonged. The truth was that Lina had secured the status that she had always secretly believed she should have.

She would buy the children and Raj expensive clothes from Harrods, and Raj was surprised to discover that the children's pushchair with all its attachments cost nearly as much a secondhand car would have. But Lina's parents would always thank him for making her so happy and her father would slap him on the back, beaming, congratulating him on his success. They were, after all, *his* family now. If Raj ever brought up her spending, Lina would point out that *she* only wore modestly priced clothes herself, often bought from sales racks or the supermarket, and this was true.

Lina piled on the weight after her pregnancies, and would complain of sore knees and feet, and Raj would often come home to a bomb site. Lina would be sitting in front of the TV, toys strewn everywhere, with the children in dirty nappies, running amok. She'd rarely have anything prepared for the children's meal, and Raj would find himself giving them cheese on toast, and then bathing them, ready for bed. "What a day it's been," Lina would say, "I'm exhausted." She rarely cooked now, and Raj either cobbled something together or they would have a takeaway. Lina would be in bed by 9pm, snoring away. How different things were from just a few years ago – but Raj just put it down to the pressures of parenthood.

When it was Lina's turn to host a mother and child coffee morning, however, things were very different. The house would be gleaming. The children would be dressed in their best clothes, hair shiny and neat, and Lina would have made her own cookies, cakes and pastries, which would be laid out in tiered displays on her dining room table. Tea would be drunk out of the fancy china cups that she had always aspired to own, with matching side plates. Lina even had tasteful cake forks and crisp cotton napkins at the ready. "Oh this!" she would say with coy modesty,

"It's nothing! Please – do try a millefeuille! Or perhaps one of these Indian sweets?" She made it look easy on the surface, but no one had seen the stressed days of preparation that had preceded such events. And it was Raj who was always tasked with the clearing up, once he had returned from work.

And when it came to the children's birthday parties, Lina would really pull out all the stops. Children's entertainers, jugglers, bouncy castles and face painters would take up residence in her enviable garden. She would prepare an impressive buffet, and everyone would comment on her wonderful hostess skills. The thought that they were secretly jealous pleased Lina, but she would never dream of saying anything, other than to her mother. "You're a lucky man, Raj!" his friends would tell him.

But Raj did not feel so lucky. Apart from when anyone else was looking, Lina was lazy and messy. Both spare rooms were piled high with clothes that didn't fit, that she had bought in the sales but couldn't be bothered to return. The kitchen was always in a state, the bins overflowing and the dishwasher not loaded. The interiors magazines that she was so fond of were strewn about, open, and the doorbell would constantly be ringing with deliveries of things they didn't need, including clothes and shoes for himself.

Raj also noticed that Lina really didn't like it if he didn't wear the exact combination of clothes she had put out for him to wear the night before. She considered it to be part of her role, as a wife and mother, to remove this burden of having to choose what to wear from her family. He tried to feel grateful, but sometimes he just wanted to wear what *he* wanted to wear without having to justify it, and without being made to feel guilty for not appreciating Lina's efforts. As the children got older this became a problem for them too, as their own choices in clothing were deemed to be 'common' and 'low class'.

In the toddler years Raj would often come home to find that Lina was out shopping, and his mother-in-law was babysitting, washing, ironing and sweeping. Raj was mortified at times like this, but Lina refused to let him get a cleaner. "I don't want strangers coming in here," she would argue. "I have my pride…" Raj felt as though they were exploiting her ageing mother, however, and took even more upon himself to assuage his guilt.

Even though Raj was run ragged, if he was so much as to leave a damp towel on the bathroom floor by mistake, Lina would sulk. "I do so much for everyone," she would sniff. "Nobody appreciates what I do." "I've only ever supported you in whatever you want," she would say, tearfully, feeling well and truly taken advantage of. She would follow this up by moving to the spare room for two or three days, barely speaking to Raj, so deep was her resentment and hurt.

And Raj didn't like the way she could be with the children either. Arun, the oldest, was the apple of her eye. "One day you are going to be a dentist, just like your Daddy!" she would tell him, from the day he was born. "Or maybe even a doctor! Even better!" Whatever Arun did, he was the best at, in her view. She enrolled him in cricket lessons as soon as he could walk, and got him into the junior chess club from the age of five, where he did very well, much to Lina's delight.

But it was a very different kettle of fish for their daughter, Laila. Laila was a skinny little girl, who needed glasses from an early age, and had the great misfortune of having darker skin than her brother. In Lina's culture, fair skin was associated with beauty and status, and Laila was a desperate disappointment in this regard. Where Arun could do no wrong, Laila could do no right, and Lina would shame, ridicule and criticize her constantly. "Arun was reading fluently at your age," she would say, when Laila was just five. "I suppose I shouldn't be surprised that you didn't win," she once sighed, when Laila came second in the egg and spoon race. "So unathletic…"

Arun's drawings would always get pride of place on the fridge, whereas Laila's would be tossed into the recycling with barely a glance, and a 'hmmph' at best. "You'll never amount to anything if you keep going like this," she would tell her all the way through her childhood, slathering sun lotion on her all year round, in a desperate bid to stop her from getting even darker. "Eat, eat!" She would shout impatiently at her, even when she was being spoon fed in her highchair, "People will think I am starving you with those skinny legs…"

Today Laila is fifteen and suffers from anxiety, depression, and anorexia nervosa, but Lina refuses to believe these diagnoses. "You are just a moody teenager…" she will tell her dismissively. "Happiness is a *choice* – you should just snap out of this nonsense." "Stop pushing your food around on your plate and JUST EAT. Do you know how long it took for me to make this? I have toiled all of your life, just giving, giving, giving, and *this* is how you repay me?"

When Laila rebelled against her mother's insistence that she wore her hair long, getting it chopped into a pixie crop one day after school, Lina was predictably apoplectic with rage, but the usual pattern followed, as Raj stepped in on Laila's behalf.

At these times, Lina retreats into hurt mode, piling on the guilt. "What did I do wrong? Tell me where I went wrong? I have sacrificed so much for this family, for you. Only Arun appreciates me. You would all be better off without me. Is that what you want? For me to just go? You will be sorry when I am dead…" she sobs, as if her whole world has come tumbling down. At these times everyone jumps to console her, ashamed that they have hurt her so badly, proffering tissues, tears and hugs.

But whilst Lina is intolerant of anyone else's illnesses, her own are a different matter, and she groans and sighs with every minor movement. She is in constant pain from her knees and feet, although the doctors haven't been able to find the cause. "I am an enigma," she regularly says, shrugging with a hopeless air. Lina also insists that she can't eat wheat or dairy, that caffeine doesn't agree with her and that she is pescatarian.

If she goes out for a meal, in addition to these dietary requirements, she will always ask for an alteration in some way, smiling sweetly at the waiter. "I'll have the fish, but could you put the parsley in a little dish on the side, finely chopped?" "Would you make sure the baby new potatoes are peeled?" And could I have rocket in the salad instead of the lamb's lettuce?" The more salubrious the restaurant, the more modifications will be required.

When Raj's 40th birthday came round, Lina's mystery aches became too bad for her to be able to organize a celebration, so the staff at the dental practice decided to throw a surprise evening party there instead. Laila and Arun were enlisted to help, and the practice manager ran things with military precision, organizing food, music, decorations and tasteful invitations.

Somehow, however, Lina let it slip to Raj that this was being arranged, spoiling the surprise, but Raj was delighted anyway. Lina had been tasked with getting Raj to the party, but on the day, everything seemed to go wrong. Raj's car keys had somehow fallen under the sofa, and took ages to find, and Lina couldn't decide which dress to wear and kept changing. She curled her hair but then decided it would look better straight, and so had to re-wash and dry it. Raj was getting more and more impatient as the time ticked on, and an argument ensued, much to his regret. When they eventually arrived at the party, they were over an hour late – but all was forgiven when Lina limped in on crutches, ahead of Raj, smiling shyly. Raj duly feigned surprise, and the party was off to a start.

Brave Lina, incapacitated by pain, was waited on hand and foot by the practice staff, who even opened up the drug cupboard to get her some painkillers – but in the end the pain won out and she was driven home early, by one of the nurses. When Raj returned from the party she was in the spare room again, refusing to answer him in anything other than monosyllables. Days later he found out that he should *never* have danced 'in that way' with his receptionist.

In spite of the terrible time Lina had had, she was still able to post lovely pictures of the event on Facebook, with the caption "My wonderful husband's surprise 40th birthday! Thank you to everyone who came!" The 'likes' came flooding in, as they always did for Lina's posts, which portrayed her family life as one of wealthy, happy perfection. It was interesting that she didn't correct anyone who assumed that *she* had planned the party, though. And why was it that, although Lina had hundreds of friends on Facebook, they were conspicuously few and far between in real life?

Technology has been a mixed blessing for their family. Lina insists upon tracking everyone through their phones, on the grounds that she is 'worried about them', and will ring and message them several times a day. If they don't reply immediately, and she can see that they are online or have read her message, her texts will become more insistent and demanding. Lina is not very good at being on her own in the house, and every now and then she will imply that there is an emergency, and then switch her own phone off. One of them still rushes home, worried that this could be the time she's not actually crying wolf.

Even though she's still young, Lina has given up driving completely. It happened slowly – first she said she was too scared to drive at night. Then driving on motorways was out. After this, turning right became an issue, leading to tortuous lengthy routes having to be planned out. Raj wonders whether he is being uncharitable when he feels a bit used and controlled by Lina's insistence that he drive her everywhere. "Jenni's husband doesn't mind driving *her* around" she will say, of one of the dads from school, who looks like a younger version of George Clooney. In fact, Raj has noticed that it's always 'Jenni's husband this' or 'Jenni's husband that' these days – but he knows that Lina would never have the courage to speak to the man, and he is just the latest in a line of men that she has worshipped from afar. *She just needs more attention and sympathy from me*, he chastises himself at these times, disappointed with his own inadequacy in making her happy.

Lina sees herself as the very model of empathy and generosity. If someone she barely knows dies, she will comfort the relatives with zeal, taking meals to the widowed person and trying to help with the funeral arrangements. She will visit the bereaved family daily and speak to their other relatives on the phone, choking up as she offers her condolences. She will mourn their loss as one might mourn the loss of a best friend, and Raj and the children know better than to question this, even though it seems odd and over-the-top. They just wish that she could be quite so understanding when one of *them* is poorly – and it hasn't escaped their notice how her *own* ailments increase at these times, inevitably requiring much fuss and attention from everyone.

The Closet Narcissist – the poor put-upon victim, who struggles on in the face of adversity, caring and giving. Secretly needing to believe themselves to be special and important, but staying away from the limelight. Basking in the glow of another's status and specialness. Disguising control as 'worry,' and seeking attention in covert or sneaky ways, such as through mystery illnesses and dietary fads. Portraying an image of the perfect family life, whilst intolerant and dismissive of any of the children's imperfections. Favoring a 'golden child' over the other. Concerned about image and appearance. Jealous of others, but at the same time believing others to be jealous of them. A propensity for social climbing. Selfish, with a belief of being entitled to special treatment. Happy to exploit others behind closed doors, and to take the credit for other's hard work. Although afraid to openly seek attention themselves, resentful when others do. A lack of real empathy for others. Manipulativeness, disguised as 'rescuing' and a desperate need for approval and validation. Do you recognize these features in your partner?

THE DEVALUING NARCISSIST

Oonagh Campbell-Jones is now 51, and you will never see her without a full face of makeup and perfectly coiffed hair. Born as just plain Oonagh Campbell, she firmly believes that the best thing her poor, put upon husband Geoff ever did for her was to give her a way to hyphenate her surname. Oonagh was brought up on a small farm in Ireland where money was tight, but she knew she was destined for greater things. When she announced her engagement and intended new surname, she was met with squeals of delight from her many younger sisters. "Campbell-Jones – it sounds dead aristocratic!" and "Our Oonagh's an *English lady* now!"

Her father, always one to pour cold water on things, simply looked up from his paper and muttered "Well girls, our Oonagh's always had ideas above her station, so she has…"

And indeed, Oonagh *had* decided that she wouldn't be sticking around in rural Ireland for the rest of her life. She left school aged 16 and, much to her father's disgust, rather than help on the farm, she secured a job in the university library. Come rain or snow, she would cycle three miles down to the bus stop, lean her rusty old bike up against the hedgerow, and catch the first of the three buses she had to get on, in order to reach the city. She quickly became an expert at piling on her make-up on the way there, and wiping off all traces of it on the way home, and she'd spend the rest of the journey absorbed in the books she had borrowed from work. Oonagh was on a mission to 'better herself', and no one was going to get in her way.

After two years, Oonagh's persistence finally paid off. She quite literally bumped into Geoff in the student library, when he took a few steps backwards into her, causing her to drop the enormous pile of books she was carrying. Englishman Geoff was older than Oonagh, and had come to Dublin to do a PhD in Biology. But despite his age, Geoff was awkward and shy, and had never had a real relationship. Flustered, he helped Oonagh pick up the books, thinking that such a beautiful girl like her would never be interested in someone like him.

But Geoff was wrong – she was indeed interested, and he couldn't believe his luck. She was everything he had ever dreamed of. Well-read with a sharp wit – and stunning too, with her flame-red hair, which fell to just above her tiny waist, in natural corkscrew curls.

They soon started spending every lunchtime together, and meeting later too, at the library after she finished work. They'd often go back to his student flat for an early dinner, eating to the soundtrack of his favorite classical music (which no other girl had ever been interested in), until it was time for Oonagh to catch the bus home.

By the time they met, Oonagh had learned how to dress to emphasize her physical attributes. She'd carefully observed the city girls, and devoured the fashion magazines in the staff coffee room where she had been eating her sandwiches. Her hemlines and heels were carefully chosen to show off her long, shapely legs, which she would cross and uncross provocatively, and wide necklines would 'accidentally' slip every now and then, to give a tantalizing glimpse of an alabaster shoulder or cleavage. Oonagh was the sort who just could not stop playing with her red locks either – twirling them in her fingers or pinning them up, only to release them a few minutes later to toss around. And when she ate – well, it was sensuality personified. Geoff, quite understandably, found himself driven wild with desire.

Oonagh made Geoff feel manly and sexy – with her he felt like the best version of himself. She listened to his hopes and his fears, with rapt attention. She even adored listening to him play his violin (he played first violin in the university orchestra and was very accomplished indeed). Geoff had met his soulmate, and according to Oonagh, she had too.

After a month, Geoff took Oonagh to England to meet his parents, who were utterly charmed by the Celtic beauty with the soft accent, who hung upon their son's every word, and gazed at him adoringly.

NARCISSISTS IN DIVORCE: FROM LOVE-LOCKED TO LEAVING

Looking back, Geoff now knows that he missed a red flag in those early days of their courtship. When Oonagh's younger sister got engaged to her childhood sweetheart of five years, Oonagh was incensed. "How *dare* she? I'm older than her…She should have waited for *me* to get married first…"

Geoff's attempts to rationalize with her, and to calm her were met with footstamping and tears. "You English people don't know anything about it! It's how we do things in Ireland. Who does that Billy White think he is, proposing without even checking with me first? How *dare* he? He's made an utter fool out of me…"

Was she right? Perhaps he *didn't* have the right to comment about her culture. As she raged and ranted, lovestruck Geoff found himself telling himself that she was just a fiery redhead, and that that was what he loved about her. Was he being a fool, getting down on one knee and proposing to her, right then and there, in the university park, with a ring pull from a can of cola for a ring? Was two months just too soon? It didn't feel like it, especially when her tears of frustration turned to those of joy and she declared her undying love for him.

Oonagh got her way, and they married before her sister, just six months later, in a small ceremony in front of only their parents and Oonagh's immediate family. When he asked her why she wasn't inviting her old friends (whom he had never met), should he have considered her responses more carefully? "They're jealous of me. They can't stand the fact that I'm leaving this shitehole and moving to London. They just don't know how to be happy for me. They are all losers anyways. I just wouldn't want them there, spoiling our day. Honestly Geoff, they'll just be embarrassments, so they will."

Geoff decided that if she wasn't inviting her friends, he wouldn't invite his either, in solidarity. They'd be able to celebrate properly with them once they were living in England, he told himself.

Oonagh's sister's wedding took place two months later, but Oonagh continued to refuse to be her bridesmaid. "Sure Geoff, I can't condone it – I really can't. That Billy White is just a nobody. She deserves so much more. I just can't go against my principles. I've got to be true to myself, you know?" Geoff was still blinded by love, and decided that it was not his place to interfere. But did he genuinely believe that Oonagh was 'just making an effort for the wedding' when she booked a hairdresser and make-up artist for herself for the day, and put on a show-stopping, figure-hugging white dress? Today he'd hang his head in shame and tell you that he was so smitten that it really did not occur to him that Oonagh was upstaging her sister, on the biggest day of her life.

These days, 30 years on, things are a far cry from those heady days of youth. In fact, things began to change on their honeymoon. Just the day after their wedding, Oonagh started criticizing Geoff's prowess in the bedroom, when she'd never complained before. He was utterly wretched – why was she saying these things? She started ogling other men on the beach, commenting on how muscular they were, knowing perfectly well that Geoff was a bit touchy about his lanky frame. She'd always been more interested in his intellect than his looks – so why the sudden change? But when he looked hurt she just laughed it off dismissively. "Sure Geoff, stop being so oversensitive, will you? It's very unattractive, you know. And anyways, there's nothing wrong with just looking." And she was right. Wasn't she?

Once they moved to London, little by little things continued to deteriorate – so slowly that Geoff just accepted them as normal. The occasional weekends that the couple had enjoyed visiting Geoff's parents got further and further apart. Oonagh would always have something else to do, or worse, cancel at the last minute. Geoff tried everything to encourage her to go, especially as his parents thought *she* was wonderful, and he was their only child.

When Oonagh gave the excuse that the food they served was unpalatable, he'd suggest going out for dinner with them instead. When she said that they were boring, he'd try to entice her with a designer shopping trip at the outlet mall near to their house. When he suggested that they came to visit them instead, so that she could do her own thing whilst they were there, she'd mess up the house in the preceding days and refuse to help him tidy it in preparation. And if Geoff went to see them on his own, Oonagh would be cold and silent toward him for at least a week afterwards, all the while claiming that 'nothing was wrong.' These silent treatments were agonizing for Geoff, and he found himself fawning over Oonagh to try to get back into her good books – bringing her cups of tea, cleaning her car, buying her flowers – but nothing worked. These moods were so destabilizing and upsetting that Geoff started to see his parents less and less, effectively allowing Oonagh to isolate him from them – one of his biggest regrets today.

It became obvious early on that Oonagh was an ambitious lady, and despite her lack of formal qualifications, she climbed the corporate ladder in marketing quickly. It also became clear that, to her, Geoff's job came second. When he was promoted to Head of Pharmacokinetics at a big pharmaceutical company, he came home with a special bottle of champagne, sure that Oonagh would want to celebrate. When he got the text from her saying that she would be a little late, he decided to start making a special celebratory meal – steak, Oonagh's favorite. Although lateness was what he had come to expect from Oonagh, he was sure that today would be different. But he waited. And waited. And waited. She seemed to be receiving his messages on her phone, but she wasn't responding to them, and he was starting to get worried. What if she'd been mugged on the way home, and someone else had her phone? Anything could have happened, especially as no one was answering the office line.

By the time Oonagh rolled in at 10.30pm that night he was so beside himself with worry that he didn't notice that her normally perfect lipstick was a little smeared. Whilst it wasn't unusual for her to work late and not tell him what time she would be home, this was a *special occasion,* and he was sure that something bad must have happened. But no. Oonagh just yawned and said that she'd had important work to do that night, and that it wasn't her fault that it had taken so long. "If I hadn't had to read all those messages from you, I'd have been finished way sooner..." she even had the gall to say.

"God almighty. This steak's dry as a bone. I can't be eating this." Oonagh then complained, prodding it with a knife. "Why'd you keep it in the oven for so long? Anyways, we had pizza in the office, so I'll pass and head on up to bed. And can you turn that bloody classical music off? You know I can't stand it..." Geoff was utterly deflated, and the champagne remained unopened until Oonagh grandly presented it to her company's CEO at his summer barbecue, to much appreciative 'oohing' and 'aahing'.

When other people congratulated Geoff for his promotion in front of Oonagh, she would wrap her arm around him, beaming, and say how proud she was. *Phew!* Geoff would think, relieved – *she does appreciate me after all! I was just being touchy before.*

But then, behind closed doors, she would scoff, with a snigger, "Ah Geoff, I think we both know you're not a *proper* scientist."

These occasional public displays of affection, interspersed with humiliations, were all very confusing for Geoff. But Oonagh had had a terrible childhood of harsh poverty, made worse by a vile father. She was *wounded*. Geoff had made his vows – he just had to love her more and everything would eventually be okay. Besides, he was pretty sure that Oonagh was a bit autistic and this explained why she could behave so oddly at times.

But why, although *she* was often late back from work, would *he* be questioned at length about his whereabouts, if he was even five minutes later than expected? At first Geoff had been flattered by this, thinking that it showed how much she cared and worried about him. But as the years wore on, the hypocrisy of it did slowly dawn on him. He would often have to put up with embarrassing tirades over the phone from her, whilst his colleagues tried not to exchange glances at each other, pretending not to hear her vile accusations that he was 'f**king some slag'. At those times he really wished the ground would just swallow him up. And when he did get home, did he know just how abnormal Oonagh's interrogations were? He knew he was terrified of her at these times, that's for sure, especially when she would tell him that his fast breathing rate and increased swallowing was proof that he was lying to her. "Don't think I don't know exactly what is going on in that tiny mind of yours, Geoff" she would say to him at these times, with an intense and chilling steeliness.

At some point in their relationship, Oonagh completely stopped taking her house keys out with her when she left the house, on the grounds that they jangled annoyingly in her bag and the sound gave her intense migraines. In reality, this meant that Geoff had to be home before Oonagh, to let her into the house, if he was to avoid her wrath at being made to wait outside. He had suggested hiding a key for her outside, or giving a key to a neighbour for the rare occasions when he couldn't get back in time for her, but she was adamant that this was completely unsafe and that they would be asking to be burgled. Geoff never did cotton on to what an excellent way she had found to covertly control his movements.

One year he resolved to join a cycling club, after she accused him of 'letting himself go' by putting on a bit of extra weight. The people were welcoming and fun, and he realized how much he had let his social interactions slide. Oonagh didn't actively discourage him until she realized that women were also involved in the club, and that after the cycle ride they would all eat lunch together at a cafe. She was furious with him, and told him that the reason she had agreed to him joining was on the grounds that he would be attending purely for his physical health, and that having lunch with them ('if that was even what he was *really* up to') was ruining their own 'quality time' together. He doesn't quite know when her jealousy stopped feeling like love and turned into an inescapable oppressive weight, but he remembers feeling as if he had no choice but to leave the club, and to forget about ever doing anything outside of work that didn't involve her.

Speaking of social interactions, Oonagh had the remarkable knack of being able to completely change her accent, and her range was impressive. She could go from southern Irish farm girl to English landed gentry in the space of a heartbeat, with all the gradations in between. She could speak softly and liltingly, or at great speed, with machine gun precision, depending on what was required. "Oonagh is like a box of chocolates," Geoff once tried to explain to his mother, misquoting a famous film, "You never know what you're going to get next…"

But one thing never changed – Oonagh believed herself to be vastly intellectual, and she had the bookshelf to prove it. "I'm living proof that university is an utter waste of time," she would declare, in clipped British tones, at the dinner parties they were rarely invited to. "Geoff will tell you – won't you Geoff? What I haven't read simply isn't worth reading."

Oonagh would then go on to quote obscure poetry and literature to prove her point, and then feign incredulity when people didn't recognize the source. "Surely, you can't be telling me that you don't recognize *Ulysses*? Seriously now? And you've a *Master's* degree?" During one such conversation she even proclaimed "I made a decision a long time ago that the day Geoff reads Proust *in French* will be the day that I take his intellect seriously!" She'd then let out little peal of laughter, "And I think we all know that *that* day won't be coming anytime soon, don't we?" Needless to say, the invitations dried up almost completely over time.

She got even worse after a few glasses of wine. At Geoff's pharmaceutical company's Christmas dinner, which she felt very aggrieved at having to attend, she loudly held court. "Tell me, do all of you with PhDs call yourselves 'doctors'? Geoff does. Honest to God, people actually think he's a *real* doctor. I tell you, we were on a plane this once, and he was asked to revive a woman who'd collapsed. It was utterly mortifying, having to explain that he's just in pharmaceuticals. I nearly died *myself* – of the sheer embarrassment!"

And what could Geoff do, other than to sit frozen and red-faced, when she leant conspiratorially over to his boss, with her ample cleavage in full prominence, and whispered, sotto voce, "You know, I used to think that with Geoff, 'still waters run deep'. But I've come to realize that those waters are actually just still…Tell me, Brian…are *you* deep? I bet you are…"

Geoff tried harder and harder, but no matter what he did, as the years wore on he, and almost everyone else they knew, was treated with increasing ridicule and contempt. Nothing anyone did or said was good enough, apart from the occasional new person at work or in the neighborhood, who Oonagh would idolize, and talk about endlessly in glowing terms – until they too fell off their pedestals and became 'losers'.

She would complain ruefully about anything she could, looking up from whatever classic masterpiece she was reading, as Geoff cleaned up around her, or brought her wine and snacks, tiptoeing around her. One time, she knocked the wine glass (that he'd carefully set in the usual place on her side table) with her elbow, spilling red wine everywhere. "Oh you idiot!" she roared at him, "What a stupid place to put it – that close to me, when I'm busy reading!" Everything had to be his fault, even innocent accidents.

If he ever asked for help with the household chores, she would reply, "I will not be stereotyped Geoff – you know that. We women have to make a stand. We've been the underdogs for far too long, and you should respect my position as a feminist." Was she right? Geoff couldn't tell for sure these days.

But every now and then everything would change, and Oonagh would make him a romantic dinner, and her criticisms would stop for a while. They'd even curl up on the sofa together and watch movies, just like they used to, and go for walks, hand in hand. Oonagh would even ask Geoff to play her something on his violin at these times, something he rarely now did because of her 'sensitive ears.'

See Geoff? he used to say to himself at these times. *Everything is okay after all!* It took decades to accept that these reprises would never last – and that her scorn and mockery would inevitably return.

Geoff's greatest sadness was that they had never had children. When they first met, Oonagh had told him that she dreamed of having a boy and a girl, just as Geoff wanted. She painted a picture of wanting to be a stay-at-home mother, at least for a few years whilst the children were young. They had even talked about baby names in that first year, and they bought a house that had enough rooms for the children. But as the years wore on it became clear that Oonagh's career was more important to her than a family. At first, she simply said that she was not ready to have children, but later, when she was 35 and time was running out, she delivered her biggest blow.

"Oh, come now Geoff, you call yourself an intelligent man. The world's overpopulated for God's sake. It's *unfair* to bring children into it. You're thinking about it all wrong – and you've absolutely no right to tell me what I should do with my womb. Just get a bloody dog if you're that broody…"

Heartbroken, Geoff did just that. And it was from Maisie, a dainty black and white mongrel that he, at last, received the unconditional love so missing from his marriage.

"She never comes to meet *me* at the door when *I* come in…" Oonagh would complain, jealous of their bond. When Maisie grew old and grey, she would tell Geoff that it was 'cruel' to keep her alive. "If it were down to me, I'd just shoot the bloody thing…" she'd say every time she saw Geoff giving Maisie her thyroid tablets. But when the time did eventually come for Maisie to be put to sleep, Oonagh made a big show of tearily leaving work to go home to say her goodbyes.

And when the vet and nurse arrived at the house, brimming with kindness and sympathy, Oonagh took one look at them, and curtly said, "Listen. I grew up on a farm. You don't have to pretend to be sad on my account, okay? So how about I give you permission to drop the act?" Did she notice their eyes widening in dismay? Yes, she did. But she smugly misattributed this to her belief that she had correctly called them out on their insincerity.

At least Oonagh had the decency to stand back and allow Geoff to rest his head on Maisie's and whisper reassuringly to her as she fell asleep for the final time.

But when he let the tears roll down his face, something he had been careful to avoid doing in front of Oonagh for decades, she just stared at him, as though he was a science experiment.

"It's just a *dog*. You can't *love* a *dog* for God's sake…" he heard her muttering incredulously, as she left the house to go back to the office, where she sniffed and dabbed her dry eyes, and basked in the glorious sympathy of anyone who felt brave enough to approach her.

Oonagh has threatened to leave Geoff countless times. He used to feel as though he simply couldn't live without her, and so each time he would beg her to reconsider. But he has finally made his mind up. The next time she brings up leaving, he will agree with her. After years of being told by Oonagh that 'no one else would ever be able to love him', he fully expects to be alone for the rest of his life, but he's accepted that. His bigger problem is his fear of how she will react when she realizes that he is actually leaving but even he, familiar though he is with her rages and cruelty, won't be prepared for just how bad things will inevitably get when he does finally make a break for it.

The Devaluing Narcissist. Critical and demeaning. Invalidating other people's achievements. Putting people down in order to feel more special themselves. Name-calling ('losers'). Gaslighting others so that they question their own self-worth, their emotions and their opinions. A sense of entitlement resulting in not having to pull one's own weight. Exploitative behavior. A need to believe that one is intellectually superior. Lateness as a devaluation and control tactic. Silent treatments, as a method to punish and control, and to acquire narcissistic supply from the fawning that results. A cyclical pattern of abuse followed by a period of respite. Love bombing occurring at the beginning of the relationship. A tendency to see people only as either 'all good' or 'all bad'. A pattern of isolating the victim from others. Nonsensical assertions, made with absolute conviction. Control and jealousy. Rage when things do not go their way, or their image of themselves is threatened. A profound lack of empathy, and inability to care about the feelings of others. Derision, ridicule and contempt. Future faking, inventing a dream of shared goals and visions, but never delivering upon it. Destroying the victim's self-esteem so that they feel too weak to leave the relationship. A complete inability to love.

THE COMMUNAL NARCISSIST

Marcus is now 30. Being mixed race is a big part of how he sees himself, and you'll be mesmerized by his unusual blue eyes, which he uses to great effect by holding your gaze for just a little too long.

If you ask him about himself (and even if you don't) he'll tell you, in his deep slow drawl, that he's 'one of life's good guys'. He'll nod earnestly as he speaks, and occasionally flash you a disarming smile, revealing all his perfect white teeth. It can feel a little discombobulating, for some reason.

"You know, I've done a lot of things in my life…" Marcus likes to arrange his athletic 6 ft 4 frame on the chair with deliberate intention, leaning back, and resting one ankle on the other thigh. It's an open posture, one you might find yourself unconsciously mirroring, as he continues, "but it's time for me to 'give back', you know?"

And indeed, Marcus's social media profiles corroborate his varied skills. He has a 'broad range of expertise in a variety of fields.' He's an 'innovator', a 'thought leader', an 'entrepreneur', a 'family man', a 'philanthropist', and a 'sportsman'. "But I'm a Christian first, you know? That's what keeps me on the path – the righteous path…"

Marcus married fairly young, as he believes all good Christians should. "Irina is like…she's like a guiding light to me, you know?" he speaks with great fervor about his Romanian wife, who is six years his senior.

Irina was a struggling single mother when they met, balancing cleaning jobs with caring for her eighteen-month-old son, Janis. But handsome Marcus was not put off, and swooped in to rescue her and Janis. When Marcus's grandmother died, she had left her four-bedroom Victorian home in Camberwell, South London, to him. It was the house both he and his mother had grown up in and was, by this time, worth a very sizeable amount. They'd only known each other a month when Marcus asked Irina to move in.

If you mention this generosity, Marcus will nod thoughtfully and say "Yeah, well you know – if you've got empathy, that's all you need in life. Yeah. I guess I was lucky like that – I've got empathy levels off the scale."

NARCISSISTS IN DIVORCE: FROM LOVE-LOCKED TO LEAVING

These days Irina runs a small cleaning firm, with four staff. They clean affluent South Londoners' houses, but it's a stressful business which nearly went under during the COVID-19 pandemic. The clientele can be rude and demanding, and they frequently complain and withhold payment. Irina also often finds herself having to step in for absent staff members at the last minute.

She'd like to go to university and then train to be a psychotherapist, but Marcus tells her that even if she *did* have the brain for it, they wouldn't be able to afford it, even though they have no mortgage. And it's true – they can't afford it. Money just seems to drain away, as fast as it comes in. She knows that his penchant for all the latest designer trainers isn't helping, and she despairs at the size of his collection (which has taken over the spare room). But Marcus is clear on this point. "They are an important part of my cultural identity as a black man," he tells her, with absolute conviction, making her feel as though she is a racist. She hasn't heard of 'gaslighting'.

Marcus is keenly involved with the local football club, where he coaches the youngsters, including twelve-year-old Janis, every week. To onlookers, he's taken on the role of stepfather admirably.

His voice is naturally deep and resonant and so travels great distances without him having to shout. "That's it Janis, my main man…hook it under, yeah, cool one…" "Harris, dude – you've got this…save! Result, man…badass…" There have definitely been more mums on the sidelines since Marcus started football coaching in his shorts and tight T-shirt.

Janis finds these public displays of 'encouragement' excruciating, and he's fully aware of the fact that his 'cool' stepfather is nothing like this when no one else can hear or see him. When he picks him up from school, Janis usually finds him intensely interacting with one or other of the mums, who usually seems flustered or giggly. Marcus takes his kit bag from him as he fist-pumps him, and then encases him in a giant, over-the-top bear hug, which Janis surrenders to. He knows that the car journey home will probably be in silence.

Marcus talks a lot about his work, through his church, in helping disadvantaged children – although if you actually followed him around for a few days, you'd be hard pushed to work out what he actually does in this regard.

You might note that he has worked his way through various churches, falling out with the pastors and other members. The last time this happened, Marcus insisted that he could take over from the lead guitarist of the church band, who was emigrating. No one questioned his ability until their first practice, when it became painfully clear that, although he had an incredibly expensive handmade guitar, he could barely play it, and just mis-strummed chords randomly. The pastor was enlisted to ask him to step down, but Marcus raged so frighteningly that the police were nearly called. He accused the terrified pastor of racism, and of using his white male privilege against him. "God is going to pay you back for this, you f**king nobody…" were his parting words as he stormed off. But when he got home, he was so depressed he could barely speak, and he didn't get out bed for three days. He told Irina that the luthier, who had made the guitar specially for him, had 'made it wrong' on purpose, to sabotage him, and that it was all his fault.

He's the sort who gives twenty-pound notes to the homeless (if he happens to have an audience) with a "Peace, brother…" and when you comment on his generosity, he'll dismiss it modestly, with a wave of his hand.

NARCISSISTS IN DIVORCE: FROM LOVE-LOCKED TO LEAVING

But Marcus feels his greatest altruistic achievements have come through Instagram, where he has over 100,000 followers. Every other day he posts a short video starting with the words, "Greetings, fam. Marcus Brown here, sharing with you my thoughts. It's my intention to make the world a better place, by spreading peace and light."

Marcus mostly lifts his content from other people, including from his own pastor's weekly sermons. He is so good at passing off other people's work as his own that he even gets away with using old or obscure poems or song lyrics, which he delivers slowly and with great intensity.

Irina doesn't quite know what to make of the fact that he has set up a permanent studio in a corner of the dining room, with lighting rigs, a boom microphone and an eye-wateringly expensive camera and teleprompter. She and Janis know to tiptoe around the house whilst he's 'in session', as he calls it, recording himself time and time again until he gets it just right. But then again, she hasn't been allowed to put her own stamp on any part of the house since she's lived here, on the grounds that she'd be 'violating the memory of his grandmother' if she did.

Marcus ends his videos with a little outro. "I hope that's given you either food for thought, or comfort or joy. Once again, I'm Marcus Brown. Follow me here or on Twitter, if you'd like to be part of my growing community of thinkers and changers. Peace and love, fam."

Marcus makes sure he responds to every single comment he receives in response to these videos. "It's practically a full-time job," he once told Irina, when she had the audacity to ask him if he could load the dishwasher. These days she can't help but feel irritated when she comes back from work and finds his cereal bowls and mugs littered around the place, the washing not done and the fridge bare. There's only so much his winning smile can make up for, she has realized in recent years. It's particularly annoying as she knows he's very capable – if anyone visits he will make a big show of wiping down surfaces and drying dishes, or whipping up a delicious meal. But as he points out, she should be *grateful* to be living there. "Don't forget where you'd be if it wasn't for *me*," he growls at her, if she steps out of line.

When Irina heard rumors that Marcus was having an affair with Loretta from their latest church, she was confused, and nearly brushed it off as ridiculous. Marcus had always displayed a zero-tolerance approach to infidelity in everyone he came across, so she was stunned when he eventually came clean and admitted that the unlikely gossip she'd been hearing was true.

Irina was absolutely distraught, her pain amplified by the humiliation of realizing that everyone in the community had known except her. But, somehow, Marcus had persuaded her to give him another chance. In couple's therapy, he blamed his indiscretions on the fact that Irina was often working, leaving him feeling lonely and isolated. The therapist agreed with him and spoke of the value of forgiveness. Irina felt terrible guilt, and agreed to try again.

Only she knew how loving and sweet he could be when he was on form, and how he had begged her not to break-up their family unit, even saying that he didn't think he would be able to go on living without her. It got to the stage where he was so scared about her leaving that he would whisper into her ear, when he thought she was asleep, over and over again "You will *not* leave me…"– proof of his enormous regret, or so she thought.

"He's such a great dad!" the other mums will say to her, who know him from his football coaching. But Irina knows that Janis only plays football because it is what *Marcus* wants. Marcus is always trying to 'bulk' Janis out too, breaking raw eggs into glasses of milk for him to drink, which he hates, and mercilessly criticizing his match performance once they get into the car.

And when Janis broke his leg in a school football match that Marcus was watching, Irina was appalled to hear that he had refused to call an ambulance, instead making him wait in the car for an hour until the match was over, with no painkillers. "The body is a miracle of God" he had drawled, when she had confronted him about it that evening. "It produces *natural* painkillers, and heals itself…"

Irina also can't understand why Marcus is so disbelieving of Janis's asthma. He sometimes has an attack when exercising in cold weather. If there are people present, Marcus will rush over to give him his inhaler, concern etched on his face. But once, when he didn't think she was around, she heard him saying angrily, through gritted teeth, "Just breathe *normally*, you little idiot…" When he turned around to see her standing there, with a horrified expression, he quickly laughed it off. "I was only joking!" he said, with his trademark winning smile.

And why, if he is such a charitable man, is he always so very rude to waiters? Why does he get fidgety and edgy if he ever has to wait in a line? Why does he always point out overweight people in restaurants, and tell her that they put him off his food? Why, on the rare occasions that she goes out with a friend for lunch or a glass of wine after work, does he text her continuously throughout, and ask her for a blow-by-blow account of the conversation afterwards? Why is he so damned *jealous*? Forever suggesting that he has seen her looking over at some man or other with interest, or that she is having an 'emotional affair' with someone she barely knows. He seems so sure that she's even started to question herself, even though she knows, deep down, that she's never been unfaithful to Marcus.

Every evening Marcus insists that Irina sits with him to watch TV, because 'time spent together is essential to keep a marriage healthy'. She used to think that this was a sweet sentiment, but the sports programs that Marcus makes her watch are just not her cup of tea at all, and he never lets her choose what they watch. The one time he acquiesced, and she put on a period drama that she'd been dying to watch, he shifted around impatiently, yawned loudly, and kept looking at his phone. She felt terrible that he wasn't enjoying it, and after twenty minutes she handed him the remote control, when she could bear the guilt no more. Irina realizes that it is easier to just sit beside him and let her mind wander. And if he happens to fall asleep on the sofa, as he frequently does, she can sneak off to get on with the piles of business invoicing and paperwork that is necessary to keep funding their lives.

In recent years Irina has also noticed that Marcus just doesn't listen to her any more, dismissing her worries or feelings as ludicrous or invalid. If she tries to state a point of view, he will always have the opposite view, and she finds this exhausting and predictable – every conversation is hard work. In fact, nowadays he goes through cycles of being frosty and dismissive when behind closed doors, although she has noticed that, if she ever meets him in public, he will grandly kiss her on the cheek, hold her hand and smile affectionately at her once again, as if they are the world's biggest love story. In her heart of hearts, Irina feels completely unloved and uncherished.

This type of narcissist, also known as the Altruistic Narcissist, hides beneath a facade of being a do-gooder but, sadly, their wonderful image is merely skin deep. They often derive their all-important feeling of specialness by portraying themselves as the most kind, the most empathic, the most generous, the most pious or the most spiritual person you will meet. So whilst they *do* carry out good deeds, their motivations are far from pure – because, yet again, they are driven by their need to secure narcissistic supply. You'll find them in all sorts of environments and in all sorts of roles – in charitable, religious and environmental organizations, and as therapists, spiritual teachers, vicars and doctors. This sort of narcissist often loves sitting on committees and fundraising, but they are highly territorial about their philanthropic endeavors. Beneath the false persona, the usual narcissistic behaviors are in play – in Marcus's case, a sense of entitlement about not having to work or do chores; degrading others; a lack of empathy for another's pain; denial or invalidation of other people's feelings; lying, gaslighting, and using the family as image props; a tendency to play 'devil's advocate'; seeing children as mere extensions of themselves, so being unable to tolerate their imperfections; exerting control over others; applying high moral standards to others but not to themselves; blowing hot and cold; a marked tendency to be easily angered; and a masterful ability for impression management.

3

A deeper dive into NPD

So now you've met our four types of narcissist, it may be that some lightbulbs have gone off in you regarding your partner (or even a family member, work colleague or friend). You may be struck by a sense of relief, or horror, or both, if what you've discovered so far has resonated with you. You'll probably be hit by intermittent guilt (as no one really *wants* their partner to be a narcissist, even if it does explain a few things).

But most likely, even if you have moments of certainty, you will be doubting yourself at other times. This is completely normal at this stage, and remember, we still have some things to look at before you can even *start* to feel sure about whether your partner is a narcissist – so, desperate though you might be for an answer, try not to pressurize yourself too much. The truth will make itself known in time.

However, it may be that *none* of what you have seen so far has any relevance to your partner, in which case, you may be one of the lucky ones, and perhaps we'll be able to bid you farewell, fairly soon. If this is you, please, please count your lucky stars. Your break-up, if that's what is on the cards, may be acrimonious to begin with, but there is a real chance that things will improve with time, and you'll be able to find amicable solutions. But please do stick around if you are still unsure, because we are now going to consider the official diagnostic criteria for NPD, and then we will take a look at all the other real-world behaviors of narcissists.

A textbook diagnosis

According to the Diagnostic and Statistical Manual of Mental Disorders (5th ed.; DSM-5; American Psychiatric Association, 2013), at least five of nine criteria need to be met in order to diagnose NPD. To paraphrase these, the things to look out for are:

- Grandiosity with an exaggerated sense of self-importance. This can show up in outward behaviors, or can be in fantasy. For example, they might exaggerate their talents, or expect others to recognize them as being superior, regardless of their actual achievements.
- Being wrapped up in thoughts of success, beauty, power or a romanticized notion of love.
- A view that their specialness and uniqueness means that only other people who are special (or who have high status) can understand them, and that they should only be involved with people or institutions of this nature.
- Feeling entitled to special treatment, and for people to simply comply with their wishes.
- Exploiting others, taking advantage of them for their own gain.
- Low empathy, with a limited understanding or concern for other people's needs or feelings.

- Being envious of people, and/or believing that other people are envious of them
- Behaving in an arrogant and haughty way, or having attitudes of this nature
- Needing excessive and constant admiration from others.

Think back to our Devaluing Narcissist, Oonagh, if you will, and reconsider this list. It's pretty clear that she qualifies for a diagnosis of NPD – there is very little that is subtle about *her*, and she scores well over 5 out of 9. The same can be said for our Exhibitionist Narcissist, headmaster Jonathan.

But what about Lina, our Closet Narcissist, who you also met in the last Chapter? The Closet Narcissists don't want others to see them as obviously arrogant or haughty, but we can see that the 'yeses' for Lina include that

- she married Raj, a dentist, because of his high status
- she doesn't really have true empathy (shown by her unwillingness to care for others when they are ill)
- she exploits her mother and Raj who do the housework for her
- she needs to be admired by the other mothers (so hosts impressive coffee mornings and children's parties to gain this admiration)
- she believes that people are secretly jealous of her

It gets a bit trickier when it comes to Lina's 'grandiosity' and 'exaggerated sense of self-importance', because the Closet Narcissists try to hide this from the outside world, but you do get a sense that Lina wants to be recognized as being superior by others, and probably fantasizes about it. We can see that she goes about getting this sense of superiority in sneaky ways, such as through 'bigging up' her son's achievements.

Lina's sense of entitlement also makes an appearance through her manipulation of others. She expects her family to respond to her messages immediately, and ensures that she gets special treatment by feigning mystery illnesses.

You may wish to have a go at applying these nine criteria to your partner, now that you have a good idea of what they are all about. Also, the DSM-5 has an alternative model for diagnosing NPD, which you might also want to try out. Let's have a quick look.

This alternative model describes NPD as a moderate or severe impairment in personality functioning, with difficulties in two or more of four areas (identity, self-direction, empathy and intimacy). Grandiosity and attention seeking behavior also has to be present.

So, how this might apply to Marcus? We can see that he is grandiose from his social media profiles, where he describes himself as a 'thought leader' and an 'innovator', amongst other things. His Instagram videos are clear attention seeking behaviors, and it is also clear that his sense of identity is abnormally dependent on how other people view him, and can fluctuate wildly, depending on what they think of him. His rage at being seen as not good enough for the church band, and his subsequent depression, alludes to this.

He also has difficulties in 'self-direction'. This can play out in two ways. Some narcissists set standards for themselves which are very high, and can be extremely motivated to achieve them. These high-achieving narcissists do this so that other people see them as exceptional, once they have achieved their goals. And this, in turn, allows them to *see themselves* as exceptional. Jonathan and Oonagh fit into this type. However, the opposite can also be true: some narcissists, like Marcus, have no motivation to achieve. This type believes, as a result of their sense of entitlement, that *others* should provide for them. This explains why narcissists can either appear to be high achievers or parasitic spongers – which, on the surface, might look like a bit of a paradox.

And what about empathy? We discussed this core feature of NPD in Chapter 1, and it's quite clear that Marcus has low empathy, given that he left poor Janis waiting in the car with a broken leg for an hour. The irony is that Marcus himself has no idea at all that this is the case, and openly describes his empathy levels as being 'off the scale'.

Difficulties in intimacy is another area to be considered. This isn't really about sexual intimacy, but emotional intimacy. Narcissists simply *cannot* genuinely emotionally connect to other people in a vulnerable way. Narcissists see others simply as objects; 'its.' There's a good chance that if you ask your narcissistic partner why they love you, they won't be able to come out with any deep and meaningful reasons that demonstrate any level of emotional connection with you. The answer you get is likely to be very telling indeed, and may range from superficial reasons, such as "You are sexy," "You make people laugh," or "You make a good lemon drizzle cake," all the up way to a slightly confused "I don't know – I just do."

All of a narcissist's relationships are superficial, although, as you might know from experience, at first, it's easy to be fooled otherwise. Narcissists only have relationships to make them feel good about *themselves* – they don't really care about others' experiences. The big clue here is how Irina feels unloved and uncherished by Marcus – the latter being something you are highly likely to relate to, if your partner is a narcissist.

The shortcomings of being a narcissist

Narcissists are very limited individuals indeed, in some respects. There are certain things that they simply cannot do as well as non-narcissists, some of which we have already alluded to, but let's take a closer look. You may wish to jot down any examples of these shortcomings that you have noticed in your partner.

They cannot truly care about others

It stands to reason that, because narcissists have low emotional empathy, and so cannot actually feel another person's emotions (positive or negative) they can't really care about them. They might make over-the-top demonstrations of 'caring' behavior, when they have an audience, or if they stand to benefit in some way, but that's as far as it goes, and they can even appear to be cruelly callous at times. This inability to care about you (and the children you might share) will rear its ugly head if you split up, and the extent of it can leave you reeling in shock.

They can't truly love

Again, we have touched on this previously, but the point I want to emphasize here is that narcissists cannot really even love their children, which is absolutely vital to know in separation, when you are trying to decide how to split the time you each spend with the children. We look at the relationship narcissists have with their children in Chapter 7, but I wonder whether you've ever had suspicions about your partner's ability to love? Some narcissists even openly admit to their partner, as time wears on, that they 'can't love', or that they 'don't know how to love.' Remember how Oonagh gave her own limitations away (regarding her capacity to love) when she told Geoff that "you can't love a dog"?

They can't maintain deep, long-term friendships

The inability to be emotionally intimate with other people means that, although many narcissists might know a large number of people, their friendships tend to be superficial, and limited to mere acquaintances. They rarely have deep, long-term friendships, which are on an equal footing, because friends tend to drop away over time, as a result of the narcissist's emotional limitations, lack of empathy and tendency to view other people as two-dimensional objects. They may well have a fan club, often made up of subordinates however – but don't mistake this for true connection.

They can't cope with imperfection

Narcissists need the world to see them as perfect (and unique and special), so that *they* can see *themselves* that way. Some might also need their environment to be perfect, their work to be perfect, their outward appearance to be perfect, their children to be perfect and their colleagues to be perfect. Lina's fancy tea parties were a testimony to how, if she did anything public, she had to do it perfectly. Oonagh learned early on how to dress and do her make-up to present herself as flawless, and never had a hair out of place. Carefully curated images on social media are also often used by narcissists to present an image of the perfect life.

And, as you might already know from experience, narcissists also demand perfection from their partners and their children, who cannot help but disappoint them at times. To add to this, because narcissists don't see their children as being separate from them, their 'flaws' are felt deeply, as being flaws in *themselves*. Remember how Marcus couldn't deal with Janis having asthma? And how deeply disgusted Lina was with her daughter Laila's anorexia nervosa? These imperfections were utterly unacceptable to them. You can see why this might cause you problems if you share children with a narcissist, and are unable to protect them from their narcissistic parent's unrealistic standards, once you are divorced from them.

They can't genuinely feel happy for other people

Narcissists exist in a very hierarchical world, meaning that they compare themselves to other people constantly. If someone else has more of something they want (looks, power, status, money, success, a perfect marriage, clever children, to name a few) they are unable to be genuinely happy for that person, *because they feel that it detracts from their own success*. That is part of the reason why they devalue others, by shaming them, criticizing them and putting them down – so that they can feel better about themselves by comparison.

You can see why 'schadenfreude' (taking pleasure in other people's misfortunes) is a feature of narcissism – because if someone else *fails*, the narcissist automatically *succeeds*, boosting their own self-image, which, as you know, they so badly need to believe in. This doesn't bode well in trying to find a compromise in divorce – after all, to a narcissist there can only be one winner (and that had better be them).

Jealousy is a huge feature of narcissism as a result of this hierarchical thinking, and incredibly, narcissistic parents can even be jealous of their children. I recall a middle-aged narcissistic mother who was wildly jealous of her sixteen-year-old daughter for her youth, slim figure and her talents as a singer-songwriter. The irony was that *she* had pushed her child relentlessly to achieve musically, because she had never been able to gain fame in this area herself.

She would outwardly bask in the glory of her daughter's successes, taking the credit for them, to gain narcissistic supply. But in truth, she actually *resented* her daughter – because her *own* position in the hierarchy was pushed down by her daughter's achievements. At times, she tried desperately hard to compete with her, getting plastic surgery, dieting obsessively and making repeated attempts to find fame herself. At other times, she would resort to putting her daughter down, telling her that she was fat, ugly and of 'average musical ability'.

Causing much confusion, narcissists will also be jealous of their *partner's* successes – or at the very least, will downplay them, so that they don't have to actually *feel* their jealousy at being comparatively inferior. Remember how Oonagh reacted when Geoff was promoted, sabotaging the celebratory meal he had prepared, by deliberately not turning up for it? You can't expect a narcissist to cheerlead you, unless there is an outside audience, or you are in a love bombing phase.

Even narcissists who have achieved great things, who are rich, well-regarded in their field and powerful, will be jealous of seemingly the strangest things, which can seem quite bizarre at times. Do you recall how Oonagh was jealous of Geoff's relationship with their dog, because it seemed to favor him by always greeting him at the door, when he came home? Narcissistic parents are commonly even jealous of the other parent's relationships with their *own children*, and may even try to sabotage them.

When it comes to intimate relationships, a narcissist will *always* baselessly accuse their partner of having affairs, and will be intensely jealous of anyone who they feel might be able to take away their primary source of narcissistic supply. Partners often incorrectly perceive this jealousy to be 'love', and even feel flattered by it, but as you now know, nothing could be further from the truth. I wonder, how much does jealousy feature in your partner's behavior towards you?

Most narcissists also need to believe that other people are envious of *them*, as this bolsters their sense of superiority. You may recall how our Closet Narcissist, Lina, took pleasure in her belief that everyone attending her lavish children's parties was secretly jealous of her. And what about Jonathan, who was envious of another headmaster who regularly discussed education on the TV and radio? In order to cope with his jealousy, he convinced himself that this headmaster was actually jealous of *him* – projecting his own feelings onto another person so *he* didn't have to feel them.

They can't admit defeat

Narcissists need to see themselves as 'winners' to maintain their feelings of specialness and superiority. They can be openly competitive with others, even needing to beat their toddlers in games. They are usually terrible losers, and will often blame their failure on someone, or something, that is out of their control. Narcissists may also rewrite history if they lose, and even deny that it actually happened, even lying to others about the outcome of their divorce. I remember this happening to a client of mine, who had actually come out of her divorce with a reasonable outcome. Her narcissistic ex told everyone they knew that he had 'destroyed' her financially in court. She wasn't surprised, and told me with a resigned shrug, "Even when he loses, he wins."

Needing to win often plays out horribly in the divorce process, where a narcissist will feel the need to annihilate their spouse in order to come out on top. A word of advice: if you are trying to negotiate with a narcissist, and they don't get what they want, it is always best to at least *let them have the last word*. This way they can leave with their defensive shield partially intact. Otherwise, their lasting resentment is likely to cause episodes of rage, which will be directed at you, for *years* to come.

They can't feel most emotions deeply

A narcissist's emotions are often only superficial, and as a result they may come across as 'insincere'. Because they are shallowly held and not deeply felt, some narcissists also seem able to switch between their emotions disconcertingly quickly.

A narcissist who is upset with someone for a perceived misdemeanor is likely to act in a cruelly cold way towards them, to show their displeasure and punish them. But upon receiving a text message, or seeing something on TV, that same narcissist might quickly switch emotions and laugh heartily, as their victim, who is still suffering, looks on, confused as to how they were able to recover their spirits so quickly. Your narcissistic partner might go, from a huge row with you, straight to the pub, where they are able to banter with the other regulars, as if nothing untoward had happened with you, just moments before. Do you recognize this ability to quickly shift emotional gears in your partner?

It's probably the case that different narcissists actually feel their emotions to different degrees, some more than others. But with many, particularly the ones who aren't particularly theatrically gifted, it can seem as though they are just 'play-acting' their emotions, without feeling them at all. They may even over-act, making extreme facial gestures, such as inappropriately giant smiles, or sob loudly with suspiciously dry eyes.

Narcissists may also claim to be feeling a certain way which isn't congruent with how they actually outwardly appear. It's not uncommon for a narcissist to tell you that they are depressed, suicidal, grieving or stressed, whilst only momentarily appearing to look sad, if at all. This is a common ploy to try to suck you back into the relationship, if they suspect that you are thinking about leaving. Does this sound familiar to you?

As you will discover later on, in the early stages of divorce, narcissists ramp up their abusive behaviors towards their spouse, in order to scare them into not leaving them, and this may even escalate to physical abuse. You can be sure that when the police arrive, the narcissist, who has just been snarling at you, with their hands around your neck, will instantly be able to turn into a completely calm and rational-looking person, whilst you, shaken by the incident, look like the crazy one. This is a story that I have heard far too many times.

Of course, this works in reverse too – positive emotions can turn into negative ones, at the drop of a hat (as you will be only too familiar with, if you have been in a relationship with a narcissist).

They can't say 'sorry' and mean it

I don't think I have ever come across a narcissist who has apologized for their behaviors and actually meant it, and this a big red flag of a narcissistic relationship.

Narcissists *can't* accept blame, because that goes against the very point of what their narcissism is *for* – to protect them from feeling shame, worthlessness and inadequacy. If they do accept the blame for something, they risk feeling that shame – the intensely painful feeling of believing that one is flawed and unworthy of love.

Because narcissists rarely accept blame, they also rarely feel guilt, which often leads to them showing a distinct lack of remorse for their behaviors.

So how do narcissists *avoid* accepting blame for their behaviors and feeling shame? Firstly, they often *fool themselves* by denying, justifying or minimizing their behaviors. 'It didn't happen', 'it wasn't that bad' and 'they deserved it' are common narcissistic mantras.

It's also particularly interesting to watch a narcissist engage in the techniques of 'blame-shifting' and 'shame-dumping'. Here, with lightning speed, a narcissist will shift the blame onto someone else, or, in the case of shame-dumping, try

> *"Narcissists can't accept blame, because that goes against the very point of what their narcissism is **for** – to protect them from feeling shame, worthlessness and inadequacy"*

to shame the other person for behaviors that *they themselves* have perpetrated. When Marcus suffered the humiliation of being asked to leave the church band (because of his poor guitar skills) he blamed the luthier, who had handmade his expensive guitar for him, for 'making it wrong' – a classic case of blame-shifting.

Narcissists will blame others for everything, from the biggest disasters to the most inconsequential of events. When Oonagh spilt her wine by knocking it with her elbow, she was incensed with Geoff, who she blamed for it without even a moment's hesitation, even though he'd been careful to put it in its usual place. In reality, it really didn't matter whose fault it was – Oonagh simply couldn't accept culpability, even for this small mishap.

Of course, if your relationship is on the rocks, this will be entirely your fault, which is one reason why couples counseling is a pointless exercise with a narcissist. And during divorce, a narcissist will believe that their horrendous behaviors towards you are entirely justified, so they will never ever say sorry, and you will never be able to get closure in that sense. This is not an easy thing to come to terms with.

They can't be alone

This goes back to the fact that narcissists need to be continually receiving narcissistic supply. Remember that a narcissist stores their narcissistic supply in a metaphorical bucket with a hole in it – which means it *constantly* needs topping up.

Narcissists can only get their narcissistic supply from *other people*'s attention or adoration, from their emotional reactions to drama and conflict, and from their fear.

Of course, narcissistic supply can, these days, be easily gained from social media at any time of the day or night, so narcissists don't ever really need to be alone. Twitter, Facebook, Instagram, Snapchat, TikTok and the others serve as extensions to the narcissist's false persona. Carefully taken photographs, and accounts of their lifestyle and opinions can be shared with thousands of followers with minimal effort and, when comments and likes come flooding in, narcissistic supply is boosted nicely. Marcus, our Communal Narcissist, posts daily videos of himself sharing 'his insights', precisely for this reason.

Trolling people on social media is another great way to get supply from the comfort of your armchair, and I often wonder what proportion of trolls would actually qualify for a diagnosis of NPD. Propagating conspiracy theories is also a favored narcissistic pastime, with all the debate and attention that it generates.

Instant messaging and forwarding memes to others are also great ways to secure supply from people who aren't in the room, and dating apps are even better.

Narcissists often can't even do journeys alone, and often phone people to interact with when driving, or on the train. Like Marcus, many don't even want to watch TV on their own. Remember how he would make Irina feel obliged to sit with him, to watch programmes she didn't even like, just to get narcissistic supply from her being there?

The better a source of supply you are to a narcissist, the fewer extra sources they will need. But you would be very hard pushed indeed to find a narcissist living a completely isolated life, with no social media, and no opportunity to gain supply from even work colleagues.

But even with these various methods, narcissists still tend to need *actual people* for the really premium grade supply. I'm afraid they are rarely out of intimate relationships for long because of this, and so, if you do break up, you'll need to be prepared for them finding a new partner, as you are still grieving their loss. Remember, this is no reflection on you, and their new partner is simply an alternative source of their desperately needed narcissistic supply (hard though I know that is going to be to accept).

The things that narcissists are abnormally good at

Just as narcissists are severely *limited* in many ways by their brain wiring, there are things which they *can* do, practically effortlessly, to great effect. It's no coincidence that these 'narcissistic super skills', as I like to call them, are often what make narcissists such frightening adversaries in divorce. If you think your partner may be a narcissist, you'll definitely want to take note of these, because they will ramp up every one during your divorce, to dizzying levels.

Controlling others

This is a big feature in many narcissists, which is conspicuously missing from the DSM-5 diagnostic criteria for NPD. There are various areas in which different narcissists excel at being in control.

Many control the *people* around them, dictating how they spend their time, where they go, who they see, even what they eat. They can also be overly controlling when it comes to money, and demand receipts or check bank statements.

Narcissistic parents often control what activities their children do, what subjects they take at school, and even what career they choose. They might refuse to let them see certain friends, or not allow them to come to their home. One narcissistic mother I knew of wanted to know exactly what her teenage son was up to at all times, and insisted that he always kept the door to his room open, even whilst he slept. Marcus, our Communal Narcissist insisted that his stepson Janis play football, because it was *his* interest as a football coach, and Lina controlled what everyone in her family wore, even putting their clothes out ready for them the night before. She even felt she had the right to dictate how her 15-year-old daughter wore her hair, and was incensed when she sneakily went to the hairdresser, to have it chopped into a crop.

Remember how Jonathan insisted that Brigitte drove a hybrid car, but wouldn't let her turn the radio or heating on, because it would start using petrol, instead of electricity? Things got so bad that she stopped driving it completely, and just took the bus, which limited her freedom significantly. And what about how Oonagh refused to take her house keys out with her, so that Geoff would always have to be home before her, to let her into the house?

Narcissists also shine at putting their own stamp on special occasions, to subtly wield control. If not actually organizing the occasion, at the very least you can expect a degree of sabotage. Remember how Lina loved to organize other people's funerals, even if she barely knew them, but when she didn't organize Raj's 40th birthday party, she made him late for it, and hogged the attention by feigning being in pain? To spoil things further, she then refused to speak to him for days afterwards, accusing him of dancing inappropriately with a work colleague. Birthdays, Christmases, weddings and any special occasion can be ruined by any narcissist who needs to be in control.

Interestingly, some narcissists need to be in control so badly that they actually develop genuine fears (and even phobias) of things they can't control, such as a fear of heights, or of flying. Some are scared of driving, because they don't feel completely in control of the other motorists around them. They may try to stop driving altogether and make their partner do all the driving instead, as Lina did.

You can see how some of these examples of exerting control are quite subtle, particularly those that can be dressed up as 'helpfulness, or being in another person's 'best interests'. And if, you divorce a narcissist, you can be sure that they will attempt to control the whole process in every possible way. They'll refuse to move out, insist upon mediation, withhold your contact with the children, shift the goalposts when agreements have nearly been reached and cause as many delays as possible, to name just a few. You will need to be ready for this.

Lying

The truth to a narcissist is what they say it is, at the time they are saying it. They completely believe their own lies, and do not see truth as a fixed entity. They are especially good at lying because they are so practised at it – their whole false persona, which they hide behind and use as a shield, is an invention – a lie which they need to maintain 24/7.

When people eventually leave a narcissist's orbit, they often find themselves questioning everything the narcissist ever said to them (with good cause) – and the real truth about the lies that

> *"The truth to a narcissist is what they say it is, at the time they are saying it."*

they fell for can keep surfacing for years to come.

It is really important to mention smear campaigns here too. If a narcissist gets wind that you are about to leave them, they will begin this campaign against you, telling lies about you to important people. Your family, friends, work colleagues and potential employers will be told that you are an alcoholic, a stalker, a prostitute, an embezzler, an abuser, a plagiarizer and more, in utterly convincing tones, and you may well lose your support network (and even your job) at a time when you need them the most.

In divorce, a narcissist's ability to lie will be a big problem. Allegations of abuse against you are common, and can draw out court cases, and you can fully expect the narcissist to not be honest about their finances.

Interestingly, neither lying nor gaslighting, which I talk about next, are mentioned as diagnostic features in the DSM-5 – another glaring omission, in my view.

Gaslighting

Gaslighting is a key feature of narcissistic behavior, and it's quite a frightening method of draining you of your self-confidence and self-belief, to alter the power dynamic. The narcissist actually alters their victim's *reality*, so that they are unable to see things as they really are. Confused, they lose confidence and trust in themselves, *and they come to trust the narcissist instead*, which is how they gain even more power.

So what exactly is gaslighting? To give its proper definition, it's the 'act of undermining someone's reality, by denying facts, denying the environment around them, or denying their feelings.' But let me simplify that. Basically, if someone is lying to you in a way that makes you question or stop trusting your own perceptions, memories or beliefs, they are gaslighting you. Make no mistake – this really is a very dangerous form of psychological abuse.

Gaslighting versus lying

You may be wondering what the difference is between gaslighting and 'normal' lying, so here's an example to illustrate.

If we'd agreed to meet for dinner at 7pm, but I'd left the house late because I just couldn't get my act together, I could lie to you and tell you that the traffic had been awful, and that that was why I didn't arrive until 8pm. Here I'm not making you question or doubt yourself – I'm just telling you a lie.

But, if I was gaslighting you, I could tell you with absolute conviction that *you* had got the time wrong, and that we had agreed to meet at 8pm. I might then embellish that further by telling you that I'd noticed that you seemed to be forgetting small things, and 'losing your thread' in conversations. I could even then ask you whether you'd considered talking to a doctor about it.

It's gaslighting *because it would make you question yourself*, and make you doubt whether you had got the time right, or whether you are, in fact, making mistakes and forgetting things. Gaslighting is itself a two-step procedure – first you are made to think that your thinking or feelings are distorted, and then the

> *"If someone is lying to you in a way that makes you question or stop trusting your own perceptions, memories or beliefs, they are gaslighting you."*

gaslighter tries to persuade you that *their* ideas are the true and right ones.

The term gaslighting originated from a 1938 thriller in which a husband makes his wife think she is 'going mad' by dimming the gas lamps in their home to just a flicker, and then denying that they are flickering when she questions him.

Gaslighting your memories

One of the most common forms of gaslighting is when a narcissist denies a person's *memory* of events, by saying something along the lines of "That didn't happen". This is incredibly common, and narcissists are known for rewriting history, completely denying that things have happened. They might say "I never said that – actually what I said was this…" Or "I never did that – actually what I did was this…" During a break-up, when gaslighting is likely to become even more prominent, it's common to find yourself wanting to record every conversation you have with your narcissistic partner, to prove what was said.

A client of mine told me that her narcissistic ex would make himself a cup of tea in front of her, and then tell her, with absolute conviction, that it was actually coffee he was drinking, and that she had remembered it wrong. After years of this, she began to doubt herself – although, after she eventually left, she came to understand how bizarre this behavior had been.

Gaslighting your feelings

So how can gaslighting be applied to a person's *feelings*? Anyone who has had a relationship with a narcissist will be familiar with expressing their emotions to them, only to have them trivialized, minimized or invalidated.

Imagine the scenario where a male narcissist has been caught in a compromising position, perhaps with a prostitute, perhaps on an office night out.

Quite justly, their partner will feel betrayed and upset – but a narcissist might tell them that *all* the men who work in his office regularly do this, and that it is normal. They might tell their partner that they are 'thinking about it incorrectly', and that they are *not* actually being unfaithful, because they are paying for the service. They might assert that, in truth, they are helping someone in need (the prostitute) to pay their bills and make their way in life, and that this should be seen as a 'good thing'. They may tell their partner that using prostitutes has no bearing at all on how they feel about *their* relationship, and the two things are completely separate. They may even try to make their partner feel guilty, perhaps suggesting that *they* are a bad person for not allowing the narcissist to help the prostitute to do her job, to keep her family in food. They may accuse their partner of intruding on their private life, or they may blame them for needing to visit prostitutes in the first place, because they always seem too tired to service their needs themselves. A narcissist might even demand an *apology* – and if the victim has been gaslit enough, for long enough, they may actually *feel guilty* and do just this – apologize, even though, in their heart of hearts, they know they have done nothing wrong.

Do you remember how, when Geoff's dog was put to sleep, Oonagh tried to tell him that his feelings of grief were wrong, because 'you can't love a dog'? Classic gaslighting.

Do you recall how Marcus invalidated Irina's distress about how he had made Janis wait in the car for an hour, with a broken leg, without painkillers? "The body is a miracle of God," he had gaslit her "It produces *natural* painkillers, and heals itself…"

Gaslighting often happens in conjunction with other narcissistic behaviors as well, such as 'projection', which we will look at separately.

What effect does gaslighting have on the victim?

As with other abusive behaviors, the narcissist turns up the volume on their gaslighting so slowly that the victim barely notices. It's not hard to understand why, in a relationship that has gone on for years, the victim actually *believes* what the narcissist is telling them – even though anyone looking in from the outside would find the narcissist's assertions utterly ludicrous.

I'm reminded at this point of the true story of the famous opera singer, whose narcissistic partner eroded her beliefs and thinking about herself and the world so much, that she actually came to believe that she couldn't sing. Even though the whole world celebrated her ability, the narcissist had managed to get her to question herself. The years of gaslighting had led her to accept what he was telling her as reality.

And that is actually one of the major points of gaslighting – it enables the narcissist to get you to doubt yourself so much that you start to rely on them – *they become your 'voice of reason'*. That means that you might start wearing what *they* tell you to, rather than what *you* think looks good. It means you might not be able to make decisions, even little ones, without their input. It means that you might become quiet in social situations, because you have been gaslit into believing that people find you irritating or boring, or that you talk too much. The ramifications are really quite varied but, ultimately, if the narcissist can undermine you and deplete your reserves of self-confidence and self-belief, you will be too weak to leave them, and so will remain a ready source of narcissistic supply, just as they want.

"Effective gaslighting has the effect of making the victim dependent on the narcissist's opinions, memories and versions of the truth."

Some red flags of gaslighting to look out for:

The more of the following that resonate with you, the more likely it is that you have been gaslit by your partner

- Do they try to persuade you to doubt the evidence of your senses, or your thoughts, or your feelings?

- Do they never accept that you have a different opinion to them – and so never stop trying to persuade you that you are wrong?

- Do they, when they are called out on something, use flawed logic to turn the tables on you, making out that you are at fault and that *they* are actually the victim, or the hero?

- Do you find yourself relying on them to make decisions for you, micromanage you, or to tell you how to behave, or what to wear?
- Do you find yourself apologizing and feeling guilty for things that you have been accused of, that you know, deep down, you haven't done?
- Do you feel more and more confused, to the point where you feel as though you might be going crazy?
- Have you stopped expressing your emotions to them because you know that your feelings will always be 'wrong', according to them?
- Is there is a big imbalance of power between you and your partner?

True narcissists will continue to gaslight you (and everyone else) in the divorce process. They will claim that your memory is at fault and that they provided information to you that they didn't, and they will rewrite history. They will even gaslight the court, often through documentation, claiming that what they have provided is evidence of something that it actually isn't (eg. a job application as 'evidence' of a job contract, or a completely normal X-ray report as evidence of a 'disability'. Lawyers and judges, pressed for time, and unaware of what to look for, often fail to pick up on these.

Projection

Projection is a psychological defense mechanism that *all* people use. It's completely unconscious, and it enables the person to 'give away' their shame and guilt to someone else, for the behaviors, inadequacies and feelings which they can't accept as their own. Narcissists project with ease.

Essentially, in projection, the narcissist accuses you of doing or being what *they* are doing or being, but they do it *unconsciously* – in this way, you could view it as an unconscious form of gaslighting. Although everyone projects to some degree, to protect themselves, narcissists do it astoundingly commonly.

I remember a client of mine telling me that her husband, in a narcissistic rage, was repeatedly punching the wall, whilst screaming at her that it was *her* who was 'breaking his hand'. Here he was trying to project the blame onto her.

Narcissists will often accuse their victims of being bullies and abusers and, stunningly, they will also accuse them of *actually being narcissists*. I estimate that around ten percent of the people who consult with me are actually the narcissist themselves, projecting their own narcissism onto another person. Don't be surprised if this accusation is levied at you by your narcissistic partner – this really is a dead giveaway.

The classic projection is the false accusation from a partner that you are having an affair. They are handing the guilt and shame of their own affair, or fantasies about it, on to you, so that they don't have to feel it. But if you have been in that relationship for a long time, and have been gaslit enough, you may actually start to believe that the narcissist is right, and that you must be having an affair, just like they say. This is known as 'projective identification' – you actually come to believe the thing that is projected on to you. You can see why people in narcissistic relationships often feel as if they are 'crazy'.

And if you do leave a relationship with a narcissist, you can expect the projections to increase. "You are mentally unravelling," "You need serious help," "You can't cope," "You are stealing from me," "You want to abduct the children". All of these are projections, and are highly informative as to what the narcissist is up to, or how they are feeling. In divorce, these projections often appear in legal documentation as accusations against you, which you could feel you have to defend through expensive lawyers.

Toxic positivity

Toxic positivity can also be thought of as a subtle form of gaslighting. Many narcissists (when it suits them) will paint a picture of the perfect life. They will tell others that their home lives are idyllic and that their jobs are everything they could have hoped for. Whilst this might sound like quite an admirable attitude to have, the problem with it is that everyone involved will have to play along. And if you are the partner or child of a narcissist, this will include you.

This means that you will not be allowed to express anything other than *positive* emotions, regardless of how you are really feeling. Disappointment, worry, anxiety, frustration, anger, sadness and even grief will be invalidated by the narcissist, who will give you a multitude of reasons why you should not be feeling the way you are, and dictate how you *should* actually be feeling.

It's not hard to see how this can have the effect of making you feel as though your negative emotions are 'wrong'. Often, if you do dare to express them, the narcissist will feel personally criticized, and will berate you for your churlish and ungrateful attitude. The message from narcissists who do this is clear – you will be positive and upbeat at all times. Remember, you are simply a two-dimensional object – an 'it'– who exists to serve the narcissist – and 'killing the narcissist's vibe' will simply not be acceptable.

Even as a very little boy, Janis, who was crying when he hurt his finger, instantly stopped, as soon as he heard Marcus coming through the front door. Hurriedly wiping away his tears, he said to Irina, "Quick Mummy – act happy – Daddy's home." You might remember how Marcus also used toxic positivity when he left Janis waiting for an hour in the car with a broken leg, with no painkillers. He later invalidated Irina's outrage by claiming "The body is a miracle of God…It produces *natural* painkillers, and heals itself…"

Narcissistic pseudo-logic and word salad

You have already learnt how very convincing narcissists can be, and how excellent their gaslighting and lying skills are, as a result. But a particularly fascinating facet of this is what I call 'narcissistic pseudo-logic'. Even those narcissists who don't have high IQs can employ a tone and manner which give the impression of great intelligence and speed of thought. They will throw what sound (on the surface) like reasoned arguments into the mix, which most people won't question in the moment. But if their listeners were to play back recordings of the narcissist, they'd probably be quite shocked at how little sense they actually make. This is narcissistic pseudo-logic at play – a narcissist's rationalizations and explanations as to why one plus one doesn't make two/why the earth is flat/why there is 'no such thing as global warming' may pour forth with great fluency and conviction, but the logic behind their assertions will be stunningly flawed.

Think back to Irina's concerns about Marcus's spending, and the size of his ever-expanding designer trainer collection. Remember how Marcus justified it with great conviction? "They are an important part of my cultural identity as a black man," he had told her. She came away confused, and feeling as though she was somehow being racist. This was narcissistic pseudo-logic. Marcus's assertions, if you examine them, made no sense, but they did what they were supposed to do – cause Irina to question herself, and accept his version of reality.

The loose associations and odd conclusions you see when a narcissist is using pseudo-logic become even more pronounced if the narcissist has experienced a profound drop in narcissistic supply. In divorce and separation, it is really common for the narcissist's style of communication to descend into what is known as narcissistic 'word salad', because of this. Here the narcissist makes even less sense than before. They will speak at great speed, contradicting themselves from one minute to the next, making ranting, accusatory assertions about you. They will project their own feelings and behaviors on to you, go round and round in circles, blatantly re-write history, and deny saying things that they said just moments beforehand.

Most people who are in the final breakdown phase of a relationship with a narcissist will find themselves recording their conversations with them, to try to reassure themselves that they are not losing their minds. Thankfully, narcissistic pseudo-logic and word salad are much more obvious in the written form, such as in text messages and emails. In divorce, you can even expect to find them in your narcissistic partner's lawyer's letters to you (as their lawyer will often just follow their instructions to copy and paste their nonsensical assertions into their legal letters).

I am reminded of one of my clients who, upon leaving her narcissistic husband, was receiving messages from him in full meltdown. At one point he was accusing her of 'not letting him into the marital home' – but he was actually sending the texts from the comfort of the marital bed, which he was occupying at the time. You can see how, if you don't know that you are simply dealing with word salad, you could find yourself utterly confused, and even wondering whether you (or your partner) are 'going mad'.

Boundary trampling

Narcissists don't like the word 'no' and will tend to bulldoze over anyone who tries to exert a boundary, either by completely ignoring it or trying to persuade the person that what they want is 'wrong'. They may ignore physical boundaries, by encroaching on your space or taking food off your plate, or waking you up in the middle of the night because they can't sleep and want to chat. They might borrow your things without asking, or use them even when you have requested that they don't. Snooping on other people's computers is another common violation of privacy.

Social boundaries can be violated in many ways, such through making excessive eye contact with victims, or not leaving your friend's dinner party until 3am, in spite of their yawns and hints. They may also make socially inappropriate comments in social settings, or be excessively nosey about people's lives. Sexual boundaries are also commonly overstepped, as are boundaries to do with time. Narcissistic bosses, for example, will often expect their subordinates to answer their emails at the weekend, or work late without warning.

I recall the story of a narcissistic ex-wife who was caught on webcam, letting herself into his apartment, using the key he had given his daughter. He was shocked to see her rifling through his new partner's wardrobe and underwear drawer, and going through his desk papers, particularly as they had been divorced for four years. I've even heard of a narcissist who, when his neighbor went on holiday, climbed a ladder and prised open an upstairs window, which had been left open just a crack, just to have a look around the house.

Narcissists find it even easier to violate their children's boundaries, which can become problematic as they get older. They might read their diaries, go through their phones, and barge into their rooms without knocking, and they often subject any boyfriends and girlfriends to inappropriate and embarrassing questioning.

Narcissists are inherently selfish – only *their* needs and wants matter, and they will scale any boundary you put up if they want to get to the other side, irrespective of your feelings. What examples of boundary violations can you call to mind, regarding your partner?

As you now know, in divorce narcissistic behaviors tend to become even more extreme – so you'll need to be prepared for this. Your ex, who is supposed to have moved out of the house, is likely to come and go without warning. They might remove items belonging to you, look through your divorce paperwork, or even cyberstalk you. One client of mine returned home from work to find workmen in her loft, installing cameras throughout the house. Incredibly, neither her lawyers nor the police could do anything about it, as the house was in her husband's name.

Triangulation

Triangulation is where the narcissist brings a third person into the dynamic, either to make their victim feel jealous or insecure, or to fulfil some other function. Narcissists naturally triangulate without shame, guilt or remorse, with impressive skill.

Narcissists can triangulate anyone with anyone else. You can be triangulated with a narcissist's family members, work colleagues, or even with their favorite movie star. Remember how Oonagh greatly enjoyed flirting with Geoff's boss at his work Christmas dinner in front of him, as he watched on, ashamed and embarrassed?

If you happen to have more than one child with a narcissist, you may recognize that they triangulate your children against each other. We'll look at this in more detail in Chapter 7, but briefly, one child will be the golden child (who can do no wrong), one will be the scapegoat (who can do no right) and, if there is a third child, they will be the invisible child, who is completely ignored. All the children will want the approval and love of the narcissistic parent, and will jump through hoops to get it, sometimes even turning on each other. This is a wonderful way for the narcissist to gain narcissistic supply, and they can be warm and loving towards the golden child, whilst at the same time being cold, critical and demeaning towards the other children.

Do you recall how Arun was Lina's golden child, praised for everything he did, whilst daughter Laila was constantly shamed, put down and criticized?

Narcissists often like to switch things up in this family dynamic, by reassigning the roles to different children, without warning. The golden child suddenly becomes invisible, and so on. This is the ultimate in control and power, and the instability of the children's roles is an excellent way to keep them on their toes. Is this something you have recognized in your partner's relationship with the children?

This brings me on to another variation of triangulation, The Drama Triangle. There are three players – The Victim, The Persecutor, and the Rescuer, but their roles are not static (the victim or rescuer may become the perpetrator, for example), but at all times the three roles have to be filled. This means that if one person changes role, the others are forced to change too, usually with no idea of what is happening.

Narcissists love the drama triangle. They use it at work, in friendships and in family dynamics, playing people off against each other. The sense of control and power they gain, together with the conflict and drama it creates, are wonderful sources of narcissistic supply.

In relationship breakdown and divorce narcissists use it in in a variety of ways. In couples therapy they cast themselves as the victim, so the couples therapist tries to rescue them, unwittingly actually becoming the persecutor of their spouse. Does this sound familiar to you, if you have tried couples therapy? The same can happen in face-to-face mediation, during your divorce. Narcissists might also enlist well-meaning, but ignorant, family members or friends to try to 'talk some sense into you' during your divorce, triangulating them so that they become inadvertent instruments of the narcissist's abuse.

Playing the victim

This key narcissistic behavior, disappointingly, is another one that is not mentioned in the DSM-5. Narcissists deploy this form of manipulation with pinpoint accuracy, whenever required.

The Closet Narcissists, like Lina, play the victim all the time, but the other types of narcissist will wheel out this tactic when required too, often if they are called out on their bad behaviors, or if someone threatens to leave them.

Marcus, who was of mixed race, constantly used this fact to his advantage, implying that others (even his wife, Irina) were being racist, when things didn't go his way. Racism will also commonly be alleged by a narcissist who has been reprimanded or sacked in the workplace, as will accusations of bullying. Narcissists will also frequently allege that they had physical or mental health issues which were unsupported by their employers, and they'll happily make formal complaints (which can escalate all the way to court). Has your partner ever made complaints of this nature about their employer?

Issues with physical health will be exaggerated, or completely made up by narcissists when required, with claims of incapacitating pain, immobility, or any other health condition that works to secure them what they need – a common way to pretend that they can't work, when it comes to the financial side of divorce.

Another scarily common tactic used in divorce by narcissists is the claim that they are victims of domestic violence, and the police may even be duped into arresting their partner, especially if they are male. The 'DARVO' acronym is relevant here – if you've ever accused a narcissist of anything, you will have noticed that they will Deny, Attack and Reverse the true Victim with the true Offender.

Mothers are also often accused by narcissistic fathers of perpetrating 'parental alienation' (claiming that the children are being turned against them). Because narcissists play the victim with aplomb, they can be highly convincing to judges and social workers, and the non-narcissistic parent can even lose the children as a result. This is the level to which a true narcissist will sink to punish their ex for leaving them. You may think that perhaps I am scaremongering here. I can assure you that I am not.

Projecting a convincing outward image

By now you know that narcissists are highly practiced at projecting an outward image to the world, to act as an armor to hide behind, to stay feeling emotionally safe. You understand that how they appear to other people desperately matters – because those people's belief in this image keeps it strong enough to shield them from their own low self-esteem. They are therefore proficient at acquiring *things* that feed into that image, whether it's expensive things to show their wealth, things that make them look powerful, things that make them look clever or sexy – or whatever else they need to prove that they are who they are claiming to be.

Many narcissists are also adept at superficially appearing *cleverer* than they actually are, and so many people are fooled into believing that they are particularly intelligent as a result. It's a well known fact that tall men reach higher positions of power than shorter men, and earn more than them, because of the positive biases people apply to them – but I suspect this is also true for narcissists. I'm sure some narcissists, particularly the Exhibitionist Narcissists achieve greatness, which is out of proportion to their abilities, because of how they are perceived. Could this be true for your partner?

In divorce, this ability to project a convincing outward image can be disastrous in court. If they can maintain their image on the witness stand (usually as a 'victim' of your abuse towards them, or as someone who has falsely been accused of abusing you), then things can go very badly wrong for you. Not all narcissists do manage this, however, and there is always a possibility that they reveal themselves in court, by flying into a rage or being unable to explain away their lies.

The ability to ignore rules and laws

Narcissists are perfectly *capable* of following rules and being law abiding citizens when it suits them, but, in reality, they don't believe that the rules and laws apply to them, and so find them supremely easy to ignore. Rules are for other people, people who are less important than them.

So how does this play out? The most bizarre ways seem to relate to the laws of nature. Some really extreme narcissists behave as if they can defy the laws of physics, for example. These are the narcissists that drive at high speeds around blind corners, or literally take off in cars or on motorbikes, terrifying their passengers. They even drive through rivers – the ex-wife of a particularly grandiose narcissist once told me how her husband had done this, with a car full of pleading passengers, just to prove that he could. She said that he seemed utterly perplexed when the car did not make it through the river and had to be towed out, as if he had expected the waters to part for him.

> "Narcissists always lie under oath, because the oath is completely meaningless to them..."

The laws of biology also seem to be commonly disregarded by narcissists. It's a known fact that a person who has had to undergo multiple abortions whilst in a relationship might actually be a victim of abuse. Male narcissists often refuse to use contraception, with no regard for the biological consequences on their victim, also violating boundaries and showing a distinct lack of empathy, in one fell swoop.

Relatively minor rules are often disregarded too, such as 'no entry' or 'private' signs. I recall a client whose first date with the narcissist she eventually married (and then divorced) involved him climbing the wall of a beautiful private garden, and letting her into it. It had seemed fun and romantic at the time, but actually, it was a big red flag.

It is also surprisingly common for a narcissist to coerce their spouse into taking the blame for their speeding tickets, so that they do not lose their driver's license – which is illegal here in the UK. Illegal drug use is also common in narcissists, with cocaine as a particular favorite, on account of its ability to boost feelings of omnipotence and grandiosity.

Self-employed narcissists, and those who run small companies, are often tax evaders. They may flout employment law when it comes to their employees, sacking them if they get pregnant, for example.

Narcissists also have fluctuating morals – after all, these are just another type of 'rule' that they can bend to their own advantage. They may well loudly and publicly apply high moral standards to others, but not to themselves. Have you noticed this type of moral hypocrisy in your partner?

Narcissists have a big advantage when it comes to being able to disregard rules and laws – they can avoid feeling guilt and shame, and have limited capacity for remorse – no wonder it's easy for them to construct their own, ever-shifting, rulebook. Looking back on your relationship, do you recognize this feature?

In divorce, this trait often has disastrous consequences for their family and ex. Narcissists usually ignore court orders (mostly getting away with it) and rarely give a true picture of their finances. Narcissists always lie under oath, because the oath is completely meaningless to them, and they sign statements of truth which they know are untrue, because of their total lack of respect for the law. Am I exaggerating here? Sadly not – and staggeringly, the family justice system, certainly here in the UK, delivers no punishment for lying.

Giving unsolicited advice

Narcissists are highly skilled at giving advice, especially if you haven't asked for it. You can expect to be told to your face what you should want, what you should have, what you should be, how you should do things and what you are doing wrong. Narcissists usually do not feel that they need experience of a situation to be able to advise on it. It can present a bit like 'mansplaining,' but female narcissists are equally prone to it.

Narcissists who are not parents will tell you where you are going wrong with your children, and narcissists who have never worked a day in their lives will tell you how to manage your boss.

Closet Narcissists may do things slightly differently. They may hide their opinions about how you are living your life from you, but instead criticize you to other people, behind your back (often under the guise of 'worrying about you'). They often enlist other people to pass on their opinions to you, sneakily triangulating them with you.

You might also have noticed, if your partner is a 'real' narcissist, that their opinions don't always seem fixed, or grounded in any real values or beliefs. They often change them at the drop of the hat, and many narcissists relish playing the rather exhausting game of 'devil's advocate', taking the opposite view to whatever is currently being expressed.

In divorce, your narcissistic ex will advise you that you don't need a lawyer, and that the two of you should be able to sort things out between you. If that doesn't work, they will advise you to attend mediation with them. They will advise you that your lawyer isn't very good, so that you start to lose confidence in them, and will make various suggestions as to how you should divide your time with the children, and split the finances. They'll sound calm and reasonable at these times, and you may even be tempted to believe them. After all, you don't want to be giving all your money to the lawyers, as they rightly say. Unfortunately, narcissists are never going to be fair, and they'll never consider your needs to be equal to theirs.

Behaving in an entitled way

Most people would cringe just at the *thought* of behaving as flagrantly as narcissists do in this regard. Narcissists feel absolutely *entitled* to use and manipulate other people. They feel entitled to be late for people. They feel entitled to special treatment. They feel entitled to take the credit for other people's work. They feel entitled to not have to pull their weight, at work, at home or anywhere else, if they don't feel like it, or if it doesn't bring in narcissistic supply. They feel entitled to violate other people's boundaries. They feel entitled to spend other people's money, to be rude to them and to upset them. They feel entitled to lie, cheat and steal if they feel like it. They feel entitled to your undivided attention and your lifelong loyalty. They feel entitled to complete transparency from you, but total privacy for themselves. They feel entitled to be hypocritical. They feel entitled to be utterly selfish in the way they approach everything.

Another big area where this shows up is in wills. Narcissists may challenge wills that they didn't benefit from, or try to convince elderly parents to change their wills to favor them. It's also really common for adult narcissists to extort money from their aging parents for years before their deaths, without their other siblings' knowledge. Has your partner behaved in this way, to your knowledge?

The Closet Narcissists can hide their sense of entitlement under a veneer of 'niceness' and shyness. They get what they feel they are entitled to in sneakier ways than the other types of narcissist. For example, they may believe that they should be first to board the airplane, and so feign a disability, so that they are driven in an airport buggy to the boarding gate, rather than loudly making demands at the check-in desk.

In divorce, narcissists believe that they are entitled to all the money, and that their spouse is entitled to nothing. This classically wreaks havoc in the divorce process, as they hide and spend the marital pot of money. They also feel that they are entitled to punish their former spouse to the point of near annihilation, in any way they so choose, nicely topping themselves up with premium narcissistic supply in the process. They may even feel that only they are entitled to spend time with the children, and try to prevent contact with the other parent. This sense of entitlement becomes a huge issue when trying to negotiate fairly with them, and cases often end up in court. In the UK, around 5% of all divorces reach a final hearing in court, because agreement could not be reached beforehand. According to many lawyers, it's probably not unreasonable to estimate that at least 50% of these involve a narcissist.

Exploitation

I briefly mentioned this core feature of NPD in Chapter 1, but it deserves another look here. It's a doddle for narcissists to shamelessly exploit others, partially because they don't view them as actual three-dimensional people. They see others merely as objects – 'its' – over whom they have a permanent sense of ownership – and this is particularly noticeable for those close to them. The people who revolve around them are there to be used in whatever way best suits the narcissist – it doesn't really occur to them that other people think differently. It's a sort of vampiric relationship in this way.

So narcissists exploit everyone to some degree, with the ultimate aim of securing narcissistic supply, whether directly, or indirectly. For example, they might have chosen to be friends with someone because they are particularly attractive looking, and so are good to be seen with, leading to indirect supply from the admiring glances of others. Perhaps they have chosen friends because of their social network or contacts, which can get them into the best restaurants – so making them feel special and important. Perhaps they hired their secretary because she gazes at them adoringly, or hangs upon their every word, so giving them narcissistic supply in this direct form. Narcissists, particularly of the exhibitionist variety, can be experts at making the people they hang out with think that they are their best friend, when actually they have no genuine feelings for them at all. You may well recognize this in your partner.

Taking credit for other people's work is another big feature of exploitation. Remember how Marcus pretended his pastor's sermons and obscure poems were *his* original content, in his videos? It is highly likely that, if your partner is a narcissist, they have a reputation for workplace exploitation of this nature.

Even children will be exploited by a narcissistic parent as a way to secure narcissistic supply – Lina's children were a way for her to gain narcissistic supply from others by throwing spectacular birthday parties for them, which were the envy of the other mothers. And Janis was simply a tool for Communal Narcissist Marcus to publicly play the role of doting stepdad to the outside world, securing praise and admiration from everyone around.

Partners will be exploited and taken advantage of in all manner of ways too, including financial exploitation and even sexual exploitation. I'm sure you can see why a divorce would present a narcissist with even more opportunities to exploit others, including by using your children as weapons against you, which we will look at in Chapter 7.

Passive aggression

There are many ways in which a narcissist can employ this tactic, and the beauty of it is that it's often about '*not* doing something'

> *"Stonewalling is commonly employed in the divorce process..."*

– which makes it quite subtle and hard to pinpoint. The silent treatment is the classic example of passive aggression – when, hurt and confused, you ask the narcissist why they are not speaking to you, they can simply tell you that they *are*.

Stonewalling is another passive aggressive tactic – narcissists will often simply refuse to respond to issues you bring up, or deliberately appear to misunderstand the issue, and respond to that instead. Stonewalling is commonly employed in the divorce process, and narcissists will often enlist their lawyers to adopt this approach towards you, by simply refusing to engage. It causes delay, increases your frustration, and runs up your legal costs, as your lawyer haplessly writes to their lawyer to demand responses. If your lawyer doesn't know what they are dealing with, they will often make the mistake of imposing a deadline by which the narcissist must respond, inadvertently handing themsomething they can ignore, which hands *them* the control and power – the very stuff of narcissistic supply.

Backhanded compliments are also passively aggressive – Jonathan's devaluation of Brigitte during his wedding speech, when he cheerfully announced that she had 'scrubbed up well' for her big day, was such an example.

Putting people down

It stands to reason that it's pretty difficult to put a person down to their face, if you care about their feelings. But, of course, narcissists don't – which is why they excel in this area.

NARCISSISTS IN DIVORCE: FROM LOVE-LOCKED TO LEAVING

We've already talked about the ways in which narcissists will devalue others, to weaken them so that they cannot escape the relationship. They also put people down in order to elevate themselves within their own hierarchy of importance, so that they feel better about themselves. You also know about how they intersperse these devaluations with idealizations to cause trauma bonding, which make their victims addicted to them.

Even children are subjected to these devaluations, with criticisms, ridicule, and name calling. They can expect to be body-shamed by their narcissistic parent and called too weedy, or too fat. The Closet Narcissist might be less obvious about this, but may come across as the ever-giving parent, whose child disappoints them over and over, no matter how hard they try. This is simply a more covert way of making the child feel 'not good enough', and a failure.

Narcissists always devalue people behind their backs too – a very big warning sign. I recall meeting a vicar at a party, who, drunk, didn't hold back with his criticisms of people he disliked at all. He already had a reputation in the parish for being attention seeking and for hogging the limelight – he'd deliver sermons that went on forever, with anecdote after anecdote, and sing solos during hymns. He was also known for being a bit of a control freak in his role on the parish council. It is thought that there is a relatively high proportion of Communal Narcissists in the clergy, and I suspect that this chap may well fit the bill.

If your partner puts you down, and you repeatedly suffer from a sinking heart when they do (even if they tell you that are 'only joking'), take note.

Of course, just as with all narcissistic behaviors, divorce will make a narcissist devalue their ex even more. Expect to be called 'lazy' in court as they try to justify why they shouldn't have to support you financially whilst you try to get a better job. Expect to be called the worst parent – neglectful, cruel and unsupportive, so they get more time with the children (for appearances sake, so they don't have to pay you child support and so that they can hurt you where it hurts the most). Expect to be called every name under the sun, to your face and behind your back, and expect to be openly jeered at and ridiculed, maybe even in front of the children.

Manipulation

It's probably pretty obvious from everything you have read so far that narcissists are excellent manipulators. They have learned to manipulate at an early age, and so do it completely unconsciously and effortlessly, because it is second nature to them. Even these narcissists are likely to be at least five steps ahead of any non-narcissist. However, some narcissists are also able to *consciously* manipulate, making them all the more difficult to manage. Trying to out-manipulate a narcissist can be like trying to play three-dimensional chess wearing a blindfold, with heavy metal music blaring straight into your brain, so you can't think straight. This becomes even more difficult in the divorce process, when the narcissist will be able to run rings around your lawyer, if they have no idea what is coming next, because they don't even recognize that your ex *is* a narcissist. How

> *"Most narcissists do not plot and scheme late into the dead of night – their manipulations are effortless"*

good is your partner at manipulating others? What examples of this spring to mind?

Do narcissists know that they are narcissists?

I think we have reached a good point to tackle this important question, because many people believe that all narcissists 'know exactly what they are doing'. But in fact, the vast majority of narcissists do not actually know that they are narcissists. The occasional chest thumping braggart of an Exhibitionist Narcissist may know that they are a narcissist (because they have repeatedly been told that they are) but, to them, this is actually something to be *proud of*, as it works to their advantage.

Whilst narcissists may know *what* they are doing to some extent, the vast majority don't know *why* they are doing it — they are unaware of the subconscious programming that is driving their behaviors. Contrary to popular belief, most narcissists do not plot and scheme late into the dead of night — their manipulations are effortless. However, a minority most certainly do consciously manipulate — and these are the really frightening ones. The behaviors described in this book are merely a description of the narcissist's operating manual — which most narcissists don't even know exists.

I conclude this chapter with a summary list of narcissistic traits and behaviors. You might find this useful to refer to in the coming months (or even years), regardless of what conclusions you have drawn about your partner's personality — because, as you will doubtless discover, narcissists are actually *everywhere*.

Summary Table of Narcissistic Traits and Behaviors
Low empathy
Inability to truly care about others
Sense of entitlement
Exploiting others
Love bombing in initial stage
Cycles of devaluations and ations ('nice/nasty narcissist')
Need for attention/adoration/drama/conflict/to scare others
Invalidating other people's feelings, beliefs, successes
Inability to take the blame/blame-shifting
Shame-dumping
Projection
Inability to see people as a blend of good and bad ('hero to zero')
Selfishness
Gaslighting and lying
Jealousy
A preoccupation with outward image
Manipulativeness
Triangulation
A need to be in control
Playing the victim
'DARVO' Deny, Attack, Reverse the Victim with the Offender

Summary Table of Narcissistic Traits and Behaviors
A need for perfection
Violating boundaries
Flouting rules and laws
Moral hypocrisy
Highly sensitive to criticism
Tantrums
Rage
Aggression (and passive aggression)
Silent treatments
Stonewalling (completely ignoring you or your communications)
Narcissistic pseudo-logic and word salad
Schadenfreude (taking pleasure in others' misfortunes)
Need to win/have the last word
Needing to appear clever
'Knowing best'
Superficial, easily changeable emotions
Only conditional/transactional love
Difficulty being alone
Lack of deep, long-term friendships
Seeing their children as extensions of themselves
Future faking

4

Let's talk about you

So now you are aware of all the behaviors that are the hallmarks of NPD, and we have also touched upon how those behaviors will increase during separation, divorce and often beyond. I'm sure you are now in no doubt as to why it is so important to know if your partner really is a true narcissist (someone who would qualify for a diagnosis of NPD).

I know only too well that I have presented you with a huge amount of information, and that can be overwhelming, but even so, if your partner is not a narcissist, by now it is likely that you will know that, and this may be the juncture at which we part company (unless you want to find out more). Although a *few* of the behaviors will have been recognizable in your partner (which would be *normal* to find – because, as I've mentioned previously, NPD is simply the presence of extreme variations of *normal* personality traits), you wouldn't have been emphatically nodding at *most* of the behaviors described.

But if many the features of NPD in the previous chapter *have* been resonating with you, I know you will have been experiencing a number of powerful emotions.

I understand how painful this process can be, and how it is far from just a quick tickbox exercise. This is not a linear process. At times you will be sideswiped by grief. You may find yourself paralyzed by shock, as the realizations dawn. You might be hit with memories at the most inopportune times, and you will have to hold back tears until you can get to a private place. You may struggle to focus at work, and start to obsess. You may wake in the night, and find it difficult to get back to sleep, as the thoughts (and doubts) swirl around in your head.

If your partner is a narcissist, your brain will have been complicit in shielding you from seeing the behaviors for what they are. Unfortunately, that's what our brains do, to protect us. As you prise open the lid of NPD, and peer in, the brain stops hiding the information you are looking for from you, because it now recognizes that it is relevant to you. But the hidden memories, and the things you saw (but didn't consciously register) don't just flood out of Pandora's Box in one huge rush.

They creep out, little by little, slightly dazed, and they sneak up on you and whisper in your ear, or tap you quietly on the shoulder, often when you are not even thinking about them. When you are on the train, blankly staring out of the window. When you are taking your morning shower. This is a veil that doesn't lift over hours or days. It happens slowly, over weeks, or even months. And this is not process that you can force.

So, for now, we have to let your brain do its thing, in its own time. When memories surface, you may wish to write them down in a journal to get them out of your head and onto the page. This can also be very useful in helping you deal with the doubts and confusion that will arise as part of this process (the so-called 'cognitive dissonance' that we will look at later on).

You might want to structure a journal, perhaps dedicating a page or a double page spread to each of the behaviors described in Chapter 3, for you to add to, as and when. Or perhaps you are more of a 'stream of thought' type of person. You might prefer to write on an iPad, or write notes on your phone. But whatever you do, please make sure that your partner cannot get hold of your writing. I will explain later why it's best for you not to share your suspicions of narcissism with your partner.

But in the meantime, you may be wondering how on earth this happens to people, and how it happened to you. How did you end up in what I call 'the narcissist trap'?

Why You?

Most narcissists need victims who will enhance their status in some way, so they will have considered your social desirability when considering you as a potential victim. But in addition to this, *all* narcissists need victims who are going to be compliant with their wishes, who will put up with their behaviors, and who will be great sources of narcissistic supply. Please note that you are absolutely not to blame for this – narcissists take advantage of other people's kind natures – the 'fault' lies with them.

Your status enhancing properties

Closet Narcissists are particularly attracted to people who appear 'special', so much so that their targets can range from minor local celebrities to A-listers. But *most* narcissists are attracted to people who have something different or special about them, that reflects well on them.

It may be that you were particularly attractive when you met, or young (relative to them), and so were seen as a 'trophy'. Perhaps your success at work was attractive to them. Maybe you were seen as rich or you came from a background which enabled the narcissist to 'social climb'. Perhaps you impressed them with your intellect, or your abilities as a conversationalist, or as being the life and soul of the party – all traits which they would have enjoyed being associated with. Maybe you were a wonderful cook and homemaker, or a dab hand at home renovating – skills a narcissist would enjoy flaunting to their acquaintances. Or maybe you just had great potential for the future, obvious to all who met you.

> *"All narcissists have hierarchical thinking, and constantly compare themselves to others..."*

You already know that all narcissists have 'hierarchical thinking', and constantly compare themselves to others, which explains why they often need partners who will lift their own status up, in their own mind. But if you *were* targeted for your status enhancing qualities, the narcissist will inevitably have become jealous of those qualities, and will have tried to sabotage or destroy them, as time went on – often successfully, as you may know only too well.

But your status enhancing qualities are only one part of the draw – a narcissist will also usually be looking for someone who will have been primed for a narcissistic relationship by the life they've led – and this is where your background will give them plenty of information.

Your background

Did your narcissist ask a lot of deep questions when they first met you – about your relationships with parents, family and friends? Or did they self-disclose *first*, revealing what you assumed were their vulnerabilities, so that you felt safe to do the same? Narcissists are often looking for partners who fit the following profiles, as they may be more susceptible to accepting a narcissistic relationship – so you may wish to consider the following questions:

- **Had you been in a previous abusive relationship before you met your partner?** It doesn't matter what that relationship was – it may have been that you were taken advantage of by a co-worker, or bullied by a boss. Perhaps you had been in a romantic relationship with an abuser, or perhaps you had a narcissistic friend who destroyed your self-worth, or badmouthed you. It may even be that you were still in an abusive relationship when you met your narcissistic partner, which *they* would have been able to pick up on, even if *you* hadn't realized it at the time.

- **Were you brought up by a narcissist?** If you have a narcissistic parent, you would have made the perfect victim for another narcissist, because, as the saying goes, 'You find the person whose teeth fit your wounds.' But not only would the narcissist have been attracted to your wounds, but *you* are likely to have felt strongly attracted to the narcissist. You see, all people are subconsciously drawn to people who remind them of their primary caregivers, and what you might have felt to be a soulmate connection, or an instant feeling of 'having known your partner your whole life' might actually have been the subconscious pull of the familiar. It's incredibly common for those with narcissistic parents to end up with a narcissistic partner. And your narcissistic partner may superficially be very different to your narcissistic parent – a Closet Narcissist versus a Devaluing Narcissist, for example, making the similarities very hard to initially see.

- **Did you have a 'caretaker' role in any previous relationships?** Did you look after a substance addict, or someone with a chronic illness? As a child, did you have to look after a sick parent, or one who was an alcoholic? People who come from relationships like these often need the *other person* to feel okay for *them* to feel okay. They are used to putting the other person's needs ahead of their own – making them perfect for a narcissist who sees their *own* needs as paramount. This is the essence of co-dependency, which is a type of relationship addiction in itself – you *need* the other person just as much as they need you, but in this unhealthy sort of way.

Your personality characteristics

Some people find it difficult to accept that their personality characteristics might have contributed to their falling prey to a narcissist, and may even feel that this is 'victim blaming'. Once again, I want to stress here that, in fact, the blame does *not* lie with the victim, but with the narcissist, who is hunting for people who happen to have these characteristics. This was never your fault. Just as the narcissist has certain personality characteristics, their victims also do. If you think of a narcissist and their victim as two interlocking jigsaw pieces, it might help make sense of why certain character traits would make a good fit for a narcissist. Can you see any of these in yourself?

- **Being naturally trusting.** If your default position is to trust people, until they give you a reason not to trust them, you are an ideal target for a narcissist.

- **Believing that all people are 'basically good'.** This is a great footing on which to begin a relationship with a narcissist (for them, that is – they will exploit this belief time and time again).

- **Believing that 'love conquers all'.** In romantic relationships or friendships with narcissists, this mindset allows the narcissist to behave badly, knowing that they will be forgiven by you repeatedly – and that you will try to make things better by loving them even more.

- **Being 'too' easy-going.** I'm talking here about people who come across as easy-going because, in fact, they have no preferences or needs. These people may actually have come from co-dependent relationships, where they have put the needs of the other person above their own. They may have no idea what *they* actually want, and may not even realize that they are *allowed* to want anything, or to have a preference. If you don't mind which type of food you eat, where you sit in the office or bar, which movie you watch, or whether you'd prefer a tea or coffee, a narcissist could easily wish to set their sights on you. Does this resonate with you?

- **Having an aversion to feeling special.** How do you respond to compliments? Can you accept them graciously, or do they make you feel uncomfortable? If you are the sort of person that bats compliments away (perhaps by telling the person who is complimenting you that they are actually wrong, and that your hair is looking terrible at the moment/you've actually put on weight/you had a lot of help with the presentation), this could be very attractive to a narcissist. If you receive a lovely gift, do you ever feel that it is too good for you, so you give it away, or save it for a special occasion with others? This again can be a sign that you feel undeserving and unworthy. It means that you are the polar opposite to a narcissist, who is always looking to try to feel special – and as we all know, opposites attract.

- **Being highly empathic.** A narcissist will play on this attribute time and time again, telling tales of woe so that their poor behavior is forgiven and made excuses for by the empathic person. If you are the sort of person who cannot watch the news because you find it too upsetting, or if you work in a caring profession, rescue animals, or are involved with charities, unfortunately, narcissists will be drawn to you like moths to a flame.

- **Being a people pleaser.** People pleasers are also prime targets for narcissists, because their focus will be on pleasing the narcissist, and they will be unable to see their situation objectively. Do you always need other people to like you and to positively accept you? Do you desperately avoid conflict with others, including by apologizing often, even for things that are not your fault? Do people take advantage of your giving nature? Do you find it difficult to say 'no' to doing what others ask of you? Do you struggle more than most with criticism? Do you find it difficult to disagree with other people? Do you feel as though you are 'not enough' as you are? Are other people's opinions of you more important than your own? Do you fear not being liked or accepted? If so, you might be one such people pleaser.

- **Having 'rescuing' tendencies.** Rescuers are easily taken in by a narcissist's pity plays and exploited. They may need to rescue others to feel needed and to matter, and this is a trait that has developed in their own childhoods, perhaps as a result of abandonment, or because they had a parent to rescue, perhaps from drug or alcohol misuse. If you are a rescuer, you might only feel good about yourself when you are saving others, something a narcissist will use to enable their abuse, drawing you in, exploiting your kindness and claiming dependency on you. Did you find yourself rescuing your partner?

- **Being loyal.** If you are a loyal person, and you do not badmouth others, a narcissist will know that you will keep *their* bad behavior towards you under wraps. Narcissists need others to see them as perfect and special, so that they can see themselves as being that way, and they know that you will be complicit in this – a highly attractive trait to a narcissist. It may be that even your closest friends don't know how unhappy you are in your relationship, and it's really common for people who leave narcissists to be met with shock and surprise from those around them, because they thought they were 'the perfect couple'.

- **Having poor boundaries.** A boundary is where you end, and another person begins. Setting and sticking to solid boundaries enables people to protect and take care of themselves, by defining what they will and won't be responsible for. Boundaries can be physical, professional, personal, emotional, sexual, to do with time, or a combination of these. You might be good at exerting one type of boundary (professional, for example), but not so good with other types. If you have poor boundaries, you may be unable to say 'no' and mean it, and you might feel resentful for much of the time. People might repeatedly cancel you, or fail to show at agreed meetings without warning, if you are a poor boundary setter. Narcissists are flagrant boundary violators – they will not take 'no' for an answer, so those with poor, porous, weak, moveable boundaries are ideal targets for them. My clients often tell me that they didn't even know what a boundary *was* until after they left their narcissistic partner.

It's easy for anyone to fall into the narcissist trap

Even if you happen to have the type of background and characteristics which made you a relatively 'easy' target for a narcissist, you might be tempted to chastise yourself for allowing yourself to be lured into the narcissist's trap. So let me remind you of the following: Even people who don't have those susceptibilities can be taken in – for a variety of reasons. But firstly, because narcissists look 'normal'. The very nature of narcissism means that most narcissists superficially appear to be not much different to 'ordinary' people – people like us – which is just one of the reasons why they fly under our radars so very effectively. The exception is the subtype of narcissist who appears to be much *better* than average. They are better looking, funnier, cleverer and more successful than everyone around them, and often fall into the exhibitionist category – and let's face it, who wouldn't find these qualities attractive?

And regardless of subtype, narcissists don't have two heads, or come with warning symbols tattooed on their foreheads, and nor do they speak in an alien tongue. And we assume that, just because they *appear* to be like us, they must *think* like us, and their values, beliefs and motivations must be like ours. We believe that

> *"Relationships with narcissists usually progress at a very fast pace – this is a big red flag for narcissism."*

they hold the same moral principles. That they are guided by the same star.

But those with Narcissistic Personality Disorder do *not* think like us, behave like us, or feel like us, *because underneath they are completely different from us, no matter how similar they may superficially appear to be.* There is no way you could ever had known this when you were targeted by your narcissistic partner. Once again: This is not your fault.

The standard entrapment tactics that *anyone* could fall for include love bombing, future faking, and rescuing, and all of these are hard to recognize in the moment. A big red flag is that relationships with narcissists usually progress at a very fast pace, but even as children we are sold the 'love at first sight' type of romance, through those pesky Disney-type cartoons and films.

Society has set us up – so try not to be too hard on yourself if, within a month of meeting your partner, you had discussed baby names and thought you had met your 'soulmate'. On that note, we discussed love bombing earlier, but let me remind you briefly about it here.

Love bombing

If you remember, the whole point of love bombing is to make you feel so special that your neurochemicals skyrocket – the first stage in making you become addicted to the narcissist (which is known as trauma bonding). A narcissist will put you on a pedestal, and tell you how great you are. They will laugh raucously at your jokes (even the rubbish ones). They will hang upon your every word, ask you for your opinions and appear to agree with them.

Exhibitionist, Devaluing and Communal Narcissists will go on an all-out charm offensive as part of their love bombing, which may involve super-attentiveness, gifts and lavish meals. But Closet Narcissists may be less obvious in their love bombing. Remember how Lina, our love bombed Raj by cooking for him, and providing him with emotional support?

'Mirroring' is also an essential part of love bombing. Narcissists will often mirror their target's likes and dislikes at the beginning of a relationship, so that they can appear to be the perfect person for them. Think back to how Oonagh would love listening to classical music with Geoff, and would ask him to play his violin for her at the beginning of their courtship, and how heavily this contrasted with later on.

Because narcissists often grew up having to tiptoe around a difficult parent (more on that later), as children they learned how to become hyper-aware of other people's moods and sensitivities, so that they could stay safe. You already know that narcissists have limited 'emotional empathy' (which means that they are unable to step into someone else's shoes and *actually* feel what they are feeling, rendering them unable to really care about them). However, many narcissists have excellent 'cognitive empathy' and are able to intellectually pick up on a person's emotions. So narcissists can be very well attuned to other people's desires, and can deliver upon them, as part of the entrapment process. Remember that a narcissist's false persona is an invented outer shell, and is basically a lie – it's not hard to make some temporary tweaks when required.

Narcissists become whoever you need them to be at the time – until you are safely in their trap. I'm sorry if this is all sounding horribly familiar to you, as you look back.

Rescuing

Related to this, is rescuing, a terribly common way for a narcissist to trap their victim, by riding in on a big white horse, and scooping them up, when they are at their most vulnerable. Were you having a tricky time in life, when you met your partner? Do you remember how Lina, our Closet Narcissist, even told Raj that she believed that Parvati, the Goddess of Love, had sent her to save Raj from his grief? And how our Communal Narcissist, Marcus, saved single mother Irina and her young son Janis from poverty, by moving them into his sizeable London home?
Another oft-employed entrapment tactic is where the narcissist gets *you* to rescue *them* (if you happen to have the rescuing personality trait, and are highly empathic). Think back to Oonagh's meltdown in the university park, in reaction to her sister getting engaged before her. Geoff fell for it, and got down on one knee and proposed there and then.

Future faking

Future faking is often used by narcissists as part of the lure. Did your partner, early on in your relationship, offer or promise you things that simply didn't materialize? Perhaps a wish to get married, have a white picket fence or move abroad with you? Or to start an exciting new business with you, which would be certain to make millions? Remember Geoff's bitterness when, after several years of marriage, Oonagh went back on her proclamations of wanting to have children? Did your partner uncover your future wants and promise them to you, early on in your relationship? It's easy to look back on this and feel like a fool, if they did. But how on earth could you ever have known? Narcissists are utterly convincing, and would have played the game for just long enough that even the most mistrustful person would have been taken in eventually.

So the upshot is that I would really like you to have some self-compassion here. You absolutely deserve it.

Why did you put up with their behaviors for so long?

And here is another question that you might be beating yourself up about. As we've already discussed, if you were brought up by a narcissist then you are not likely to recognize that toxic behaviors are even occurring, particularly if your narcissistic partner is very different outwardly to your parent. A fun Exhibitionist Narcissist partner is going to look like the polar opposite of your sour-faced Devaluing Narcissist mother (on the surface), for example. If you have previously been in any sort of co-dependent relationship, then you will consider it normal, through no fault of your own, to put your own needs last. And if you have any of the personality traits we previously discussed, then you will be wired to keep forgiving and making excuses for narcissistic behaviors, and possibility even trying to heal the narcissist by giving them endless empathy and love.

But on top of that, there is a much more sinister sounding reason why you might have been blind to your partner's bad behaviors for so long – and that is because narcissists can take advantage of a person's neurochemistry, brain mechanisms and psychology to keep them in the dark. And please don't for one minute think that this has anything at all to do with lack of intelligence. Even Einstein's brain could have been taken advantage of in these ways. Let's look at brain filters first.

We see what our brains think we want to see

Our brains have systems to filter out incoming information that they do not consider to be relevant to us. However, when it comes to narcissists, these brain filters can often inadvertently filter out the very things the victim *needs* to be aware of, preventing them from reaching their *conscious* awareness.

If you noticed every single thing that was happening around you, you'd be pretty overwhelmed. Imagine if you were aware of every single bit of incoming sensory information, such as the feeling of the inside seams of your jeans on your legs. It's not just sensory information like this that the brain filters out – but information that is not in line with your beliefs and your view of the world, as well as stuff that just isn't relevant to you. You probably won't clock the political headline on the front page of the papers, as you walk past the newspaper stand, if you aren't interested in politics, for example. The brain simply deletes this information – a so-called 'deletion', so you never even become aware of it.

Our brains also *distort* how we see reality, magnifying or diminishing our conscious perceptions of things, and these are known as 'distortions'. And finally, the brain's mental filters

> *"We literally see what we want to see (and believe what we want to believe), but with no idea that this seriously limited view of the world is what we are actually experiencing."*

lead to 'generalizations', where we make automatic assumptions, based on our past experiences, such as 'all nurses are kind'. Some of these filters are formed by our life experiences and the beliefs we have formed as a result of them, and they produce unconscious (or conscious) biases.

It's not hard to see how your brain could have been inadvertently stopping you from seeing things as they really are, when it comes to your partner's behaviors (especially if you believe that people are 'basically good', which leads your brain filtering out anything that it not in line with this belief). *We literally see what we want to see* (and believe what we want to believe), but with no idea that this seriously limited view of the world is what we are actually experiencing. You can hardly blame yourself for not knowing that until now, can you?

'Cognitive dissonance'

Our brains also work against us when it comes to the narcissist's bad behaviors that it *has* let in through the filters. The problem is that the brain feels uncomfortable holding two opposing beliefs at the same time (for example the two contrasting versions of your partner as they go from 'nice narcissist' to 'nasty narcissist'). So what the brain does, to resolve this discomfort, is to choose just one belief. It does this by *completely denying* that bad behaviors ever happened ('he didn't really smack our daughter'), by *minimizing* how bad they were ('it was only a tiny little thump'), by *justifying* them as being reasonable under the circumstances ('she had been acting like a spoilt brat for the whole day'), or by *making excuses* for them ('he's been having a bad week at work and his nerves are frayed'). Here the brain is choosing to believe that your partner is still 'nice narcissist'.

In practical terms, this means that your brain does a very good job of convincing itself that *nothing is wrong,* quite automatically, with no help from you.

Addiction and Trauma Bonding

You now understand how it's the cyclical nature of the so-called 'cycle of idealization and devaluation' (or 'nice narcissist, nasty narcissist'), that causes your addiction to your narcissistic partner, as the brain chemicals alternately (but randomly) soar and then plummet.

These days we are all familiar with how addicted we can get to a pinging phone, notifying us of social media likes and comments, and most people are aware that every ping causes a little boost in our brain chemicals (dopamine being the most commonly cited one). But narcissists have been doing this since time began, without truly knowing how their victims become addicted to them, to the point of being so hooked that they become grateful for any crumbs of attention the narcissist throws their way. Everybody knows that addicts can't see things clearly, due to the nature of their addiction. Is it any wonder that you put up with the things that you did, blinded by your need to get the next fix of 'love' from your partner?

You no longer trust your own perceptions

Our old friend 'gaslighting' makes another appearance here. If you've been lied to in such a way that you have come to doubt your version of reality, then you are hardly going to be able view your partner's behaviors and your relationship with clarity. You might find yourself questioning all sorts of things – your memory, your beliefs, your values, your perceptions, even your emotions. As I explained in Chapter 3, gaslighting leads to a shift in the power dynamic. You stop trusting yourself, and start trusting your narcissistic partner instead. You might find yourself needing their opinion on everything, because you are not sure that yours is valid, or right. You might come to rely on them as your 'voice of reason'. So, if they have become your barometer of what is right, there's no way you could possibly have seen their behaviors as being unacceptable.

You have been in a cult

This might feel incredibly embarrassing, or even shocking, but being in a cult is exactly what being in a narcissistic marriage or partnership is like, with good reason. The methods that cult leaders use to ensnare their victims and keep them trapped are exactly the same as those used by 'everyday narcissists'.

It is also highly likely that you were isolated from your support networks – the family members and friends who would have been able to keep you grounded and lend a sense of perspective regarding your situation. Narcissists use lots of methods to do this, including 'just not getting on' with these people, claiming 'they are jealous' of your relationship, badmouthing them to you, or openly falling out with them. They may guilt-trip you for allowing these people to encroach on your

"The methods that cult leaders use to ensnare their victims and keep them trapped are exactly the same as those used by 'everyday narcissists.'"

precious time together as a couple, or get you to buy into their 'romantic' notion that it's just 'you and them against the world'.

And if this resonates with you, then we may as well tackle another facet of your relationship, at this point. It is highly likely that you have been, and maybe still are, your narcissistic partner's enabler.

So what is an enabler? An enabler is someone who allows and even helps the narcissist to carry out their abuse, usually unwittingly. If you have children with a narcissist, this is likely to be the area in which you have found yourself unwittingly playing this role. Enablers have absolutely no idea that they have been sucked into a narcissist's trap.

At the beginning of your relationship, you will have been fueling your narcissistic partner with huge amounts of narcissistic supply, by lavishing them with attention, admiration and adoration. You would have been so invested in the narcissist's false persona, so utterly charmed by it, that you might have even carried out abusive behaviors on their behalf, without understanding what was really happening. Looking back, did you ever do something you shouldn't have, as a result of falling for one of your partner's sob stories? Have you ever noticed your narcissistic partner's bad behavior towards another, but chosen to deny it, minimize it, or justify it, because it felt better that way? Or because you wanted to stay as their number one? Or just because it was *easier* that way? Are you cringing, red-faced as you read?

I mentioned the children earlier, and this is one of the greatest bugbears of the adult children of narcissists. They often feel great resentment towards the parent who wasn't the narcissist, for not only exposing them to the narcissist's bad behaviors or abuse, but for *excusing* it. How many times have you turned a blind eye to things that haven't felt quite right to you, or even been *enlisted* to punish your child in a way that feels wrong? How many times have you allowed your partner to blatantly favor one child over another, and not stepped up to compensate for this? How many times have you let things go to avoid having an argument in front of the kids? How many times have you invalidated your children's pain at the hands of their narcissistic parent, by telling them that they 'didn't mean it'? Or that they were just 'tired' or 'stressed'? And how many times have you mistakenly told them, with the best intention in the world, that Daddy or Mummy 'loves them very much'?

Am I judging you? No, I am not. Because this is a story that I hear from *every* parent I speak to who has had children with a narcissist. You are treading an impossible tightrope, trying to balance everybody else's needs. You are trying to prevent drama and conflict, and you are hoping that things will improve, because at times, your partner does seem able to be a good parent. But now you know that this only ever happens if they are rewarded with instant or future narcissistic supply, in some way – whether it comes from the children themselves, or from onlookers. We will discuss the effects of narcissistic parenting on children in Chapter 7, because this is essential to consider if you may be thinking about leaving your narcissistic co-parent.

And before we leave this excruciating section, I'm going to reluctantly deliver my final shame-inducing blow. If you have come to rely on your narcissistic partner's opinions, values and judgments, because you have been gaslit for years, you have probably taken on some of their behaviors too. You have probably become more narcissistic in the ways that you might have treated others, as people in cults often do.

It's just as important to face these uncomfortable truths about your own behaviors, even though they were probably semi-conscious at best, as it is to look at how your narcissist behaves. But remember that, ultimately, this was a *trap*, that you were lured into.

And if you recognize that you have taken on some of the narcissist's behaviors, and also enabled them, take heart from this: there is a cure. Awareness, and self-compassion. The first of these is already increasing exponentially, with every passing day, as you gain more knowledge. It's the second which you are likely to have to work on. And I strongly suggest that you do – because you have the rest of your life to live. The first step to finding the beauty and joy in that life (that you completely deserve), is forgiving yourself for the things you could never have known.

5

The narcissist tests

The following chapter is designed to help you to really gain some clarity on what might be going on in your relationship. I include two tests, the first of which is to help you to work out if your partner is a narcissist. The second is to help you to answer the question that, by now, you will almost inevitably be asking yourself – 'am I the narcissist?'. The first test is split into three parts. Please note that it assumes that you have been in your relationship for long enough to have experienced or noticed the relevant behaviors – it's less accurate for shorter relationships.

These tests are not diagnostic, but just for your own interest – only a specially trained clinician can make a formal diagnosis of Narcissistic Personality Disorder.

Is your partner a narcissist?

To what extent do you agree with the statements that follow?

Strongly agree – 5
Agree – 4
Neutral – 3
Disagree – 2
Strongly disagree – 1

Write the relevant score next to each statement and add them up to get a total. If you do not know an answer, score 3, for neutral.

PART ONE Let's talk about you	Score 1-5
Do you feel uncherished and uncared for by your partner?	
Have you lost self-esteem during your relationship?	
Do you feel as though your feelings do not matter or are invalid?	
Do you feel as though you have to 'act happy' around them, to keep *them* happy?	
If you express unhappiness or dissatisfaction to them, do you end up feeling guilty for expressing your own negative feelings?	
Do you feel that you are either 'hero' or 'zero' to your partner, with little in between?	
Do you feel that you have to be perfect for your partner?	
Do you feel as if no matter how much you give of yourself, you can never 'be enough' for your partner?	
Do you find yourself jumping through hoops to try to keep your partner happy?	
Do you feel unseen, unheard, or not truly known by your partner?	
Do you feel like a supporting actor in their show or a mere prop/accessory in their life?	

PART ONE Let's talk about you	Score 1-5
Do you find yourself jumping to attention when your partner demands it?	
Do you feel as if you are looking after a needy child with regards to your partner, at times?	
Does your partner purposely flaunt other people in front of you, making you feel insecure in your relationship?	
Do you feel as though you are walking on eggshells or unable to relax when your partner is home?	
Do you feel run ragged with your partner's requests, demands and expectations of you?	
Do you feel unsupported by them when it comes to your hopes, dreams and ambitions?	
Do you feel as though you can't quite trust your perceptions, feelings or memory of events, and so trust your partner's judgment of situations over your own instead?	
Do you feel as though, if you reveal your vulnerabilities, your partner will use them against you?	
Have you ever felt addicted to your partner, as though you couldn't possibly live without them?	
Do you feel as though your partner is the only person who can rescue you from your pain (even pain *they* have caused you)?	

PART ONE Let's talk about you	Score 1-5
Have you suffered from anxiety, depression, low moods, moods swings, irritability, or being on a short fuse since becoming involved with your partner?	
Have you had unexplained physical symptoms, such as chest pains, headaches, swallowing problems, tiredness, joint or back aches and pains, which have been put down to stress?	
Have you developed any chronic physical illnesses during your relationship with, including cancer or autoimmune conditions?	
Have you tried to leave the relationship, but found yourself going back to your partner?	
Do you feel dependent on them in some way (perhaps financially, socially or emotionally)?	
Do you feel 'controlled' by your partner?	
Do you feel resentful or taken advantage of by your partner?	
Do you feel as though you have never had a meaningful apology from them?	
Have you ever been unsettled by flashes of a completely different side of your partner's personality showing through, as if a mask has dropped?	
Total Score	/150

If your total score was over 100, you may be in a narcissistic relationship. However, it's important to note here that part one of the test may not be as relevant in short relationships as in longer ones. Parts two and three will give you more clarity.

PART TWO Your relationship	Score 1-5
At the start had your partner just come out of another relationship (or did you overlap with a previous relationship of theirs)?	
Did they tell you that they had been treated unfairly or poorly by their ex, or that they were 'crazy', 'mean' or unfaithful?	
At the start did they rescue you from difficult circumstances, or did you rescue them?	
Were you love bombed at the beginning?	
Did you think you had met your soulmate?	
Did your partner seem almost too good to be true at first?	
Did the relationship progress at an abnormally fast pace, with early declarations of love or commitment?	
Did they disapprove of or make you feel guilty about spending time without them, or on your hobbies, so that you became isolated from friends and family?	
Do you find it difficult to say no to them, and if you try, do you find yourself giving in to them anyway?	

PART TWO Your relationship	Score 1-5
Do they use your belongings without your permission, treat your things without due care, or spend your money without consultation?	
Do they make you feel small with criticisms, perhaps disguising their comments as jokes or telling you that you are being oversensitive?	
Do they badmouth you, ridicule you or call you unflattering names?	
Do they subject you to silent treatments?	
Are they jealous or dismissive of your successes?	
Do you find yourself putting their wants, needs or career above your own?	
Do they have episodes of rage?	
Do they accuse of you having affairs or flirting with others?	
Do they seem threatened by or jealous of your relationships with others, such as platonic friends, family or children or even pets?	
Do they neglect you when you are ill, unless they have an audience or are expecting something in return?	
If you try to discuss relationship issues, do they completely refuse to engage, 'stonewalling' you?	

PART TWO Your relationship	Score 1-5
Do they treat you differently in public to how they treat you in private, perhaps making only public displays of affection?	
Do they only pull their weight with household duties if they have an audience, or consider themselves to be too important to do mundane tasks?	
Do they control you with their money, by either not allowing you access to it or by being over-generous with it (but with expectations of something in return)?	
If they allow you access to their money, are they critical of your spending?	
Did they promise you a future which has never materialized?	
Do they deny that things have happened and rewrite history?	
If you've ever come close to leaving them, have they claimed to be depressed, suicidal, stressed or ill, playing on your sympathy?	
If you've ever come close to leaving them, have they turned into the perfect partner, effortlessly changing their ways (but only temporarily)?	
Do they falsely accuse you of things which you later realize are actually things that they themselves are doing or being?	

PART TWO Your relationship	Score 1-5
Do they 'play the victim' when you call them out on their bad behaviors, or as a way to get attention?	
Total Score	/150

If your score was over 100, you could be in a relationship with a narcissist. The higher the score, the more narcissistic your partner is likely to be. Part three looks at your partner in detail.

PART THREE Your partner	Score 1-5
Do wealth, status, power or perfection seem important to them?	
Do they seem to need the stimulus of new purchases a lot of the time?	
Do they go through numerous 'fads' (hobbies, dietary fads etc.)?	
Are they particularly vain?	
Do they lack deep, long-term close friendships?	
Do they have sycophants or admirers, or a fan club?	
Are they overly critical of others behind their backs or to their faces?	
When others achieve success do they seem jealous or upset, or are they dismissive of the person's success?	
Do they say that other people are jealous of them?	

PART THREE Your partner	Score 1-5
Do they say how good they are at things, exaggerating their talents and achievements?	
Do they charm others with ease on first meeting?	
Do they like to play 'devil's advocate' in discussions, taking the opposite view to others regardless of their actual beliefs?	
Do they change their views at the drop of a hat, and argue the opposite to be true?	
Are they highly moralistic when it comes to others, but hypocritical when to comes to their own behaviors?	
Do they seem to not know or care when they are embarrassing or humiliating someone, or making someone feel uncomfortable?	
Are they poor listeners, preferring to hold court when in company?	
Do they seem to find it difficult to be on their own?	
Are they often late?	
Do they demand respect, but rarely give it to others?	
Do they behave as though rules and laws do not apply to them?	
Are they arrogant, haughty and superior, either overtly or behind closed doors?	

PART THREE Your partner	Score 1-5
Do they get angry or upset when people don't seem to realize how special they are?	
Do they expect people to do things for them that they should do for themselves?	
Do they seem excessively opinionated, tend to 'know best', or 'have a better way of doing things'?	
Do they come across as insincere, as though they are putting on a show for others, almost like 'playacting'?	
Do they have an extreme, unrealistic, view of romantic love, or the very opposite – a belief that love isn't real?	
Do they always seem to need to 'win'?	
Do they lie convincingly, appearing to completely believe what they are saying?	
Are they good at manipulating people and situations to their advantage?	
Do they justify and rationalize things in ways that sound logical on the surface but that are actually contradictory, illogical, or nonsensical?	
Total Score	/150

Once again, a score of over 100 indicates that your partner is high in narcissistic traits. The higher their score, the more narcissistic they are likely to be, and the more problematic their

Are you worried that you are a narcissist?

At this stage, it is absolutely normal to be worrying that *you* might be the true narcissist in your relationship. After all, as you know, it is not unusual for narcissists to have absolutely no awareness of their personality disorder.

But another important thing to mention here is that even non-narcissists are going to recognize some of the traits of narcissism in themselves – so if this is what is happening to you, let's tackle it head on, because it's vital to understand what is known as the 'spectrum of narcissism'.

The spectrum of narcissism

Personality disorders are actually extreme manifestations of *normal* traits. In other words, all narcissistic traits exist on a 'spectrum'. It's where you *are* on that spectrum that determines whether you have narcissistic personality disorder or not.

Of course, this idea can muddy the waters a bit, until you really understand the spectrum. So you might be worried that you have a sense of entitlement because you don't like waiting in queues, or because you prefer to take cabs rather than the underground. Or you might suspect that you have low empathy because of that time your child was ill, and you were impatient with them, after you'd been up for three nights straight with their teething baby sister. Or you might think you are a control freak, because you really don't like it when your partner doesn't put their plates in the dishwasher. Or that you have a false persona, because you rarely leave the house without making an effort with your appearance.

So, let's take a look at the spectrum, which lies on a scale of zero to ten. Now, where you want to be, in order to be a healthy person, is right in the middle of the spectrum, at four, five or six. Here you know what your needs are and are able to get them met by yourself and others, but without exploiting anyone. You know what your boundaries are – what you are prepared to do for other people, and what you are not prepared to do, as well as where you draw the line as to what behaviors you are prepared to accept from others. You have a good sense of where you end and others begin. You are able to stand up for yourself, because you know that you are worth standing up for, but you also have empathy for other people, and see them as real, three-dimensional entities, with wants, needs and lives, who you can genuinely care about. You do like to enhance your outward image to a degree, but it's not all-encompassing.

Your sense of self-worth mostly (around 70%) comes from an intrinsic self-belief that you are worthy and enough, with a lot less (around 20%) coming from what other people think of you, and even less (around 10%) coming from how you feel you measure up to other people. People in the middle of the scale like this have what is known as 'healthy narcissism'.

Now let's look at the people lower down the scale – at zero, one, two and three. These people actually don't have *enough* healthy narcissism to be living optimally – and they are actually very attractive to narcissists.

They have a real aversion to feeling special, and try to bat off any feelings of specialness, often finding it difficult to accept compliments. They feel undeserving of gifts or offers of help. They may avoid self enhancing activities to do with image. They put their needs below other people's needs, and don't actually feel entitled *enough*, perhaps even feeling that they shouldn't take up space in the world. They may be people pleasers and rescuers, with a tendency to prioritize endlessly giving to others. They may have poor boundaries, and find it difficult to say no and mean it, and they may be almost overly empathic, caring 'too much' about others at the expense of being cared for and caring for themselves. These people are unofficially termed 'Echoists' after Echo, from the ancient Greek myth of Echo and Narcissus.

"Personality disorders are actually extreme manifestations of normal traits."

Those with pathological narcissism have traits on which the volume has been turned up too high. They are the people who would qualify for a diagnosis of NPD, and they lie at seven, eight, nine and ten on the scale, with increasing amounts of pathological narcissism the higher up the scale they are.

Moving up the scale from seven through ten, they are increasingly concerned with getting their own needs met, even at the expense of others. They have less and less empathy for others, and feel more and more entitled to the best of everything, and to special treatment. This increasing entitlement and selfishness means they exploit people increasingly, the higher up the scale they sit, and have a greater capacity to actually abuse others for their own ends. Image enhancement, and how they are seen by others, also becomes increasingly important. They don't see themselves as separate from other people, and so violate their boundaries, but at the same time, they do not view people as fully real equals, but rather as mere objects, about whom they cannot really care.

Their sense of self-worth comes mostly from what other people think of them, and how they feel they compare to others, with only a very small amount coming from their own intrinsic sense of self-belief and 'enoughness'. They chase feelings of specialness more and more, the higher up the scale they are, to compensate for their intrinsic lack of self-worth.

Narcissists can be attracted to people at any point on the scale of narcissism, but the people at the lower end are particularly attractive to them as long-term prospects – a case of 'opposites attract'.

So, with that in mind, you may now feel ready to take the next test – Am *I* a narcissist?

Am I a narcissist?

To what extent do you agree with the statements that follow?

Strongly agree – 5
Agree – 4
Neutral – 3
Disagree – 2
Strongly disagree – 1

Write the relevant score next to each statement and add them up to get a total.

AM I A NARCISSIST?	Score 1-5
Deep down I resent others who have what I lack	

AM I A NARCISSIST?	Score 1-5
I believe that other people often exaggerate their successes	
When other people achieve, I feel annoyed, threatened or envious	
I know best in the vast majority of situations	
I have a different temperament to most people	
I am not 'ordinary' or 'average'	
Everybody should respect me	
I sometimes feel only special people can fully understand my uniqueness	
I value high status people and people who are 'going places'	
It is only right that I should expect a great deal from other people	
People should automatically comply with what I expect from them	
I accomplish far more than others tend to give me credit for	
I'm not genuinely interested in other people's feelings, but can pretend to be	
Other people's feelings are often completely incorrect	
I don't genuinely care about what other people want	
What other people want is often completely wrong	

AM I A NARCISSIST?	Score 1-5
I think people are jealous of me	
It's hard to feel positive emotions for someone close to me when they have disappointed me	
I tend to see people as being either great or terrible at any one time	
It's hard to feel good about myself when I am alone	
I feel entitled to take credit for other people's work	
I feel humiliated, offended, angry or hurt by even mild criticism	
I am willing to take advantage of others to get what I want	
I often manipulate people	
I am a snob at heart	
I am better at a lot more things than most people are	
I am extremely driven to obtain unlimited amounts of one or more of the following: power, success, brilliance, ideal love or beauty	
People close to me don't have the right to abandon me	
The truth is what I say it is	
I get incensed with people who think they can take me for a fool	
It irritates me when people don't appreciate how good I am at things/mistake me for an average person	

AM I A NARCISSIST?	Score 1-5
I have hardly any deep friendships	
It's hard to admit to the weakness I feel inside	
I have never apologized and really meant it	
I often take pleasure in people's misfortunes	
If I do things for other people, it's usually because I stand to gain in some way	
Total Score	/180

If you scored 60 or less, you may not be narcissistic *enough* to be emotionally healthy, and might be a 'narcissist magnet'. Between 60 and 120, you fall into the 'healthy' narcissism range. And if you have scored above 120 in this test, you may be at a high overall risk of having **NPD**. But remember – these tests are not diagnostic, but just indicators for your own interest.

I also think, if you are starting to worry that you *are* a narcissist, that it's important to understand this one basic discriminating factor - *you cannot be a narcissist if you can genuinely feel a normal amount of empathy for others*. So, if you know in your heart of hearts that you can step into another person's shoes and truly *feel* how *they* are feeling, you can breathe a sigh of relief.

6

Now what?

"Grant me the serenity to accept the things I cannot change;
courage to change the things I can;
and the wisdom to know the difference."

– Reinhold Niebuhr

By now you may have arrived at the point where you have a pretty good idea whether your partner is a narcissist or not. Hopefully you will also have put to bed any worries you might have had about your own narcissistic tendencies. If you *have* concluded that your partner is a narcissist, then the rest of this book is for you.

For the remainder of you, I'm sorry that your relationship is in the trouble that it is. Even though you may be suffering at the hands of a partner who is violent, controlling, unfaithful, has anger or addiction issues and much more, if they do not fit the profile of a true narcissist, this book is unlikely to be the right resource for you if you are considering leaving the relationship. It may be that a domestic abuse or addictions charity will be better placed to advise you as to where to go from here, depending on your circumstances.

For many more of you, I hope you have realized that your partner is not a true narcissist, is *not* abusive, and that you are now clear on the difference between NPD and the 'buzzword' use of the 'narcissist' word. To all of you who are leaving us here, I wish you well, and hope you find the future and happiness that you are hoping for.

However, if you *are* now becoming sure that your partner is a narcissist, I want to let you know that it is highly likely, at this point, to find that your brain seems to be playing tricks on you. This is not an easy process to experience.

One minute you will be absolutely sure that your partner is a narcissist, for all the reasons that you have learnt about. As you start to question the reality of your experiences, you may start to experience flashbacks, or be repeatedly hit by intrusive memories, when you least expect it. Here the brain is allowing the memories that it previously filtered out of your consciousness to reach your conscious mind. This can be extremely unsettling, can occur out of the blue, and can sideswipe you emotionally.

At these times your emotions will be raw, and numerous. Heart wrenching grief and despair will bulldoze over you. At times, you may be taken over by rage and resentment towards your partner (and towards the 'powers that be' that let this happen to you). Towards your parents, who might have predisposed you to this, towards yourself, for allowing this to happen and towards all the people who've now come out of the woodwork to say that they 'didn't want to tell' you that they 'never really liked' you partner all along.

And how to describe that excruciating searing pain you might be feeling, at the realization that your whole relationship was a lie – that *love itself* was a lie? It can leave you gasping for air. It can rip you apart, and throw you to the floor. It can take you to the darkest place you have ever been, and leave you questioning every single thing you have ever believed to be true. Now you might understand the term 'soul rape'. Now might you know what it feels like to be broken.

But then, minutes, hours, or even days later, you may be filled with doubt, as your brain reminds you of the good times, and those memories come flooding back. You question yourself once again. You hope that things can be mended. You wonder what you can do to try again, and to be better. You might tell yourself that *this time* you will be able to get through to your partner – that this time they will be able to see their part in this mess, and learn how to repair things with you.

You might remind yourself of how strong your love was at the start, and how you felt when you knew that you had met your soulmate. You may well tell yourself that you will do whatever it takes to beat the odds, and to make everything okay. Perhaps at this point you can smile again, laugh even. But only for a while, until the darkness returns.

This flip-flopping between beliefs really is horrifically difficult to cope with, and it can go on for months (or even years) – but I want to tell you this: in spite of how it might feel, *you are not going 'mad'*. This is an entirely normal psychological process. I mentioned 'cognitive dissonance' earlier, but let me briefly remind you of it again. I'm afraid there's is nothing you can do to avoid this awful experience – with this, *the only way out is through*.

So, if you remember, the brain finds it extremely difficult to hold within it two opposing beliefs at the same time, because this feel psychologically very uncomfortable. So instead, it chooses just one belief. The beliefs it will be struggling with at this point are likely to be Belief A, 'my partner is a narcissist', versus Belief B, 'my partner is not a narcissist'. As the memories your brain suppressed (or never allowed into your conscious mind) start to reach your awareness, it will choose Belief A, with all the resulting emotional consequences for you. But, as the other memories resurface, usually of the initial love bombing phase, and the other idealizing phases of the 'nice narcissist/nasty narcissist' cycle, the brain will choose Belief B ('my partner is not a narcissist').

There's little you can do about this, other than to journal these thoughts out at these times. Having a list of all your partner's narcissistic behaviors at the ready, to refer to, can also be very useful, or you may wish to remind yourself of your answers to the tests in Chapter 5, when the doubts set in. Be assured that little by little, the brain *will* come to see the truth, and will slowly stop presenting you with Belief B.

Perhaps it is time to now consider what having NPD in your life actually *means* – for you, for your children and for your narcissistic partner. I've mentioned previously that NPD is generally considered to be largely incurable, but to understand the difficulties that treating NPD presents, let's start by considering how your partner 'got' NPD in the first place. For this, we will return to the childhoods of the four narcissists you met earlier.

How do you 'get' NPD?

Narcissistic Personality Disorder is thought largely to be a condition that people *develop* in childhood, as a result of their upbringings – although studies involving twins separated at birth also show that some people are genetically predisposed to it. Many things that we humans suffer from are as a result of the combination of nature and nurture, but it seems that, in most cases of NPD, it's the nurture element that is most important.

There are four types of upbringing that can result in a person developing NPD. To look at the first of these, let's take a trip down memory lane with Jonathan Delaney, our Exhibitionist Narcissist.

Twelve-year-old Jonathan was nervous. Very nervous, in fact. Holding his cricket bat tightly, he took up his position and said a silent prayer to a God he wasn't sure he believed in. This was the second time he had tried to get into the prestigious county cricket team, but he knew that, this time, failure was not an option. His mother would simply do her nut, and his father, who prided himself on his sporting prowess as a young man, would probably say absolutely nothing, but clench his jaw in that way he did when he'd been hopelessly let down. Jonathan didn't know which reaction he dreaded most.

The truth was that Jonathan was *tired*. Life had always seemed to be just one endless loop of activity. He wanted to be able to lie on his bed and stare at the ceiling, just for a bit. But there was always something to do and someone to compete with.

Three times a week he would be roused at 6am to be at swim club by 6.45, where he'd be critiqued, timed and shouted at by Mrs. Douglas, his swimming coach (who he'd never actually seen in the water herself). *I bet she can't even swim, the silly cow*, he always thought to himself, as he lowered himself into the pool, teeth chattering. But at least Jonathan had made it into the national squad. His mother had squealed with delight, and phoned everyone she knew, and his father had slapped him on the back, beaming. "I'm proud of you, son" he had said, after taking the obligatory photo for the dining room wall, opposite the trophy collection. But did young Jonathan *himself* feel pride? Or was *relief* the emotion he most commonly felt, each time he successfully met his parents' ever upward-spiraling standards?

Jonathan also excelled at rugby. He much preferred football, but there wasn't time to do both, and he knew that expressing a preference would fall on deaf ears, despite the fact that painful sprains and rugby injuries were a constant issue for him. So Saturdays were always spent in the car, en route to some match or competition or other, his father driving as his mother relentlessly tested him on his Latin, or his French or whatever else he needed to learn to perfection for the following week.

Jonathan was in the scholarship class at school and the academic pressures were high, but if he failed to beat Spencer Williams in every test, his mother's disapproval would be palpable. And Jonathan could have sworn that he actually saw her spitting blood when Spencer was given the lead role in the school play over him. He'd felt so ashamed on that occasion that he'd pretended to have a stomach ache, so he didn't have to face their forced conversation at the dinner table. "After all the opportunities we've given him…" he'd once heard his father complain, when he thought he was out of earshot.

And then, to top it all off, there were the extracurricular music demands. But being in the chamber choir (which he hated) and playing the bassoon in the school orchestra was not enough for either of his parents. Auditions for the city choirs and orchestra had already gleefully been put on the kitchen calendar.

But today Jonathan batted like a pro, and sailed into the county cricket team. Giant hugs and smiles were forthcoming, and neither of his parents stopped telling him how much they loved him for the entire evening, repeatedly tousling his hair and planting smiley kisses on his forehead. But Jonathan's mind was already on the next day's maths challenge, which he had to win, if he was to represent the school in the national finals.

Jonathan came to believe that he was only worthy of love and attention if he achieved great things – and specifically only things valued by his parents. He learned that parental love is *conditional.*

These hardworking children, like Jonathan, develop a sense of emptiness and low self-esteem within. They feel they need to appear perfect and successful to the outside world, and they learn to construct an image in line with this. They grow up needing the approval of their parents to feel okay. As adults, they rely upon external validation from everyone else to prop up the image they have created of themselves – so that they can feel emotionally safe. Could this have been the type of childhood that your partner endured?

To look at the second type of upbringing that can result in NPD, let's wind back the clock to visit Lina, our Closet Narcissist, in Bradford, in the north of England, just before her tenth birthday.

The sign outside Romesh Mehotra's convenience store simply said "Bradford's Best Shop." He was a man of superlatives, especially when it came to his own endeavors and achievements.

"I came to this country with one pair of trousers and a T shirt," he would tell little Lina, gesturing grandly to his surroundings, as she restocked the cramped shop's shelves with toothpaste, carbolic soap and tampons. "And look at me now, hey?"

Lina adored her father. Even aged nine she loved to be in the shop with him, watching him interact with the customers, and listening to his anecdotes. She was quite sure he was the cleverest man in the whole world.

A little bell was attached to the shop door, heralding the arrival of each customer, and Romesh would quickly arrange his features into a wide toothy smile every time it rang. He knew the names of all his customers, and had a special greeting for every single one of them. "Mr Singh, you old dog, eh?" he said every week, as he handed over a bottle of whiskey in a brown paper bag to the local tailor with a huge wink. "Don't worry, your secret's safe with me, my brother!"

"Mrs Banerjee! Welcome, welcome!" he would bow to the old lady as she squeezed her ample frame past the tinned tomatoes, "Tell me, how can it be that you look more beautiful with each passing day?" Although Mrs Banerjee would be tutting with mild embarrassment, Romesh knew that she was secretly flattered. "Just the five samosas today?"

"You see Lina?" he would say, once the shop was empty again "*This* is how you do customer service." Now run upstairs and tell Mama that we need more samosas. Quick, quick."

Lina was a sweet looking thing, with huge brown eyes, a delicate jawline and long black pigtails. One Saturday she'd got her mother to put big ribbons in her pigtails, at both the top and the bottom, and gone downstairs to the shop. Her new look had gone down a storm with the customers, and drew many comments such as "Little Lina you are too cute! I could just eat you!" and the like. But with each comment her father seemed increasingly displeased, and eventually ordered her to take the ribbons out. "What is all this, look at me, look at me, eh?" he spat meanly. "Get upstairs, now. And don't let me see you looking like this again."

Lina's father was an Exhibitionist Narcissist, and Lina's role was clear – to worship and adore him, and never, ever to take the spotlight away from him. These children are taught that seeking admiration for themselves will be punished by criticisms, and that they must never out-do their narcissistic parent, on any front. When they toe the line, they are rewarded with praise, attention and validation but, at the same time, they unconsciously learn narcissistic behaviors. They desperately want to be special, and may fantasize about feeling this way, but they learn to achieve this feeling of specialness by obtaining external validation in *covert* ways, including by playing the victim, to gain attention and narcissistic supply.

In adulthood they shy away from the spotlight, instead associating with others with status, so that the other person's specialness rubs off on them. But, because they are relying on the other person's specialness, perfection and uniqueness to feel okay themselves, they are disappointed when the other person's human flaws come out. They are more prone to bouts of depression than the other types of narcissist because of this. Would this type of upbringing resonate with your partner, do you think?

Let's now visit 1970s rural Ireland, where Oonagh Campbell-Jones, our Devaluing Narcissist, started off life, to examine the third type of parenting that can result in NPD.

Campbell's Dairy Farm had been ailing for years, and farmer John Campbell was permanently exhausted. Cows would need to be retrieved from fields and ditches at all hours, when fences came down in storms. Milking times were frequent, and at antisocial hours, and the continual hard labor of cleaning up cow excrement whilst being lashed by the rain was not for the fainthearted, leading to a high turnover of farmhands. And during calving seasons even less sleep was to be had, as one never knew when a birth would have complications.

Perhaps it was no wonder that John Campbell was continually on edge and irritable. Born and bred in southern Ireland, he came from a long line of dairy farmers, each as moody as the last, and each with a taste for liquor. But he knew where he came from, and was proud of it. John Campbell had never left Ireland, and he saw absolutely no reason to ever do so.

It continually irked him that his wife had only produced girls – and seven of them, at that. "What f**cking use is this lot gonna be to me, you stupid bloody woman?" he had angrily asked his wife after the third daughter was born, whilst she was still lying spreadeagled on the kitchen table, waiting for the midwife to finish delivering the placenta.

Oonagh was the oldest daughter, which meant that she was put to work on the farm before the others. She started by cleaning milk pails at seven years old. By the time she was 13, she hated her life, and longed to escape. She would moan to her sisters about her father's demands on her. "Sure, at least Daddy knows your *name*..." some of the younger ones would occasionally retort.

Their mother was a kind woman, but with serial pregnancies and hungry babies, she was busy, and meeting Oonagh's emotional needs was not high on her list of priorities.

There was only one thing that Oonagh could do – escape her dreary existence by retreating into a fantasy land. She was an avid reader, and read and re-read every story book in the village school. Her nose was stuck in a book whenever it could be. She'd even read whilst milking the cows, irritating her father immensely.

"Who do you think you are?" he would ask, clipping her ear if she had been too engrossed in a book to hear him. "Fancy yourself as Margaret Bloody Thatcher, do you?" "Too important to listen, are you now? UPWARDLY F**CKING MOBILE, ARE YOU?"

One day I'm going to be rich. One day, I'm going to move to England. One day I'm going to marry a Lord. Oonagh would drown out the sound of his ridicule with mantras like this, repeating them over and over in her head.

One day, when she was sixteen, her father was drunk and on the warpath once again. "Too good to be a Campbell, are you, you little bitch?" he was bellowing in her face, with the stench of whiskey on his breath. Holding back the tears, Oonagh mentally said her biggest prayer yet, begging for a solution to present itself. And the very next day, it did.

The local priest had heard about Oonagh's literary interests, and after church, he told her about a job in the university library in Dublin. The farm was in dire financial straits. They needed a steady income. If she took it, she could escape the farm life, better herself, and help her father with his financial struggles, in one fell swoop.

"It's win win, Daddy," she had told him that afternoon, crossing her fingers behind her back. It turned out that even John Campbell couldn't argue with logic like that.

Oonagh grew up in a house of ridicule and humiliation, with a father whose explosive outbursts could not be avoided. Was he himself a narcissist? Perhaps – or perhaps not. But belittling parents like these invalidate their children, who tiptoe around their moods, try to placate them or zone out. They internalize the message that they are 'not enough', 'bad' or 'useless', but try to avoid these feelings by vowing to prove to the world that their parent was wrong. It's no wonder that they are often highly driven to achieve status, wealth or power, as a way to gain the admiration of others and justify their existence. If they have learned to put other people down as a way of inflating their own shaky self-worth, they can turn out as Devaluing Narcissists, as Oonagh did – but these children can also go on to become any of the other types of narcissist too. If you have met your partner's parents, you may well recognize this as the type of childhood they must have had.

So let's now look at Marcus, our Communal Narcissist, and how his background, in London, England, demonstrates the final type of parenting style that can lead to narcissism.

When Dianne Brown told her mother that she had fallen pregnant through a one-night stand with a black man, she really didn't know how she would react – but frankly, at 37 years old, it hardly mattered. But all her mother cared about was that God had given her daughter the only gift she'd ever really wanted, and that she was radiantly happy. They hugged each other tightly as they laughed and cried.

Dianne was a midwife at St.Thomas' hospital, in London, and her busy career had meant that she had never found the right man to settle down with. It was her last day in Jamaica, holidaying with girlfriends, when Daniel, the hotel pool-boy, had flashed her a wide smile, and stuck a paper napkin under her drink, with the words 'Age is just a number, right?' scrawled on it. He was a mere 21 years old, with long dreadlocks, defined muscles and perfect dark chocolate skin.

After Dianne's announcement, mother and daughter immediately started planning. It was agreed that Dianne would move back into the house in South London with her mother, where she had grown up. She would rent out her own small flat in trendy Clapham, and this would provide the income to enable her to work part time, while the baby was little. It was agreed that she and her mother would bring up the baby together, and never divulge to anyone the story of his origins.

Baby Marcus was the light of their lives. He had Dianne's pale blue eyes, which, in combination with his brown skin, drew admiring comments from everyone who stopped to look at him. "My darling little prince!" Dianne would call him, and "My little miracle!" He was her raison d'être, and the most special person the world had ever known. When he gurgled and babbled at just a few months old, Dianne was sure that she could discern words, and she would boast about it to anyone who would listen. "He's practically speaking in full sentences!" she would excitedly say. "Oh yes, he's very musical – he was humming 'twinkle twinkle little star' in his cot the other day…" Marcus was loved like no other baby, and lauded for every single thing he did. His grandmother and mother would spend hours intently watching him, lavishing praise on him for his every movement. "Oh look! He kicked his legs! Clever boy!!!" they would coo in unison.

This was a pattern that continued throughout Marcus's upbringing. Regardless of how well he actually did, he was told that he was a 'genius', 'the cleverest little boy in the whole wide world' and the 'most talented' at everything. When he wasn't offered the part of Joseph in the school nativity play, aged five, Dianne stormed into the school to complain, and told the headmistress that 'Marcus could one day be the world's greatest actor'.

Dianne also felt that Marcus deserved the best of everything. When they went to restaurants, he would be allowed to choose the most expensive thing on the menu. If he didn't like the food, he would be allowed to choose another meal – and if he *did* like the food Dianne would insist that the chef came out to see him, so that Marcus could give his compliments in person. She liked to dress him in little buttoned shirts and waistcoats for such excursions, with the occasional bow tie, so he looked like the 'little gent' she believed him to be.

When his school grades were underwhelming, Dianne heaped praise on him, and told him that the testing system failed great minds like his, and were designed for 'just the average Joe'. When he played his guitar (hesitantly and badly) Dianne would listen with rapt attention, barely holding back her tears of pride. In company, even with adults, if he was speaking Dianne would shush everyone in the room, so that he could be heard. Dianne believed he was the wittiest, the strongest and the bravest child ever, as well as being the kindest and sweetest.

Dianne was not a narcissist, but she needed to believe that there was no area in which Marcus did not excel. It's no surprise that Marcus himself grew up needing to believe it too.

These overvaluing parents do love their children, but seem to genuinely see them as unique and superior. The child comes to believe that they are entitled to special privileges, but as they grow up, faced with reality, they struggle. They therefore develop narcissistic defenses to protect themselves from having to accept the truth. Their parents may well continue to brag about them forever, inflating their achievements and attributes throughout their adulthood. Does this sound like the way that your partner might have developed their narcissism?

Can NPD be cured?

So now you understand how these patterns of behavior became wired into your partner's brain, as a result of how they were brought up. You will, most likely, now understand why there is no drug treatment for NPD. But these stories, about innocent children, who had no choice in the matter, are incredibly difficult to hear without feeling a huge amount of sympathy. And someone like you, who is likely to be particularly high in the empathy stakes, is going to immediately be overcome with sadness for your partner as a child, and to want to scoop them up and try to heal them. But as I've already alluded to, you can't cure your partner by loving them more.

If only they could have actually been the person that they pretended to be, when you first met them, you may think. Why, if they were so convincing at *appearing* to be that person, can't they actually *become* that person? Can't they 'fake it until they make it'? Isn't being able to *act* as a certain type of person only a short hop away from *actually being* that person? Surely it must be relatively easy for a psychotherapist to treat NPD?

It's heartbreaking, but the answer is no. It really is *not* easy to treat NPD. That disconnect between a narcissist's false persona and who they *really* are, is very real indeed – and the gulf between the two is huge. This is not easy to hear, I know.

Various types of psychological therapies are showing some promise in treating NPD, but these are long-term treatments which take years, and which are super-specialized, expensive, and only likely to work for the tiny minority of narcissists who are very intelligent, have awareness of their condition, and who are highly motivated to make positive changes.

But most narcissists will *not* want to be treated, for a variety of reasons. A key problem is that, in order to make any type of change, a narcissist would have to take a deep, honest look within. And that is exactly the *opposite* of what their narcissism is for – to shield them from how they really feel, deep down.

NARCISSISTS IN DIVORCE: FROM LOVE-LOCKED TO LEAVING

Many narcissists will simply not wish to admit that they have NPD (because of the shame evoked by such an admission), and some see their narcissism (and specialness and uniqueness) as an *advantage*, that they wouldn't ever want to lose. And even those narcissists who do try therapy often find it difficult to accept the perceived power of the therapist, or else they struggle with the feeling that they might be being 'judged' by the therapist – just two reasons why therapy usually breaks down.

However, for completeness, the types of therapy that are being trialed by some therapists for narcissism are:

- Transference-focused psychotherapy
- Mentalization-based treatment
- Schema-focused therapy
- Dialectical Behavior Therapy
- Meta-cognitive interpersonal therapy

The sad reality is the vast majority of those with NPD will never be 'cured'. And, I'm afraid to say, focusing on the *hope* that the narcissist in your life will get better is unlikely to serve you, or your children. Most people in this situation find that they have been putting their partner's needs above everything else for so long, that they do it automatically. This is absolutely not their fault – they've been trained, without even realizing it, to think in this way, but it's a difficult pattern to break, and impossible if they are not aware of it.

So, it's highly likely that you will find yourself thinking about what all of these discoveries about NPD means for your partner – how it will affect *them*, how *they* will feel about it all, how much you even considering leaving would hurt *them* etc. This might sound harsh, but you are going to have to re-prioritize, and really look into what matters the most – you and the children. So, every time your mind takes you to this default empathic position of considering your partner, see if you can notice it, and then immediately (and deliberately) refocus on considering the other important people in this dynamic – not least, *yourself*.

Should I try and get my partner diagnosed?

So now you know that there is no real 'cure' for NPD, but you still might be thinking that a formal diagnosis might be useful. You might feel that *you* need a formal diagnosis to be sure that you are not making a terrible mistake, which could have serious consequences for your family, especially if you leave the relationship. Maybe you feel that getting your narcissist diagnosed will give you a sense of validation, and make them see the error their ways. Perhaps you feel that a diagnosis will be useful to *them*, because at least it will give them a *chance* to try and change, even your plan is to leave.

The fact of the matter is this – the vast majority of narcissists will never be diagnosed. At the beginning of Chapter 1 we discussed why, all over the world psychotherapists, counselors, psychiatrists and other doctors aren't actually routinely trained in Narcissistic Personality Disorder, and how difficult it can be to find someone who can actually make a proper diagnosis. That's not to say that there aren't *any* professionals trained and experienced in diagnosing NPD – there are. Some clinical forensic psychologists and psychiatrists are able to make this diagnosis, as are some clinical psychologists.

However, a narcissist would actually have to *agree* to being diagnosed (unless a court orders an assessment, or they are incarcerated). But the thing about narcissism is that it works to the narcissist's *advantage*. It allows them to manipulate and exploit people for their own gain, so that they can feel good about themselves. To a narcissist, there is nothing to fix – so you can see why they would be unlikely to agree to getting a diagnosis in the first place.

And finally, it's crucial to understand that in most cases, if a narcissist *does* agree to being diagnosed and to have therapy, their motivation is unlikely to be so that they can become less narcissistic. The sad truth is that it is more likely to be so that they can talk about themselves, manipulate the therapist (who they will see as another source of narcissistic supply) and manipulate *you*, by pretending that they are trying to 'get better', to give you false hope that things can improve.

"In practical terms, pathological narcissism is not a 'curable' condition. There's no drug treatment and 'normal' psychotherapy won't help."

Should I tell my partner that I think they are a narcissist?

Even knowing all the facts about diagnosis and treatment of NPD, you may still feel as though you at least want to tell your partner that you think they are a narcissist. After all, for years, you have probably sought their opinions about everything, and shared most things with them. It can even feel 'sneaky' and 'wrong' to keep things from them. But is telling them actually a good idea? Well, the short answer to this question is 'no' – although this advice can be really hard to follow, especially in anger or pain.

From now on, in your interactions with your partner (and with any other narcissists you might know), it's worth trying to step back before you actually do or say *anything*, to ask yourself the following question: *What good can come of it?*

'But if *I* were a narcissist, I would want someone to tell *me*', you may be surmising, quite reasonably. Or you might be tempted to hurl this accusation at your partner in anger, because you are so fed up with their toxic behaviors. Or maybe you are genuinely thinking 'what harm could it possibly do?'

Well, to answer that last one, in terms of harm, it could do quite a lot. If you are considering divorcing or separating, then telling them your suspicions is an absolute 'no no' as they will often then claim that *you* are the actual narcissist, projecting their deficiencies on to you. This could have ramifications in the divorce, and even on where your children end up living, because they may be able to convince the professionals involved that *you* really are the person with problems. But telling them that you think they are a narcissist is also likely to backfire on you because they are likely to react with narcissistic rage – because you will have punctured their shield and caused a narcissistic injury, forcing them to face the truth about themselves.

Even if your partner is already aware of their narcissism, and happily considers it to be a testimony to their superiority, you will still be left with the problem that little good will come out of the conversation. It is actually likely that you will have handed the narcissist a way to manipulate you further, perhaps by claiming that they will commit to therapy and to 'getting better' – all part of the 'hoovering' tactics that narcissists employ to suck you back into the relationship, so that you can remain as a source of narcissistic supply, which I will explain in Chapter 8.

And labelling someone as a narcissist to their face can also give them a great *excuse* for all their behaviors – "Well, I can't help it. I have low empathy, because I am a narcissist. What do you expect? You just need to accept it/love me more/get over it…"

Keeping quiet about what you know about your partner's personality is likely to serve you and your children much better in the long run, particularly if, at some point, you are likely to leave them – because you have the manual to their brain wiring, and you will be able to pre-empt their divorce behaviors. Telling them can only reduce your tactical advantage – and believe me, if you are separating from a narcissist who is wired to effortlessly manipulate, you are going to need to hold on to all the advantages you have, for the sake of yourself and your family, no matter how dishonest this might feel to you at this stage.

How about couples therapy or counseling?

I'm going to be straight with you, and tell you that couples therapy is of absolutely no use if your partner is a narcissist, not even if you are trying to use it as a way to break up amicably, rather than to try to save the relationship. And, to be blunt, it can actually make things worse for you.

Many couples therapists and counselors are not trained psychologists, and even the ones that are will be extremely unlikely to spot that your partner is a narcissist, for the reasons we've already discussed. This means that they simply will not see the true dynamics at play during your sessions, and will believe what your highly convincing narcissist will be telling them. They will not understand that a narcissist sees couples therapy as just something else to 'win' at.

In Chapter 3 I mentioned the concepts of triangulation and the 'drama triangle'. As it happens, couples therapy is actually the perfect playground for these. Like all narcissistic behaviors, it follows a very predictable pattern. You partner will begin by taking up the 'victim' position in the drama triangle, casting you as the 'persecutor'. With much dabbing of eyes, and wavering of voice, they will twist half-truths, rewrite history and make even blatantly false accusations about your behavior. The counselor will believe your convincing partner, and unwittingly step in as their 'rescuer'. And you will find yourself trying to defend yourself as the counselor patiently tries to get *you* to understand where you have been going wrong.

The narcissist will have effortlessly turned the therapist into the persecutor, and you into the true victim. It's a wonderful way to gain narcissistic supply from the attention, sympathy and drama, and the ease with which they will run rings around you and the therapist will give them an enormous sense of superiority. That bucket will be overflowing with supply – it's no wonder they will want to return week on week.

But, of course, the supply they gain from this won't just be limited to the sessions themselves. At home they will smugly remind you of all the tricks the therapist told you to try to make yourself a better partner, and of the forgiveness that you need to show them. And, if you are susceptible to their gaslighting, as you are likely to be after a long relationship, you may well believe them. After all, a *professional* is now corroborating that you are to blame. It can every confusing indeed.

> "Couples therapy is of absolutely no use if your partner is a narcissist..."

NARCISSISTS IN DIVORCE: FROM LOVE-LOCKED TO LEAVING

Remember how Irina was persuaded by Communal Narcissist Marcus to try couples therapy after she found out about his affair with Loretta, a woman from church? In couples therapy, he blamed his indiscretions on the fact that Irina was often working, leaving him feeling lonely and isolated. The therapist agreed with him and spoke of the value of forgiveness. Irina felt terrible guilt, and agreed to try again – an absolutely typical scenario.

There are also other good reasons why the whole process really is a waste of time. Firstly, in order to benefit from couples therapy, you have to be *able* to look deeply at your behaviors, to take responsibility for them, and to have the capacity to change. As you know, these are not abilities that a narcissist possesses. And secondly, let's not forget this crucial point: The reason your relationship is in trouble is largely *because* your partner is a narcissist. If narcissism can't even be reliably cured by super-specialized psychotherapy, how is a marriage guidance counselor going to cure it, when they don't even know what it is?

Having said all of that, you may feel compelled to give it a go, and I'm certainly not discouraging you from doing that. But if you do, I really do want you to be able to go into the process with your eyes wide open to what will happen, so that you can identify the behaviors in real time. This might be really helpful in consolidating your suspicions about your partner, so that you can get a realistic perspective on things – which, in turn, could be useful in helping you work out what to do next.

7

What about the children?

If you share children with your narcissistic partner, you have a whole raft of other things to think about when considering where to go from here.

You'll need to know what the *direct* effects are of narcissistic parenting on children, and what the long-term consequences are of these. You'll need to consider the fact that, at present, you may, at least, be around to combat these – but what will happen if you leave, and there is no one to protect the children from these behaviors when they are staying with the other parent? You'll need to balance that with the excruciating realization that, to some degree, in staying you have probably been *enabling* the narcissist parent's abuse of the children, for various understandable reasons, including that you were simply trying to keep the peace.

At the same time, you'll need to be aware of the adverse effects on the children of being brought up in an unhappy household. And what if the children come to see being subjected to silent treatments, walking on eggshells, and jumping through hoops to please the narcissistic parent as the *norm?* What will the risks be when it comes to *their* future relationships? Will they attract the same types of partners themselves? Or will they *become* that type of partner? You now know that NPD is passed down the generations, mostly as a result of nurture rather than nature. What could your role be here? Could you be the 'cycle breaker' who breaks the generational chains of narcissistic abuse? *Should* you be?

And what if your narcissistic partner is of the 'Disney parent' variety – the perfect parent in public, or the crazy, fun parent? Or the parent who never disciplines the children (the flipside being not setting any boundaries)? If this sounds familiar, even *you* might have been fooled into believing that your partner genuinely loves your children, and that the behaviors that you have been subjected to could never be applied to *them*.

Sadly, here again, I have to be the bearer of bad news. NPD is a 'pervasive' personality disorder – meaning that a true narcissist won't reserve their poor behaviors just for you. Narcissists abuse *everybody* that they come into contact with to some degree, whether that person ever realizes it or not, and sadly, the child of a narcissist is no exception. Children of narcissists are, like all people, simply a means of reaping narcissistic supply, directly (from their adoration of the narcissist) or indirectly (by making the narcissist look good to others).

And as to love, once again, the heartbreaking fact is this: All love to a narcissist is transactional or conditional – *including love for their children*. They may even believe that what they are feeling is love, but what they are actually experiencing is merely the effects of the adoration or narcissistic supply they are receiving from the child. Once the child starts asserting any of their own needs and wants, which are not in line with the narcissist's, this 'love' can simply evaporate, and the child can be turned upon with disdain.

Whether you choose to stay or go for the sake of the children is not a simple decision. In this chapter, I will explain just some of the ways in which a narcissistic parent will weaponize their children if you split up, in order to keep you locked in battles with them for the remainder of your co-parenting relationship. Taking these into consideration, you might even feel that it will be better to stay until the children are older, particularly if they are young. It may even be *safer* to stay in your case, depending on your particular situation.

You may be thinking, 'But surely the *court* won't let the narcissist have too much contact with the children, if their personality issues are pointed out?' Unfortunately, the court's lack of understanding of personality disorders and the adverse effect of narcissistic parenting, doesn't help here at all. In the UK there is a 'pro-contact' culture – even pedophiles, rapists and murderers are allowed to see their kids. The rights of the parent often seem to be much more important than protecting the child. You can see why the courts are highly unlikely to stop a parent with 'just NPD' from seeing their children. And if you try to withhold contact, things are even likely to go against *you* – and *you* might lose the children yourself. The system is a mess, and the people in charge are often dangerously, unconsciously incompetent.

"The courts are highly unlikely to stop a parent with 'just NPD' from seeing their children."

To understand how narcissists behave towards their children, let's revisit Jonathan, the headmaster, our Exhibitionist Narcissist, and introduce Max, his son.

NARCISSISTS IN DIVORCE: FROM LOVE-LOCKED TO LEAVING

Max is 20, and is Jonathan and Brigitte's only child. He couldn't wait to leave home and start university, mostly because he is sick of his father, who he hasn't felt aligned with since he was a little boy.

He regularly rings and texts his mother, Brigitte, who he is close to, but it annoys him when she tries to hand the phone over to his dad, or asks him to just text on the group chat, because his father 'feels left out'. "Your dad loves you very much, you know," she will often say to him, when mildly berating him for the lack of effort he makes with him.

But Max doesn't feel loved by his father. After all, he's been told so many times that he is a disappointment to him. Jonathan was angry when he chose to study Psychology at university, branding it a 'useless degree, unless you want to be a shrink, like the rest of the world'. He wanted Max to do a chemistry degree, like he did, at the same university he went to, and just could not seem to hear (or care) that Max wasn't interested.

As a small child Max struggled at school, even though he was obviously intelligent. He would talk incessantly in class and keep leaving his seat to mess around, distracting the other children. He'd always been a handful, even as a toddler, and Brigitte hadn't been able to take her eyes off him, for even a second, if she didn't want to find him climbing something dangerously, or playing with the toilet brush. By the time he was nine, she was becoming concerned, and thought that they should have him assessed by an educational psychologist.

Jonathan was completely opposed to this, and point blank refused. "There is absolutely nothing wrong with him!" he said, angrily banging his fist on the table, one morning at breakfast. "He just needs to try harder and stop being lazy. He seems perfectly able to concentrate on playing the piano, doesn't he? So it's pretty obvious that this is just a question of *motivation*. Max only does what Max wants to do, quite clearly."

When Brigitte tried to explain to Jonathan that this 'hyperfocus' was actually another reason to get Max assessed, Jonathan turned to her and snarled, nastily. "Er, I think *my* credentials, when it comes to education and children, trump *yours*, don't you?"

Brigitte was flabbergasted, but, as usual, she gave in. It had always been planned that Max would attend Jonathan's school at the age of 11, but it slowly became clear that he would not pass the entrance exam, and it was only at this point, faced with the shame of this, that Jonathan agreed to him being assessed.

It was no surprise to anyone, least of all to Max, that he received a diagnosis of ADHD, and although Jonathan still refused to believe it, his mother supported him in taking medication for it.

Max still remembers how the effect of that medication was instantaneous, slowing down his racing brain, and helping him to think clearly. He had told his mother after his first dose, "Mum – I can think in a straight line!"

Much to Jonathan's relief, Max passed the school entrance exam with flying colors but, curiously, Jonathan continued to insist that Max did not have ADHD, despite all the evidence to the contrary. Although he didn't stop him from taking the medication, Jonathan just didn't ever want the word mentioned around him. It almost felt like a 'dirty little secret' to Max and Brigitte.

Max was a was hugely creative child, with fantastic musical ability. He was naturally drawn to the piano, which he begged his parents to let him play at the age of six, before his ADHD diagnosis. Brigitte was delighted at his interest, but Jonathan hated the idea of it, and tried to get him interested in a variety of alternative instruments. "You should learn the saxophone." he would tell him, "Or the guitar. The piano is such a girly instrument – and you wouldn't want to be called a *girl*, would you?" This was another occasion when Max remembers Brigitte standing up for him. He turned out to have exceptional talent, and it was one of the few things that he was able to focus on for hours on end.

Luckily, he was so engrossed when he played that he never really noticed Jonathan putting his headphones in, if he was practicing in the house – and nor did he hear his irritated mutters, such as "That bloody boy is butchering Beethoven… He'd be turning in his grave if he could hear him…"

It was a very different story in public though, and Jonathan would make sure that Max played a solo at every school open day, and during school concerts. At these events he would beam with pride; give Max a standing ovation with loud 'bravos'; and mutter "chip off the old block!" just loudly enough for anyone around him to hear. He even had a large black and white photo of Max, seated at a Steinway grand piano, on his office wall, near to the bust of the man Jonathan claimed was his great grandfather. It was rather confusing for Max, to say the least.

At the age of nineteen, Max plucked up the courage to tell his mother that he was gay. Of course, Brigitte embraced his sexuality and was pleased that he had been able to tell her, but expressed sadness at how he'd felt he'd had to keep it from her for two years. It was an emotional day, but Max was adamant that he didn't want to tell his father himself, and that he'd rather Brigitte did it when he was back at university. He knew that his father would have trouble accepting it, and would see it as a flaw – and he was right.

At first, Jonathan was incensed that Max could bring shame upon them in this way, and called him a 'pervert', and numerous other expletives. He refused to believe that Max knew what he was talking about, and accused him of 'jumping on the homosexual bandwagon'. He had shaken with anger when Brigitte told him, full of added rage that Max had decided to tell *her*, but not him.

Max, feeling guilty that he hadn't treated his parents in the same way, phoned Jonathan several times, but he refused to take his calls. Jonathan completely shut him out for a whole year, sending only one message in response to Max's frantic communications. It simply read "You are dead to me now. I have done my grieving."

His father was also angry with Brigitte for maintaining contact with her only child, but Max knew that she would never agree to cut him off. Sadly though, she did feel she had to hide her phone calls and messages to him, which made them less frequent, and she didn't feel able to visit him at university, as Jonathan always insisted on being able to track her location though her phone 'for safety reasons'. It meant a lot of sneakiness – Max could only visit her when Jonathan was away at a teachers' conference, and they couldn't go out in public in case word got back to Jonathan.

When Max's cousin Charlotte got married, things got more awkward still. Charlotte and Max and been exceptionally close throughout their lives but Jonathan made it clear, via Brigitte, that Max should not attend the wedding, as he and Brigitte would be going. Max was in a dilemma. He didn't want to cause tension on Charlotte's big day, but he also knew that she would be upset if he wasn't there. He felt he had little choice but to come clean to Charlotte about the issues he was having with his father. She was shocked at Uncle Jonathan's behavior, but insisted that she wanted Max to be there and that she could seat them on different tables.

The day came after a sleepless night for Max, but nothing could have prepared him for his father's bizarre behavior. He acted as if absolutely nothing was wrong, hugging him with giant smiles, and proclaiming "Ah there he is, my boy!" He even looked utterly charmed when Max danced with his mother at the wedding after-party. However, when they happened to bump into each other in the privacy of the hotel lobby restroom, when no one else was there, Jonathan completely blanked him, with barely suppressed fury emanating from him. Max had known for a long time that his father prioritized maintaining a perfect facade above all else, but even he was surprised (and hurt) by this episode.

However, a year later, Jonathan had seemed to completely forget that he was ever disgusted by his son's sexuality. In fact, he was openly embracing all things LGBTQ, and insisted that the school have a morning assembly on the subject, and a special LGBTQ after-school club for pupils. He asked Max to speak at the assembly, and was genuinely surprised and offended when he declined, branding Max as 'oversensitive'. But finally Jonathan had found the subject that saw him secure interviews on the TV and radio. LGBTQ rights in schools became the subject he tweeted about the most, and he was even quoted in a national newspaper.

Brigitte, ever the enabler, was thrilled that Max was back in the fold, and told him, "See – I told you that it would all blow over. Time heals all wounds!"

Not this wound, Max thought to himself, saddened by Brigitte's invalidation of his feelings. But he knew that he would never stop hoping that he could have a meaningful relationship with his father – and maybe one day even gain his approval and love.

Becoming a narcissist's enabler

I've mentioned enabling before, but here we see how Brigitte enabled and minimized the unacceptable behavior of Jonathan towards their son. Brigitte has no idea that Jonathan is a narcissist. She believes that Jonathan is a loving father, because 'all fathers must love their children', according to her belief system.

Our tendency to project our own qualities, values and belief systems onto others works against us when it comes to narcissists. It clouds our judgment and prevents us from seeing things clearly. It means that we assume that another person's driving forces must be as wholesome as our own. And it leads us to make excuses for exploitative, uncaring, 'odd' behaviors over and over again.

I have never met a parent who shares children with a narcissist who hasn't fallen into this trap, at least for a time – and they inevitably feel horrified and full of shame when they realize it. That they have invalidated their children's feelings about their narcissistic parent's treatment of them and normalized the narcissistic parent's behaviors can be difficult to accept. There's a lot of self-forgiveness involved in being a narcissist's enabler, as a parent – but this is a vital part of moving forwards.

How do narcissists behave towards their children?

Children are extensions of the narcissist

Narcissists see their children as *extensions of themselves* – they do not see them as being separate from them. And what that means is that their children should have to *be* what they want them to be, *do* what they want them to do, and *have* what they want them to have. This is plainly evident in the way that Jonathan disapproves of Max's university choice, and his choice to play the piano. Narcissists are unable to see their children as individuals, with their own needs and wants.

This inability to recognize and prioritize their children's needs can have various consequences when the non-narcissistic parent is not around to make up for the narcissist's parenting deficiencies. Narcissistic parents might forget to feed their children until they feel hungry themselves, for example. Risk taking behaviors are also common – if a narcissist doesn't feel unsafe around a swimming pool, then why would their three-year-old be unsafe? If a narcissist doesn't see the point of wearing a cycle helmet themselves, then why would their child need to wear one? If a narcissist doesn't get scared when driving at high speeds, then why would their child? Their lack of respect for rules and laws also plays into these risky behaviors – children's car seats, required by law, are commonly seen as unnecessary by narcissists, to give an example.

But this inability to see children as being separate from themselves also means that a narcissistic parent cannot tolerate imperfections in their children. Remember that narcissists need others to see them as unique, and perfect. So if their *children* are not perfect, then this directly affects how others see *them*. Learning issues,

"Narcissists are unable to see their children as individuals, with their own needs and wants."

> "A narcissistic parent cannot tolerate imperfections in their children..."

such as ADHD and dyslexia are commonly seen as imperfections by narcissists (even ones who work in education). They simply cannot be taken on board, unless they stand to gain narcissistic supply from them in some way. Similarly, Max being gay is another 'imperfection' which Jonathan could not tolerate, until he could turn it to his own advantage.

If we think back to our Communal Narcissist, Marcus, he was unable to tolerate the imperfection of his stepson, Janis, having asthma. This is a surprisingly common feature of narcissistic parenting, which can have dangerous consequences for the child, for example when treatment for their condition is withheld. Accusing the child of 'making it up' or telling them to 'just start breathing properly' during asthma attacks whilst withholding inhalers, is a dangerously common narcissistic event.

A narcissist may even try to block a child's diagnosis and treatment (even going as far as making applications to the court, if you are separated), and should a diagnosis be obtained, they might even refuse to accept it as true. Where a child needs counseling or psychotherapy, a narcissist may also step in and forbid this, and this may also be down to the added layer of them being deeply uncomfortable with the child revealing anything they cannot control to a third party.

As the narcissist does not see themselves as separate from their children, boundary violations with children are also common. They may insist on tracking their children, as Lina, our Closet Narcissist did. She needed to know what her children were doing at all times, and expected instant responses to her intrusive messages. Narcissists will violate their children's privacy in other ways too – by insisting that they keep bedroom doors open at all times, by barging into their rooms without warning, and by breaking into their devices and looking through their diaries. In really extreme situations, sexual abuse can also be a manifestation of these boundary violations. And, if the child tries to assert their boundaries, they will cause narcissistic injury and rage and find themselves at the mercy of their narcissistic parent's wrath.

But there's also a unique, seemingly paradoxical dynamic going on with their children, which adds an extra layer of complexity. Because, at the same time as being unable to see them as separate from themselves, narcissists will also subject their children to all the other abusive behaviors that they subject everyone else to.

General narcissistic parenting behaviors

A narcissist's children are *objects* which belong exclusively to them, and so can be used in whatever ways serve the narcissist – as admirers, confidants, servants, or even as punchbags. In divorce, they will be used as weapons against the other parent. And their children will receive no empathy from them (unless there happens to be an audience), and will be unable to care when the child needs their support the most (unless the issue reflects on them in some way). Think back to how Marcus left his stepson Janis in the car with a broken leg for an hour, whilst he watched the rest of the football match.

A narcissist's children are also sources of *direct* narcissistic supply, in all the usual ways – they give the narcissistic parent attention and adoration, they place them on a pedestal, they allow them to exert power and control over them, they engage in their dramas and conflict and they live in fear of them.

But narcissists also use their children as *indirect* sources of narcissistic supply too – to obtain fuel from onlookers. Remember how Jonathan, our headmaster, couldn't tolerate his son Max being gay, until he found a way to use it to procure narcissistic supply for himself, in becoming a national school LGBTQ advocate? How, even though he didn't want him to play the piano, he would applaud him loudly at concerts, and happily take the glory for his talents?

And Marcus got immense narcissistic supply from the admiration of the mums who came to watch him coaching his stepson Janis's football team, in deliberately tight-fitting shorts and T-shirt. His outward persona of 'perfect stepdad' was much admired in the process. And Lina used her lavish children's parties simply as a way to gain the admiration (and jealousy) of others.

A narcissist's child has another important function to perform, because they also actually form part of the narcissist's false image – that of the perfect parent with the happy family.

Just as they do with their partner, narcissists will also devalue their children, as part of the cycle of idealization and devaluation. They might call them names, ridicule them, or comment on their weight, or appearance. This can be subtle, or disguised with 'I was only joking' justifications. The child's emotions, thoughts, wants and needs will also be invalidated, but the narcissistic parent will expect their children to prioritize *their* needs, and they will be punished if they don't comply, through passive aggression (such as silent treatments), or even violence.

Of course, narcissistic parents can be highly controlling, and some will find it very difficult to relinquish this control as the child grows up and individuates from them. Do you remember how Lina would insist that her children wore the clothes that she put out for them the night before, even as teenagers, and how she wouldn't allow 15-year-old Laila to have her hair cut short? Narcissists are also highly manipulative and may try to sabotage their children's attempts to leave home or go to university, and may even insist that they work for them, or make them financially dependent upon them in some way, so that they can maintain their control over them.

> *"Narcissists will also subject their children to all the other abusive behaviors that they subject everyone else to."*

A narcissist's sense of entitlement can also be hugely problematic when it comes to parenting, especially in areas which do not provide rich rewards in narcissistic supply terms. Menial, routine tasks, which are accepted as a normal part of parenting by non-narcissists, are often ignored by narcissists, who feel entitled *not* to do them. Some narcissists will engage in these tasks so that they can gain admiration from others, however, but sadly they are merely playing the outward role of perfect parent, rather than actually catering to the needs of their child. The non-narcissistic parent has often made up for these deficiencies within the relationship, but they become very obvious indeed after separation, when they are not around to pick up the pieces or take up the slack.

Very young children may have to cook meals for themselves when staying with their narcissistic parent, and bath-time and tooth brushing may simply not happen during their time with the narcissistic parent. Clean laundry and bedding for the children may not be provided at their house, and I've even heard of cases where children have been made to regularly sleep on the sofa, or even the floor (even where the narcissistic parent is affluent). A narcissistic mother I heard of felt so entitled not to do menial tasks that she would keep her 14-year-old son off school to clean the house for her whenever she was expecting guests.

Getting children to extracurricular activities on time also seems difficult for many narcissistic parents, as these are not areas of high priority for them, and it is common for children to miss out because of this. I'm also reminded here of a narcissist who insisted that his son took karate lessons, which the boy hated. The narcissist arranged for lessons to fall on the mother's parenting time without agreement, and even expected her to sew all the badges on to the child's uniform – a task far too menial for him.

Communications from the school may be deemed boring and so ignored. Homework and exam revision are unlikely to be facilitated and parent's evenings and sports days are often not attended by the narcissistic parent, unless they are desperate for continued contact with you (as some will be), when they will use these as excuses to constantly be in touch.

Routine appointments, such as with opticians and dentists, will usually fall upon the non-narcissistic spouse, but again, these may be used by the narcissist as excuses for contact with their ex, to the point where they may even insist upon being present.

Narcissistic parents are often late for their children and, post-separation, it's a common story for children to find themselves waiting around at the other parent's home, all ready to go, with their bags packed, for hours, until the narcissist deigns to show up. Of course, this is another way to exert control on the other parent, by attempting to scupper any plans they might have made for their time without the children. It can be incredibly frustrating, especially as you can be sure that the narcissist will not appreciate being made to wait for the children themselves.

It's also common for narcissistic parents to change plans at the eleventh hour and not bother to inform anyone of these changes. Many a young child has simply been left waiting at the school gates as a result, and you can't expect an apology to be forthcoming from your narcissistic ex, as you race over to the school, having cancelled your plans. Narcissists will also often bring the children back to you before they are due to be returned, or return them inappropriately late, even on school nights.

Triangulation is also commonly employed as a narcissistic tactic with children, who can be triangulated with their peers, cousins or anyone else. A variation of triangulation, the dynamic of the 'golden child, the scapegoat and the invisible child' is particularly damaging in families where there is more than one child. The golden child is the child who can do no wrong. The scapegoat is the child who can do no right and, if there is a third child, they are cast as the invisible child – the child who is completely unseen and ignored.

Narcissists love drama, and the children will be pitted against each other, all jumping through hoops in order to try get the narcissist's attention and praise, as the scapegoat and invisible child desperately vy for the role of the golden child.

The scapegoat will be subjected to all the normal narcissistic abuse tactics we have discussed, and if you remember, it was Lina's daughter Laila, who had been allocated this role, with her brother Arun cast as the golden child. The narcissist may even enlist other family members in abusing the scapegoat, and it is often this child who becomes the cycle breaker in adulthood, and cuts off contact with their narcissistic parent, and their enablers.

The invisible child learns that they do not matter. They grow up without the concept of having rights, wants or needs, and this plays out in their adult relationships, where they either develop their own narcissistic defenses in order to feel special, or they become magnets for narcissists or addicts.

The golden child, like all children of narcissists, will eventually come to know that being loved by that parent is conditional on them being who the narcissist wants them to be, rather than who they actually are. They are likely to carry this pattern into their adult lives, and often becomes narcissistic themselves. And, having idealized their narcissistic parent and been rewarded for it with praise and love, they commonly end up as the child who eventually inherits all the family money, leading to yet more tension with their adult siblings. As far too many people will know, narcissistic parents are even adept at delivering blows from the grave. An adult golden child of a narcissistic father, now in her late 50s, recently bitterly described the dynamic to me as being 'like living in a war zone, with everyone fighting for a role that they didn't know wasn't worth having'.

To add to the toxicity of this dynamic, at some point, the roles of the children may be switched. It may take months or even years, and it could be as a result of external circumstances, or for no discernible reason at all. This is an excellent way for the narcissist to keep their children on their toes. Typically, this form of triangulation goes on forever, even when the children are grown up.

A concept that always seems bizarre to non-narcissists is the fact that narcissists are also often jealous of their children, or of anyone they feel they are competing with for their children's attention. Narcissistic mothers are often envious of their daughters' talents, youthful looks and boyfriends (who they may even flirt with, driven by their need to 'win'). Even if they sing their praises and boast about them in public, behind closed doors they will put them down and criticize them.

Narcissistic mothers often also compete with their son's girlfriends or wife, and will use devaluation to raise their own importance relative to them, on their hierarchical scale of thinking. As adults, the children of narcissists often find themselves roped into making financial decisions for the parent, as their narcissist parent plays the victim and pretends to be unable to cope.

Children are often also used as confidants or companions, and may be 'parentified' and forced to take over some of the roles of the absent parent. An adolescent son of a narcissistic mother recently described to me how, during a heated argument with her, he found himself trying to explain that he 'was not her friend or her partner' because of her habit of confiding in him about her own adult issues.

The long-term effects of narcissistic parenting

With unopposed abuse, the children of narcissists may go on to

- Become narcissists themselves
- Become narcissist 'magnets', attracting narcissists in later life
- Develop 'insecure attachment styles' with others, leading to difficulties in maintaining adult relationships
- Develop anxiety, depression and self-harming behaviors

- Develop addictions
- Develop eating disorders

You can see from this list, if you do split from your children's other parent, why it will be so important to consider how much time you will be able to spend with your children to limit any potential damage from occurring. But I should reassure you at this point that it *is* possible to protect your children from these terrible consequences, even if you do split up, by consciously choosing how you parent them. We'll take a look at this next.

Protecting your children from narcissistic parenting

One of your biggest fears is likely to be that your child will go on to become a narcissist, if you leave them in their narcissistic parent's care for any length of time, so let me put your mind at rest, by explaining that you have a lot more power here than you might realize, even if the child was to end up primarily living with the narcissist.

Research has shown that if the child can form a 'secure attachment' with just one parent, the development of narcissism is unlikely. Here the child knows and trusts that they always have someone to turn to, who will always be on their side, who wants the best for them, who sees them and celebrates them as an individual, who encourages them to explore who they are and who loves them unconditionally – so let that person be you, because, sadly, it will never be their narcissistic parent.

The way to do this is by adopting the so called 'authoritative' parenting style, which is the optimal style of parenting. Authoritative parents invest a lot of effort into creating and maintaining a positive relationship with their children. They enforce rules and boundaries, but with warmth and empathy.

This is the style of parenting that you want to employ to prevent narcissism in your child.

Another important strategy is encouraging the development of empathy in your child – because if a child can develop true emotional empathy, *then they cannot develop narcissism.* *Showing* them empathy is key, by being emotionally available to them, as is encouraging your child to describe their own feelings, as accurately as they can. Making talking about feelings the norm, perhaps in relation to how people they know, or fictional characters in films or books, might be feeling is also very effective. A word of warning though – don't expect your adolescent to be high in the empathy stakes for a few years – reduced empathy in adolescents is a normal state of development, and it does *not* mean that they are destined to be a lifelong narcissist.

Bear in mind that your children's narcissistic parent will not see them as individuals, nor be interested in who they are as people. They won't be able to recognize their needs or consider their wants, and they won't be interested in celebrating their successes with them, unless they reflect well on them. They won't really listen to their fears, nor validate their dreams, and they won't be any good at commiserating with them when things don't go as they wanted. They will be late for them and they won't let them know that they are unconditionally loved for exactly who they are (because, frankly, they are not).

> *"If the child can form a 'secure attachment' with just one parent, the development of narcissism is unlikely."*

So if *you* can do all of these things effectively (knowing that you can't be perfect all of the time) then your children will eventually come to see the stark contrast between you and your narcissistic co-parent. They really will then make up their own minds about who to rely on and trust, and your modelling of these behaviors to them will be a starting-point for how they themselves learn to relate to others. It may seem too simple, but it really works.

How the narcissist uses their children as weapons

One of the most shocking behaviors narcissists exhibit is using their children in order to get back at their ex-partner, with no regard as to how that might affect the children. Using the children is a perfect way to punish *you* for leaving – one of the best weapons in the narcissist's armory, in fact – and a narcissist will try to continue this behavior for as long as they can. Narcissists use their children as weapons of emotional, financial and legal abuse, and as ever, it's because they are ultimately trying to secure narcissistic supply from you, through the drama and conflict that they are causing. If they can use the children as an excuse to see you in person, to secure the grade A supply they will obtain from feeding off your reactions, even better. What follows is a summary of the tactics they will employ to abuse you, by using the children, during and after a break-up.

Emotional abuse

During your separation and post-separation they will:

- Demand that the children spend much more time with them than they really want, to reduce *your* time with them, leading to custody battles
- Claim that you have been abusive or violent towards the children as a way to reduce your contact with them.
- Limit your contact with them to supervised visits only, by claiming to the authorities that you are an unsafe parent
- Claim that the children do not wish to see you, are frightened of you, are adversely affected by contact with you (perhaps with allegations of bedwetting or nightmares after seeing you)
- Make false allegations of poor or abusive parenting on your part to the school or the authorities
- Gaslight the children by badmouthing you to them, for example claiming that you 'had an affair', have 'taken all the money', are 'lazy', are 'not contributing' financially towards them
- Actively alienate the children from you, by making them believe things about you that are not true, so the children begin to believe that they do not want to see you
- Make false allegations of parental alienation against you, if the children don't want to see them due to their behaviors
- Threaten to move the children far away/out of the jurisdiction of the court or even abroad
- Spend time with *your* friends and family, when they are looking after the children, so violating your boundaries
- Make false allegations about your friends and family, to try to prevent the children from seeing them, to exert control
- Bombard you with constant correspondence about the children

- Insist to the children that you should be 'adult' enough to host joint birthday parties for them or to be together as a family unit at Christmas
- Turn up to the school gates on your school pick up days to 'see the children' or 'present a united front' to them
- Accompany you to the children's medical or dental appointments (when they never did so during the marriage) out of 'concern' for the child
- Insist upon attending parents' evenings and sports days with you
- Try to sit next to you at school or sporting events 'for the sake of the children'
- Fail to allow the children to have indirect contact with you, whilst they are staying with them, through previously agreed channels, such as FaceTime or WhatsApp
- Repeatedly request changes to the dates and times that they have the children
- Collect them from you late, return them early or late and make you wait when you collect them
- Take the children to *your* favorite restaurant, show, hotel or holiday, to make you feel as though you have 'missed out'
- Withhold consent for you to take the children away on holiday
- Withhold or frustrate your contact with the children by claiming they are ill
- Delay providing you with the children's passports until the last minute, before a holiday, to cause drama
- Encourage friendships with other children who they know you disapprove of
- Return the children with unwashed clothes, uniforms or sports kit to disrespect, devalue and control you

- Keep the children up late on school nights so that they are tired and tetchy during their time with you
- Insist that you attend mediation with them regarding child-related issues, as often as possibleInsist on family therapy or co-parenting counseling under the guise of wanting to co-parent more cooperatively for the sake of the children
- Introduce the children to their new partner without warning, or inappropriately quickly, to upset you
- Engineer high conflict situations with the school, resulting in the child being removed from the school, so they need to be home schooled (by you)
- Refuse to allow assessments (or treatments) of the child for medical issues or learning difficulties, to cause conflict with you
- Refuse to communicate with you regarding the children at all
- Repeatedly criticize your parenting directly to you.

Financial abuse

Expect the narcissist to use the children as weapons of financial abuse in various ways, including by:

- Refusing to pay child support, or making payments sporadically
- Refusing to continue to pay for school fees, so that they have to leave their schools, even if they can afford to continue to pay
- Refusing to contribute towards extracurricular activities, tuition or school trips
- Throwing away their clothes, shoes and uniform bought by you, so that you are forced to replace them
- Failing to return or provide schoolbooks, clothes or other necessary items, so that you have to buy them again

- Refusing to replace items which have been 'lost' whilst in their care, so that you have to buy them
- Directly financially abusing the children, even taking away their presents or their own money
- Enlisting the children to take things from your house to give to them, on the grounds that they 'belong to them'.
- Insisting that they need a private education (to be paid for by you)
- Applying to schools without your knowledge or consent
- Refusing to contribute to the children's university fees or living expenses, even if they are perfectly able to do so, so that you feel compelled to, even if you are the lower earner

Legal abuse

- Taking you back to court repeatedly over child related issues, including false allegations of abuse, false allegations of unsafe parenting, changes in school, preventing educational psychology assessments or diagnosis or treatment of conditions, and trying to increase their time (to decrease your time) with the children. Unfortunately, the court will usually take their allegations seriously, even if they are repeated, and you can be dragged back to court for years
- Repeatedly insisting that you attend mediation with them regarding the children, so that you have to pay half the mediator's fee
- Directly writing numerous letters to your solicitor to run up your legal costs, containing various false allegations to do with the children
- Enlisting their lawyer to copy and paste their own abusive allegations regarding the children into letters, to send to your lawyer, to run up your legal bills

NARCISSISTS IN DIVORCE: FROM LOVE-LOCKED TO LEAVING

The realities of co-parenting with a narcissist

So now you know exactly what you can expect if you leave your partner, with regards to the children, and you know that these behaviors could go on for years. If your relationship has been a relatively long one, you might have gleaned some useful information from the narcissism tests in Chapter 5, regarding roughly where your partner might be on the spectrum of narcissism. The higher their score, the more narcissistic they are likely to be, and the more divorce and separation behaviors you are therefore likely to encounter. The higher up the spectrum they are, the more extreme these behaviors are also likely to be.

It's important that I tell you that all is not lost, however – far from it. There *are* effective ways to deal with this type of post-separation abuse. I deal with these in the follow-on book from this, *Narcissists in Divorce: From Leaving to Liberty*, which will teach you specific communication tactics, as well as give you a really strong game plan to manage the narcissist until your children are grown up.

If the specific strategies in that book are followed, most people will be able to largely prevent these behaviors, leaving them relatively free of their narcissistic co-parent. But not all narcissists (in particular the ones who are really high on the spectrum) will leave you alone completely – and some may keep coming back to you whenever things have gone wrong for them in other parts of their lives, and they need another hit of supply from you. However, you can deal with even this effectively, once you have the right tools.

But I do need to absolutely clear about one thing, and, as a parent who hoped to bring up children with the person you loved, in a family unit, this will be a devastatingly sad thing to have to face. It will *never* be possible to peacefully and cooperatively co-parent with *any* pathologically narcissistic ex-partner. Narcissists simply do not co-parent, because their children are merely objects to be used in whatever way serves their interests. They will always be used as pawns in their parent's game of needing to 'win' against you. And not only do narcissists not co-parent, but they actively 'counter-parent' – doing the exact opposite of what you would prefer to do, regardless of what the child wants, and of what is truly in their best interests.

You will never be able to invite your narcissistic ex in for a coffee whilst the children get their bags ready to spend the weekend with them. You will never be able to go on family holidays together, or be at family occasions together without there being an awful lot of tension. You will never even be able to celebrate your children's successes together over a friendly phone call. And this will not just be due to their behaviors in relation to the children – some will be because of the other unforgivable ways in which they ramped up their abusive behaviors towards you in your separation or divorce, which I will cover briefly in the next chapter.

And, just to add even more insult to injury, very few people around you will be able to understand why you can't just 'let it go' and become friendly towards your ex, 'for the sake of the children'. People really do not understand the dynamics and limitations of NPD, and are completely unable to recognize continued post-separation abuse when it is subtle, as it often is when

"Not only do narcissists not co-parent, but they actively 'counter-parent'"

conducted by narcissists. This can be very isolating, and feeling judged by those who simply don't 'get it' can make things even harder for you. But you *will* find your tribe – those who will have your back, and who will make the effort to understand what you are experiencing.

When your child favors the narcissistic parent

Just sometimes it is not possible to prevent this outcome, which may go as far as your child no longer wishing to have contact with you, at least for a time. I mentioned parental alienation earlier, but I have to warn you that this really does happen. It may occur because their brains learn the technique of cognitive dissonance as a psychological survival tactic, where they deny, minimize or justify the difficult behaviors of the narcissist, so that they are not in mental discomfort, choosing to believe in the version of their parent who is charming, fun, rich or 'cool'.

As you know from experience, this is confusing enough for *adults* who understand NPD, so what chance does a child have in making sense of it? It may also be that the child decides that, even though they know their parent is toxic, they are going to feel safer if they side with the 'bully'.

In this chapter, I have tried to alert you to all the issues that commonly arise, to some degree, if you leave a narcissistic co-parent. I've been completely honest, and although I run the risk of being accused (by a naive minority) of scaring people needlessly, I stand by what I am having to tell you – because I want you to be forearmed.

I know for a fact that many people have left relationships with narcissists with no idea of the battlefield they were stepping into, and a good number wondered whether they would have done things slightly differently had they known what they were embarking upon.

I know that this will not have been a pleasant chapter to read, especially in the emotional state that you are likely to be in, but I want you to know that what I have told you does not have to be a bar to you leaving. If you can *predict* these behaviors, you can often prevent them, and you definitely can learn to manage the ones that do occur.

In the words of Louis Pasteur – 'Chance favors the prepared mind'. We can't change the narcissist – but we absolutely can step into our own power.

8

Deciding whether to leave

Why is this so emotionally difficult?

You might be wondering, at times, whether you are overreacting to all of this. After all, you will know people who have had difficult relationships, who have either chosen to stay, or decided to leave, and whilst they might have found the process hard, they seemed to cope better than you. Yes, they had periods of 'ugly crying on the bathroom floor', but nothing quite like what you are experiencing.

Maybe I am just weak, you might be thinking. In fact, the opposite is likely to be true. The longer you were able to stay in this relationship, the *stronger* you are likely to be in temperament, just to have been able to cope with the experience – although I appreciate that you probably don't feel that way now.

Maybe the fact that you are finding this so difficult is a sign 'from above' that you should stay? Just 'listen to your gut', people might be advising you. And yes, it is a scientific fact that there is an ancient connection between your gut and brain, which alerts you to things without you needing to engage rational reason. But you may have lost touch with those gut feelings and, given that you have ended up in a relationship with a narcissist, you probably won't be hugely trusting of any gut feelings you do have for quite a while. Once again, if that resonates with you, it's entirely normal in this situation. There are ways to get back touch with this, but that's for much later on.

It's also highly likely that your brain will still be swinging between two versions of the truth at this stage, to try to resolve any feelings of cognitive dissonance, as discussed in Chapter 4, and this probably continues to feel disconcerting. But there are other added reasons why this process of coming to terms with the truth about what your partner is (and what your relationship was) is so very difficult. Firstly, there is grief.

Grief

Regardless of whether you choose to stay (for now, or for the long haul), or whether you decide to leave, something has been irretrievably lost. The partner who you believed to be the person of your dreams, who you may have loved more deeply than you love yourself (as victims of this type of relationship often do), is no more. They are never coming back. Worse, much worse than that – they were never real to begin with.

Years, or even decades, may have passed since you first met and fell for them, and this is likely to be the first time that you have ever had to face this awful truth: your relationship was a lie. You will start to revisit every memory from a different perspective, and place upon it a different meaning.

It's worse than parting through death, because you cannot grieve the loss of something that wasn't real – or can you? What *was* real was *your* love – misplaced though you might now feel it was. What *was* real were your good intentions. Your hope for a future of togetherness, filled with laughter and shared dreams –

those were real. Everything that *you* put in was real. Everything that you gave up. You have every right to grieve.

Should you tell yourself that your partner is dead, and that the person who is probably still in your home, is *not them*? Should you look through old photographs, and revisit the good times, viewing them through this new lens, as a widow or widower might? I don't know the answer to that, but I do know that there is no way of getting out of the grieving process, and that one day, it will come to end. What I can suggest is that you turn towards it and embrace it, because, quite simply, the sooner you do that, the quicker it will be over.

There are a number of models of grief, from a scientific perspective, but the one that I feel is the closest in relevance to this situation remains the Kubler-Ross model. There are five parts to this – Denial, Anger, Bargaining, Depression and Acceptance. These are *not* 'stages' to go through in order, as originally proposed – you can experience them at the same time, and you can also vacillate back and forth between them.

When feelings overwhelm you, I want you to understand that these are *normal* parts of the grieving process, and if you can identify which of the parts you are experiencing at the time, it can be really helpful in allowing you to have a little self-compassion. These are feelings which you need to *actually feel,* so that your brain can process them, uncomfortable as they are, so give yourself permission to completely give in to them when they occur.

Denial ('this isn't really happening') will probably already be familiar to you. Anger may also be something you have already experienced, perhaps in waves. You'll probably feel anger towards yourself, towards your partner, towards anyone who enabled them, towards anyone who made you susceptible to this type of relationship (perhaps your parents) and towards life itself. Anger in this context is a *healthy* emotion, no matter what anyone tells you. Let it out in any safe way you can. Rant to a close friend, howl at the moon, scream, punch your pillow, do whatever exercise may help you to express it, or angrily write in your journal.

A word of warning here – you may feel compelled to express this anger to your partner. If you do, expect to be invalidated and blamed – they will not take responsibility, understand or care, and you will not get any closure. And if you are pushed to express it physically, perhaps by shouting at them and pushing them, you are likely to find that they will call the police. This is not something you want on record if you are thinking of leaving them, especially if you share children.

Bargaining is usually a way to try to gain some control over the situation. You may make a deal with God, if you are spiritual ('if I do this thing will you make it better?') or you may hope that therapy or couples counseling will cure your partner, or will help them to finally understand and change. In bargaining, you are clinging to the hope that you can make things as you want them to be.

Depression occurs as you see the situation as it is, coming to realize that you cannot change it – tiredness, loss of appetite, low mood, crying and an inability to enjoy anything can occur here. Acceptance is the final part, which tends to come on intermittently, in waves. Over time its presence will become a more stable feature of your life, but you cannot hasten its onset. It'll happen – all in good time.

NARCISSISTS IN DIVORCE: FROM LOVE-LOCKED TO LEAVING

Hope and guilt

We are always told to 'never give up hope', but in the case of narcissistic relationships, hope is just a trickster. All through your grieving process you are likely to be intermittently hijacked by hope, and it can feel wrong, as a positive person, to just shut it down.

I want you to know that I am not saying that you cannot stay in a relationship with a narcissist – I am merely saying that any hope you may have that it can be a mutually fulfilling, loving, equally reciprocated relationship is false. You have been fooled in many ways for a long time, and you have been made to question your judgment and your self-trust. Is it worth considering taking back your power, in this one small way, by committing to no longer being lulled into fooling *yourself*?

Guilt is another major player in the maelstrom of emotions that you will be feeling, and your Achilles heel, when to comes to being susceptible to being sucked back into the relationship, even after you've made the decision to leave.

Guilt that you made vows (if you did), in which you said 'in sickness and in health' (because NPD is a 'sickness' after all, right?). Guilt about the children not having a two-parent home. Guilt about them having to leave their schools and the house they love because the finances won't stretch, if you break-up. Guilt about having to re-home your beloved dog. Guilt about just 'giving up' and not trying harder. There might be religious guilt, guilt at letting down your in-laws, guilt at breaking up social circles and making people 'choose sides' – the list goes on.

Your tendency to feel guilt will have been exploited many times by your partner, throughout your relationship, probably through numerous episodes of victim playing. You are exceptionally good at feeling guilt. You might want to remain aware of that, as you move forwards, no matter what choices you decide to make.

Why does it hurt so much?

MRI scan studies have shown that the pain that we feel, when a significant relationship ends, lights up the same areas of the brain that light up in physical pain. The severity of that pain, which is felt as emotional distress, is equivalent to the physical pain felt from a severe burn or a broken arm – an 'eight out of 10' kind of pain, where 10 would be intolerable. This on its own would be hard to bear, but you are contending with many other added factors too, as you now know. 'Euphoric recall' is another one of these.

Euphoric recall and addiction

The victims of narcissists have a tendency to remember past events in a positive light, and to forget the negative things associated with those events. Like looking back on things with 'rose tinted spectacles', euphoric recall is defined as 'the act of remembering events positively'. This phenomenon is probably partially responsible for keeping you stuck in your narcissistic relationship, and, even now that you have an understanding of NPD, it can still play a part in confusing you, when it comes to deciding whether to leave.

As you know, it is thought that the trauma bonding to your partner that you have experienced is essentially an addiction to them, caused by the randomly alternating neurochemical highs and lows produced by their cycles of 'nice narcissist and nasty narcissist'. Interestingly, euphoric recall also happens to people with substance addictions. It is thought that addictions cause changes to an area of the brain, known as the hippocampus, which is responsible for the formation of memories, and how they are stored and retrieved. It also processes the *context* in which things happened. Addicts with euphoric recall seem to remember these contexts incorrectly, and in an overly positive light. This result in addicts being more likely to return to the contexts and environments that they remember incorrectly – and, of course, once they are there, they are likely to relapse. If you are still living with your narcissistic partner, you are in exactly the type of environment where you could relapse into your addiction to them.

You really need to understand that emotionally detaching from a narcissist is much harder than a 'normal' break-up, precisely because you have to break a serious addiction at the same time as experiencing everything else. So, if you are beating yourself up about how 'badly' you are coping, go easy on yourself, please.

The realities of leaving a narcissist

Narcissists ramp up their abusive behaviors in divorce and separation, to a level 10. I've already alluded to some of the behaviors you can expect throughout this book (which I will tackle in more detail soon) and I have explained what lies behind this sudden exacerbation, which I will briefly recap here.

Firstly, if you leave your narcissistic partner, you will have inflicted a 'narcissistic injury' on them – you will have directly pierced the shield of their false persona, which will have left it weak and unable to protect them from their own underlying feelings of shame and inadequacy, which they will now be forced to feel. Not only that, but in leaving, you will no longer be pouring your narcissistic supply into their metaphorical bucket, and because that bucket has a hole in it, the levels of supply within it will drop, to below the levels that are required to keep the shield of their false persona strong.

In these ways you will have dismantled their protection, and this will feel like an existential crisis to them. They will react with rage, to get attention, cause drama and conflict, scare you, and evoke your emotional reactions – and these top-quality types of supply will quickly replenish the bucket, and restrengthen their shield. But the bucket will still be draining away, and you, the biggest, most important source of their supply will only pour into it if they continue to drag you back into play, over and over again. That is why they just cannot let you go during divorce and separation (and afterwards). Not because they want your love, but *because they want your supply*.

Because you are no longer their partner you are also 'all bad'. You have publicly exposed the 'perfect life' that formed an extension of their false persona, as being false. Remember that narcissists can't view people (or themselves) as a blend of good and bad. You therefore deserve to be punished, and their lack of empathy for you, the person they once claimed to love, will be clearly evident, as they try to 'win' on every level. They therefore use every tactic they can to do this.

Although this might sound terrifying, you do have some advantages here – because a narcissist's divorce and separation behaviors are entirely predictable, as you discovered when we previously revealed exactly how they use their children as weapons during the process. So, to help you make your decision, let's start this section by having a look at some of the things you will have to be mentally prepared for, in the early stages of a separation.

Hoovering

Hoovering is the term given to a narcissist's attempts to suck you back into relationship, when they get the sense that you are about to leave. It's widely quoted that it actually takes seven attempts to leave an abusive relationship – and successful hoovering is mostly the reason for this. Have a think about how many times you have come close to leaving, and whether this might have happened to you.

The first thing a narcissist will try is renewed love bombing. They will turn on the charm once again, and become (very nearly) the person you fell in love with. They will flatter you, stop triangulating you with others, appear to listen to your opinions, and try to buy your affections in any way they can. They will apologize for taking you for granted, and will become involved in the menial everyday tasks that you found yourself solely in charge of. They might suggest or agree to couples therapy during this time, make heartfelt sounding promises to change, and resume their future faking.

This is usually enough to pull the grateful victim back into their orbit, and after a few days, weeks, or months, the narcissist, satisfied that their partner is safely back in their cage, will resume their previous behaviors. For them, it will simply be business as usual.

But what happens when the victim can no longer be re-lured into the narcissist's trap

"It's widely quoted that it actually takes seven attempts to leave an abusive relationship – and successful hoovering is mostly the reason for this."

by these love bombing tactics? At this point the narcissist will be starting to get scared. Remember, *they* need *you*, for your supply, and so that you can keep contributing to their image of someone who is in a successful relationship. Abandonment does not sit well with narcissists – so they need to pull something new out of the bag to keep you in your place.

At this point, they will beg you to stay, and dissolve into a messy heap. You may well see their fear, which could be genuine, but once again, this has nothing to do with love (although they will tell you that it has). They may even go into a 'narcissistic collapse' at this stage (one of the consequences of a severe narcissistic injury – do you remember how Marcus retreated to bed for two days after he suffered the injury of being thrown out of the church band?).

The next item on the agenda will be the guilt-tripping, which I mentioned earlier. "How could you not give me another chance, after all these years?", "I have been suffering from undiagnosed depression, and that is why I have been so hard to live with…" "I've been working so hard/having difficulties at work that I didn't want to worry you with", "How could you do this to our children?"

The most impressive hoovering tale I've heard was of a narcissist who went off to see her doctor once she realized that her long-suffering husband was coming to the end of his tether with her behaviors. She returned in a taxi and, looking pale and wan, told him that she had been diagnosed with a stroke and so could not drive, and would have to be looked after at home by him.

She explained that the doctor had been clear that it was the stress of her husband threatening to leave that had done it, and that she would probably die if it happened again. She had not been put on any medication, had not needed a brain scan, and was not being followed up by the doctor, but still her husband (who had been gaslit for decades at this point) fell for it. And a week later, when he was properly secured in his metaphorical compound, the narcissist went off on a high-octane girl's fitness holiday, having miraculously recovered from her near death experience. Extreme stories like this are not uncommon, sadly.

But at some point, probably as the victim is nearing their final escape attempt, even pity plays of this magnitude won't work – and then the narcissist will go nuclear. There will be threats of every conceivable nature, delivered in terrifying ways. They will threaten suicide (a big red flag of an abusive relationship), and may even 'say their final goodbyes' to the children, before disappearing for a few days, knowing that their frantic partner will be beside themselves, desperately trying to track them down.

There will be threats to destroy the house, or burn it down. To call the police, your employer, your family and your friends and tell them that you are a violent child abuser, or a drug addict. They might even get physically violent at this time, even if they haven't before, and may punch through walls to bully you into staying. You might be locked in a room, until you agree to stay, or be threatened with financial ruin or even revenge porn.

You may well feel, after all this, that you have no other option but to stay, but once you agree, the narcissist will immediately behave as if nothing untoward has happened, and suggest you both go out to see a movie/meet friends/go for a drink.

In short, I will tell you this – never underestimate the power of a narcissist's hoover. Even after you've filed for divorce, instructed lawyers and have a court hearing date, they will try to suck you back in, and they may well be successful. If you do decide to leave your partner, you will have to be sure that you are emotionally immune to these predictable tactics. This is harder than it sounds, believe me.

The smear campaign

If you leave a narcissist, you will inevitably find yourself becoming the victim of a smear campaign, even at the hands of a narcissist who prides themselves on having a 'nice' outward false persona.

Playing the victim is the stock response of a narcissist who has been abandoned, which places *you* in the role of the 'perpetrator'. Your injured narcissistic partner will not hold back on their venom, and will tell everyone you know that you are an addict, an abuser, mentally ill, a serial adulterer, and whatever else they can think of.

They will report you to your professional work body for things you haven't done, and even contact your boss. If you have children with them, they might report you to social services with allegations of child abuse, and make false allegations about you to the police. Be warned that, in this scenario, particularly if you happen to be male, you have quite a high chance of ending up spending a night in a police cell, or finding yourself in court as a result of an application for a restraining order.

"Ironically, you may also be labelled as a narcissist yourself, as the real narcissist projects their narcissism on to you."

Your family members will be turned against you, and your neighbors and people in your community might start to give you the cold shoulder. You already know that your narcissistic ex will also badmouth you to your children, and maybe even persuade them to refuse to see you. As previously mentioned, ironically you may also be labelled as a narcissist *yourself*, as the real narcissist projects their narcissism on to you.

The big problem here is that narcissists are very convincing, and people who have not yet worked out how toxic they are *will believe them*. If you leave a narcissist, you have to be prepared for this, and the fact that they are likely (at least for a time) to be believed over you.

You will lose friends

When the penny drops, and you realize that the difficult person in your life is a narcissist, the temptation may be to warn as many people as you can. But there really is little point to this, and you are likely to be labelled as 'bitter' or even 'crazy'. Tell only the very closest members of your inner circle, and no one else, and do not post anything at all about it on social media (and ideally come off social media completely for a while, to remove any temptation to vent there).

Even your closest friends may disappoint you when you tell them about the true nature of your partner, even if they initially seemed to believe you. The fact is this – you will lose friends, at the very least, when you leave a narcissist, and there will be nothing that you will be able to do about it.

If your narcissist is an Exhibitionist Narcissist, who is wealthy and powerful, your mutual friends will likely side with them, not least because of the social cachet they gain from the relationship. Frankly, trying to maintain mutual friends with a narcissist is going to be a non-starter – just the very fact that they *are* friends with the narcissist means that they do not see them for who they are, and do not believe your version of events. Those people that say "I only judge people on what I see" are essentially invalidating your experiences. You'll probably have to let them go, painful though this might be. Leaving a narcissist will inevitably show you the worst side of people – but it will also show you who your real friends are.

You will be victimized by third parties

'Flying monkeys' are the people (named after the characters in *The Wizard of Oz*) who the narcissist enlists to do their bidding for them. They might badmouth you on behalf of the narcissist. They might be recruited to try to hoover you back in ('They love you so much really – they are desperate to get back together'). They might be roped in as secret agents, pretending to support you with your divorce, but actually be reporting back to the narcissist.

These folk are usually members of the narcissist's 'fan club', and want to be special to the narcissist, so that they can feel special by association. However, they might also be narcissists themselves, thriving on the drama and manipulations (especially in families, where there are usually many narcissists in a cluster). Beware the Closet Narcissist family member who 'gets on with everyone in the family' – they might not be the ally you think they are. You will need to be on high alert for these flying monkeys when you leave your narcissist.

The narcissist will find a new partner

It is truly breathtaking how quickly your narcissistic ex will be able to secure themselves a new source of supply (although, unfortunately, they are unlikely to fully make up for *your* quality supply, which they have got so used to). Your ex could be the most unattractive person in the world, but somehow, they will still succeed in quickly finding a romantic partner – because they *have to*. Frankly, that bucket isn't going to fill itself.

They will be on dating apps before the wedding rings have come off, and certainly before anyone has moved out of the marital home. You will have to endure displays of cheerful self-grooming before evenings out, and if they arrive home at all, it will be in the small hours, and they will make sure that you are aware of their return.

If *you* go out, however, don't be surprised if you are subjected to tearful interrogations as to where you are going, and in-depth searches for 'your condoms', or similar. Narcissists are morally hypocritical, if you remember, and nowhere will this be more obvious than during the early phases of your split. And just because you left them, if you did, don't expect the arrival of this new partner not to hurt (but don't be fooled, for even a second, that your partner has finally been blessed to find the love of their life).

If you do find yourself in this situation, you may wonder whether you should warn their new partner that they are narcissist. After all, you, as a likely empathic rescuer, will find it incredibly hard not to want to save an innocent person, as you probably wished someone could have saved you, at the start of your relationship.

But I'm afraid I have to tell you that this can only ever backfire on you. Their new partner will be being love bombed by their 'soulmate', just as you were. They will be thanking their lucky stars, just as you were. They will be the happiest they have ever been, just as you were. They will be hopelessly, deeply, crazily in love, just as you were. And, they will have heard about what an awful person you are – with your serial affairs, abusive behaviors and your alcoholism, and they will believe every word.

They will have been primed to believe that you are jealous of them, and will have been warned to report you to the police for harassment, if you try to get in touch with them – because you are 'unstable', and there is 'no knowing what you might do'. Once again, these are bog standard narcissistic behaviors, and are utterly predictable.

So, I know it might feel like throwing a lamb to the slaughter, but you will have to walk away, and leave the narcissist's new 'supply' to go on their journey alone. It might even be that this will be the first time you put your *own* interests ahead of someone else's. If that is true for you, then I suggest you embrace this lesson, no matter how hard it may seem.

Now you are aware of some the challenges that you will encounter in early separation. You are fully versed on how a narcissist will use the children as weapons of abuse against you if you leave them, and I have described many other behaviors as we have progressed through this book.

In order to help you make your decision regarding whether you can (or should) leave your partner, I have summarized the behaviors to expect in separation in the next section. As with the child-related behaviors (dealt with separately, in Chapter 7) I have divided them into three types of abuse – emotional, financial and legal.

Common behaviors in divorce and separation

Emotional abuse

The following tactics are designed to throw the narcissist's ex off-balance, to punish them for the breakdown of the relationship, to gain a sense of control, to scare them, to upset them, to demonstrate their power, and to maintain contact with them, in order to make up for the loss of their narcissistic supply. Some also serve to give the outside world the impression that they are still 'winners' (even though they have lost their significant other). They include:

- Hoovering attempts
- Blackmail attempts directed at their ex-partner or anyone important to them, in return for a better financial or children related outcome
- Making or threatening to make false allegations to their ex's employer and professional bodies
- Conducting a smear campaign, to isolate their ex-partner from friends and family, including by making false allegations
- Physical stalking and surveillance, sometimes via private investigators
- Tech abuse, including cyberstalking, camera surveillance, tracking devices and listening devices (including in the car, home, computer, children's toys and via smart speakers)
- Breaking into mobile phones and computers to read messages and emails
- Falsifying messages from their ex
- Intercepting their ex's physical mail, or having it redirected to their own address
- Making false allegations of violence, abuse, mental illness or coercive control to the authorities
- Enlisting 'flying monkeys' to spread rumors or to gain their ex's trust for information gathering purposes
- Removing access to family photographs

- Removal of property from the family home without warning or agreement, including vehicles, computers and items of sentimental value to their ex
- Making frequent unwanted contact with their ex, by calling, turning up at the house or other locations, and by messaging or emailing numerous times per day
- Using their ex's address for deliveries, or failing to redirect their own mail to their new home, as an excuse to have contact with their ex
- Trying to undermine their ex's confidence in their lawyer by badmouthing them
- Making claims that their own lawyer is ridiculing or calling their ex names, or is sure that they will 'lose' to the narcissist
- Deliberately spelling their ex's name incorrectly in correspondence, or using a previously unused version of their name
- Flaunting their new partners or dating endeavors in front their ex
- Suggesting that lawyers are not required, and claiming that they will ensure a fair settlement to their ex outside of the legal process
- Refusing to move out of the family home, whilst continuing to engage in abusive behaviors
- Attempting to goad their ex into responding to their abusive behaviors whilst filming or recording them
- Threatening to disseminate videos or photos of their ex online, including revenge porn
- Searching through their ex's belongings for evidence of infidelity, even after separation
- Making threats regarding any pets, including to the children
- Threatening suicide, including to the children

- Threatening to burn down the house or destroy property
- Threatening their partner with financial ruin
- Hiding or removing their ex's financial paperwork, to frustrate the divorce
- Claiming that others are gossiping about their ex, ridiculing them, or badmouthing them
- Bombarding their ex with manipulative, accusatory, nonsensical, threatening correspondence

Financial abuse

Narcissists will:

- Unexpectedly withdraw large sums of money from joint accounts or offset mortgage accounts and spend it
- Spend huge amounts of joint money on luxury designer goods, eg. handbags or diamonds, which will keep their value, and then 'give them away' for the duration of the divorce
- Transfer shares into their parent's/relative's names
- Divert money into 'trusts for the children', so that they are removed from the marital asset pot
- Reduce their work hours to lower their earnings, so they are liable for less maintenance/alimony to their ex, or to gain more maintenance from their ex
- Falsely claim that they are ill or disabled, and so cannot work, or that they are contemplating retiring, to reduce their maintenance liability or to increase their claim for maintenance
- Reduce their income during the financial legal proceedings (especially if they are self-employed), and then increase them once the divorce is finalized
- Reduce their income in the year of the divorce, but overpay tax in line with their previous income. In this way, they will receive

a significant tax rebate the following year, after the financial settlement. A good way to remove money from the marital pot of assets
- Run up debt on joint credit cards, so that their ex-partner is jointly liable
- Transfer jointly held air-miles to themselves
- Encourage flying monkeys to invoice them, or their company, to falsely increase their business expenses.
- Undervalue their business and claim that company assets are 'illiquid'
- Undervalue their assets, and overestimate the worth of their ex's assets
- Sell properties held in their sole name and hide or spend the proceeds
- Demand the return or sale of the engagement ring or of gifts made through the relationship
- Threaten blackmail in return for a more favorable financial deal
- Delay drawing income from their business
- Forgo any company bonuses, if they are employed
- Remove financed vehicles on a lease agreement in their ex's name, to use themselves without financially contributing
- Withdraw their tax-free lump sum from their pension, so that if the pension is subsequently shared with their ex, all withdrawals will be taxable, and the annual amount that their ex can put into their pension will be reduced

If the narcissist is the higher earner of the couple, they will do all that they can to reduce the value of the marital assets, even if it means that *they* also lose money. They will:

- Increase their spending

- Give others expensive gifts, or give money away
- Give assets away, or sell them at low prices
- Invest in business ventures which are likely to fail
- Try to sell the marital home at below its market value, by publicizing that it is being sold due to divorce, to encourage low offers, or by refusing to maintain it so that it falls into disrepair
- Bribe estate agents to reduce the sale price of the marital home
- Stop contributing to house bills, school fees and mortgage payments, and
- Refuse to provide any financial support at all to their ex and the children
- Run up their ex's legal fees by making false allegations about them, which they have to defend through their lawyer or through the court
- Run up their ex's legal fees by insisting upon mediation.
- Run up their ex's legal bills by pretending to reach agreements, but then change their mind, and repeatedly shift the goalposts

If the narcissist is the less affluent partner, they will also make unreasonable demands, due to their sense of entitlement, such as demanding to keep the family home for themselves without having to pay any bills or mortgage. They may refuse to sell the house, and fail to cooperate with house viewings. They may expect to be provided with lifelong financial support by their ex, and will lie, bully and manipulate their ex, in the hope that they will capitulate to their demands.

Legal abuse

Narcissists will use the legal system to their advantage. They will use it as a tool of financial abuse, by forcing you to spend excessively on legal bills, and because of the delays inherent in the court process, they will use it to draw out your divorce or separation, in order to procure narcissistic supply from you for as long as possible. Because they don't respect rules or laws, they will refuse to comply with parts of the legal process and even court orders. The various behaviors, which inevitably overlap with financial abuse, include:

- Insisting upon mediation, with no intention of sticking to any agreements, in order to cause delays and run up your costs
- Refusing to be transparent when disclosing their finances
- Challenging pre-nups and post-nups
- Making false allegations against you (or your family) which result in more court proceedings, and more expense
- Ignoring deadlines
- Increasing your legal bills by writing to your lawyer to make accusations about you, which you will feel you need to respond to
- Lying convincingly on the witness stand, without repercussions (in the UK, shockingly, there is no penalty in the family court for lying on the witness stand)
- Using the children as excuses to make repeated court applications, for example, regarding holidays and schooling
- Forcing you into making court applications by stonewalling you and refusing to engage with your attempts to move things forwards outside of the court process
- Exploiting any loopholes in court orders, where the court orders haven't been explicitly detailed enough
- Using their lawyer as a weapon of abuse, by instructing them to write (or copy and paste their own) abusive letters to send to your lawyer. (In the UK at least, lawyers have to follow their

client's orders, and so regularly become abusers by proxy. Incredibly, there is no professional regulation of this type of behavior.)

Further considerations regarding leaving

I know that I've bombarded you with hundreds of facts, which may be difficult to take on board, especially at this incredibly difficult time. You may be utterly shocked at the divorce and separation behaviors of narcissists that I have laid out. You may be disbelieving of them, and wonder whether I am exaggerating.

We all know people who have had acrimonious divorces, who have experienced some of the behaviors I've just described. But I want remind you once again, that personality disorders are *extreme* variations of normal traits. This means that a narcissist is likely to carry out a *large number* of these behaviors, not just a few, and the higher up the spectrum of narcissism they are, the more *extreme* their behaviors will be. It also means that, because a personality disorder is running the show, they will not 'calm down' over time, and start to see sense, as 'normal' people do.

You may be feeling completely disheartened, and be starting to think that if leaving really does mean being faced with this, you might be better off staying with your narcissistic partner, and resigning yourself to an incomplete, unfulfilled life. After all, you must now be realizing that the very *process* of divorce or separation with a narcissist is traumatizing *in itself* (and here I am talking about trauma with a capital T). Given that sorting out the child arrangements and finances in divorces like this usually takes well over a year, it's pretty obvious why being subjected to sustained, high-level abuse like this could take its toll on you.

But this is why you need to be ready for it. I've already impressed upon you the advantage you will have from being able to pre-empt these behaviors, to head some of them off at the pass. But it's also vital to understand that the *stronger* you are when you begin the process, the less affected you will be by the abusive behaviors that do occur. I have dedicated the final chapter of this book to exactly this, for this very reason.

Throughout this book I have used the term 'leaving your partner'. But a better term is '*escaping* your partner', as a narcissist will do everything they can to keep you available to them as a ready source of narcissistic supply, for as long as they can. The narcissistic ex of a client of mine put it particularly well, when he stated, after she had told him that she was finally leaving for good, that he would 'refuse to be just a speck in her rear-view mirror'. He was true to his word, for a long time, until she learned how to manage him.

Now it may be that your situation at the moment is absolutely intolerable, and that staying even a moment longer will be placing you (and maybe the children) in serious danger, whether that be emotional, psychological or physical danger. If that is the case, then of course you *must* escape, as soon as you are able (even if that would mean escaping to a refuge or similar).

It may also be that you don't share young children with your narcissistic partner, in which case escaping will be so much easier, particularly if you can arrange your finances so that you can be financially independent of them. I always breathe a sigh of relief when working with clients in this situation – although there are still huge challenges, they are so much easier to navigate, and the end of the relationship really can be the end of all contact. No contact, forever, is the gold standard result when ending a relationship with a narcissist. So, if your circumstances make this is a real possibility for you, you may well be ready to escape relatively soon.

But if you do share children with the narcissist, you will be aware of the added complexities and issues that could arise, as we discussed in Chapter 7, which is why, for you, there might be some further considerations.

Firstly, the age of the children might be a factor. In the UK at least, children are able to make their own minds up about which parent they live with (and how often they see the other parent) from the age of 16. What this means in reality, is that, because court proceedings take so long, really they are 'safe' from any attempts of the narcissist to force them to live with them from around age 15, or maybe 14-and-a-half. So if your youngest child is 13, for example, and the situation at home is tolerable and not unsafe, you might wish to delay your escape for a year or so.

Also bear in mind that the older a child is, the more their 'voice' will be heard by the social workers who will report the 'wishes and feelings' of the child back to the court. So a 12-year-old's wishes and concerns will be taken more seriously than a seven-year-old's.

However, if your children are much younger than this, even though the risks of protracted litigation and drama will be higher, it is likely that you will want to bite the bullet, and make your escape early.

On the subject of social workers, who assess the situation to do with any allegations of abuse, mental health issues, or parental alienation, it is crucially important to understand that they do not receive training in personality disorders. Because narcissistic abuse is usually subtle, and because the narcissist can play the victim (and the Disney parent act) with aplomb, they are highly likely to be fooled by them.

At worst, they will believe the narcissist, and you will lose access to, or time with, the children. At best, they will think that you are 'as bad as each other', and that you need family therapy or co-parenting classes. It is relatively rare for social workers to correctly assess the situation when it comes to NPD, and given that they are the professionals (in the UK at least) who advise the judges as to how the children's time should be split between parents, the importance of their role should not be underestimated. Scarily, most judges accept their recommendations without question.

It's also worth considering how much your narcissistic partner is actually around. It might be that they gain a great deal of narcissistic supply from being seen to be successful at work, in which case they may be the sort who is barely at home, and has very little to do with the children. This might mean that their opportunity to damage them is actually fairly limited. However, it's very likely, even if they hardly ever saw or took any interest in the children through your relationship, that they will want a 50:50 arrangement if you split up. If you think this might happen with your partner, how you time your escape will also be crucial.

Some narcissistic parents are so driven by their work that they might actually not want to see the children very much at all, upon leaving, although this is much rarer than the previous scenario. This might also be true of the really lazy, entitled narcissists who find childcare impossibly difficult or boring. Remember, narcissists aren't able to truly love their children, so how much they see them after a divorce is purely a way to gain narcissistic supply, from you, from the children themselves, and from the admiration of others. If they happen to be the type who would get more supply from having the freedom to do whatever they want, unencumbered by children, then you might be onto a winner. You might feel incredibly sad for the children that their other parent doesn't want to be involved, but actually, this will be a blessing, as the damage they can inflict upon the children will be limited.

Your own age and health, and those of your partner, might also be a factor. If you are considering becoming one of the many 'silver separators' in the world, and your narcissistic partner has a terminal illness, for example, can you tolerate your life at home with them until they pass away, or will this just be too much to bear? Your adult children are also likely to be relevant if you fall into this demographic, because if you split up, you can be sure that their narcissistic parent will not give them the financial help they might have been expecting from you as a married couple. University fees or the down-payment on a property are extremely unlikely to be forthcoming from the narcissist, who will simply think of these as ways to financially abuse *you*.

A really huge consideration will also be whether, during your separation, either you or your partner will be able to afford to move out of the family home. Bear in mind that if you leave without the children, you will have handed your partner the perfect way to begin to brainwash your children into not wanting to see you, and to frustrate your contact with them. So, even if you could move out, you might want to stay until the end of the process.

Obviously this might be intolerable, especially as the narcissist will try to draw things out for as long as possible. You'll have to carefully weigh up the advantages of leaving the family home, without the children, with the mental toll that staying there, with the narcissist also present, might have on you.

You might be able to force the narcissist out of the family home through the courts, but this might be harder than you think, and will depend on the laws in your country. For some, the only option might be to escape, with the children, to a refuge – hardly an ideal scenario, but in extreme cases, it could be the most appropriate thing to do.

Your financial situation will also be important to think about if considering making an escape. If you are married, how will you finance a divorce? This type of divorce is the most expensive sort there is, and you can spend eye-watering sums on legal fees, especially if your lawyer doesn't understand or believe the nature of your partner. In your country, what are the rules as to payment of legal fees? Does each partner have to pay their own, or is there a way they can be split between the couple, or even contributed to by the more affluent partner?

How do the courts in your country view loans from family for legal bills? Do they see them as legitimate, and something that will need to be paid back to your family? In this UK, this depends on the individual judge – some see loans from family members as being gifts, which can be a nightmare for you, if you really do have to pay them back. Would you better off getting a specialist 'litigation loan', which can be factored into any financial settlement made?

Do you have any savings to pay for legal bills, or will you need time to build some up, before you make a break for it? Is there any provision in your country for free legal help? In the UK, victims of domestic abuse who fall into certain strict categories can try to get 'legal aid', but often the victims of narcissistic abuse fall through the cracks here, due the subtle nature of the abuse.

It may even be, if you are married, that it might be best for you to separate, move into separate homes, but not divorce until the children are older. I have seen this work where the non-narcissistic partner is affluent enough be able to fund their narcissistic ex's lifestyle, keeping them relatively sweet for a few years by complying with their financial and childcare demands. It requires developing good boundaries and a lot of mental fortitude, but it might actually cost you less overall, financially and mentally, to do this for a few years. This definitely isn't for everyone though.

And what are your financial rights if you are not married, but cohabiting? The law on this differs between countries, and in certain countries, including England, many people mistakenly believe that cohabitees have the same financial rights as married couples – when in fact they do not, even if they share children. Wherever you are in the world, it's essential that you do your homework on this, early, so that you know your rights. (Bear in mind that the narcissist will be the last person to ask, if you want a truthful answer).

In Chapter 7 we discussed the benefits to the children of you ultimately escaping. We also delved into how their being able to live in two contrasting households, with you no longer having to enable their other parent's behaviors, is likely to give them a clear perspective on their narcissistic parent, and a healthy model to emulate in their own adult relationships. But what if, knowing all you now know, and whether you have children or not, you feel you just can't leave, and that you might never be able to? What do you need to know, should you choose to stay with your partner for the long haul?

Choosing to stay in the long term

A fair number of people choose not to leave their narcissistic partners, for a variety of reasons. You might have financial reasons, religious reasons, reasons to do with your family or community, or you might just not be able to face the repercussions if you do leave. I want you to know that this is absolutely okay. You have to do what is right for *you*, and that could be very different to what is right for the next person. But it's crucial that you make this choice with your eyes fully open.

You know that your narcissist is a severely limited individual, and that the shield that they hide behind doesn't only prevent their true feelings about themselves from getting *out*, but it also prevents much of the outside world from getting *in*. You know that no matter what you give, how much you try and how much you love them, you will never change their underlying personality disorder, and you know that you will never truly be enough for them.

You know that true emotional intimacy is never going to be possible with them, and that, from that perspective, your relationship is always going to a lonely, unfulfilling one. You know that you are merely a fuel source, but you now know how admiration and positive attention will work just as well for them as drama and conflict, and that may well be something you can work with. You know that, in some way, you are being exploited by them, and that you will have to simply accept this fact.

You will understand that they will lie to you and gaslight you, and that there will be absolutely no point trying to call them out, as doing so will just fan the flames of conflict. You know that, in fact, there will be no point hoping for accountability with the majority of their behaviors, as they cannot accept responsibility or blame, and will therefore simply shift the blame onto you.

If you are to stay, there will be a lot you will have to learn. You will have to be able to identify when you are being pulled into the drama triangle, so that you can step out of it and leave the vicinity. You will need to learn how to exert your boundaries (although this might not always be effective). You will need to be able to recognize and mentally label their narcissistic behaviors, in real time, so that you do not take them personally, understanding instead that they are simply the products of a miswired brain. You will need to come to terms with the fact that their version of love is merely transactional, find ways to work with that, and accept that as being enough. You may have to turn a blind eye to infidelity, and work to dial down your own jealous reactions.

You will need to cultivate strong friendships outside of your relationship, with people who do cheerlead you, listen to you and validate you. If your family members are mentally healthy, you might wish to strengthen these bonds (which the narcissist may have tried to sever) so that you can be accepted for who you are; treated with care and empathy; and loved in spite of all your glorious imperfections. You will have to tolerate the narcissist wishing to intrude on or sabotage these relationships, and you will have to find a way to maintain them, in spite of that. You may even have to be sneaky – something that might not sit well with you – so that you can do the things you love without the narcissist being able to exert their control onto them.

There will be a lot that you will have to accept, and a lot that you will have to let go of, including resentment, if you are to stave off future issues with your mental and physical health. You will have to learn how to erect a forcefield around yourself, for all the toxicity (which will be an inevitable part of your life) to bounce off.

And knowing what you know about how your narcissist became this way, as a result of their childhood, could you learn to manage them, within the confines of who they are, without judging them? Could you dial down your own rescuing and people pleasing tendencies, and learn to prioritize and meet your own needs? Could you recognize any co-dependent traits in yourself, and work on dissolving them? Could you come to be more mindful of when your own empathy might be being used against you?

Could you, in spite of everything you know about the partner you have chosen to stay with, learn to see not only the bad, but the good? Because narcissists are not *only* narcissists – there is more to every one of them than just that. Their narcissism is the huge green monster who is driving their bus. But on that bus, there are other, much smaller, thinner creatures too, of all shapes and colors, each with different qualities and traits. And some of them are truly amazing. They are there, if you learn to look for them – but you do need to know this: they will never, ever grow big enough to drive that bus.

9

Becoming strong

"If you drink much from a bottle marked 'poison' it is certain to disagree with you sooner or later."

– Lewis Carroll, Alice's Adventures in Wonderland

It may be that you have now made your choice, and have decided to stay in your relationship (at least for the time being). Or perhaps you have resolved to leave, and are trying to come to terms with the momentous nature of your decision. Or maybe you are feeling *relief*, because although you hadn't previously been able to find the strength to leave for *yourself*, understanding the risks to your children led to the decision practically making itself.

But not everyone will have been able to reach a conclusion by now, and no matter how desperate you might be to know which future to embrace, you might have to just accept that this process is not something you can force – and that that is okay.

Understanding NPD, and the consequences of it (not just on you and your immediate family, but on future generations too) takes time to assimilate. It's a bit like throwing a penny into deep well, full of treacle-like fluid. Eventually that penny will sink to the bottom, but it cannot get there without slowly dropping through the layers.

And even as the penny drops, you may find yourself vacillating between your options. This is entirely normal, and just like with grief, the vacillations will become smaller, and occur less often with time. That penny will eventually reach the bottom of the well.

In this chapter, regardless of where you are in this assimilation process, I want to offer you some simple strategies to combat the effects of what you have been dealing with. These will be useful for you regardless of your final decision, but if you do plan to escape, and you can reserve a little time before you do, they could be exactly what you need to set you up emotionally, so that you are much better able to cope with the behaviors that will be coming your way.

Depression, anxiety, complex PTSD and addictions

It's incredibly common for victims of narcissistic abuse to be out of touch with themselves. After all, years of gaslighting and becoming used to not focusing on themselves, can easily mean that they are no longer really aware of how they are feeling, both physically and mentally.

It may be that you are suffering from anxiety, perhaps with physical symptoms, but don't recognize it as that. Diarrhea, stomach cramps, or just a permanent sinking feeling in your gut might be things you are so used that you just consider them to be normal. You might not have realized that even headaches, chest pains, back pain, swallowing difficulties, skin problems and allergic reactions can actually be a manifestation of chronic stress or anxiety.

Or perhaps the stress you are under *is* showing up in ways that you recognize as being connected to your mental health, such as through bouts of panic, or depressive symptoms; like low mood, tearfulness, inability to enjoy anything, lack of energy, and more. You might have noticed that your sleep might be affected, and you may be eating more, or less, than you used to. You may even have turned to unhealthy behaviors as a way to self-medicate, perhaps using alcohol or various drugs.

Of course, it's no wonder that those who have been stuck in relationships with narcissists can develop anxiety, depression and addictions, but something you may not have heard of is 'complex PTSD', and it's important to mention it here, as this is something that can get worse over the divorce and separation period, if you are exposed to repeated traumatic experiences.

Complex post-traumatic stress disorder is fairly common in the victims of narcissists, and it is caused by the abusive tactics that a narcissist uses to keep their victims in their orbits, regardless of whether they are still officially together. It differs from PTSD (which most people have heard of) in a few ways.

When we think of PTSD we usually think of the sufferer having experienced one very big traumatic incident – a serious car crash, or a horrific episode when fighting on the front line in a war zone, for example. They wake in the night, or are sideswiped at various times by the incident, which they re-experience as if they were actually back there. Visual flashbacks are a very common part of PTSD.

In complex PTSD, the person has experienced a series of much smaller traumatic incidents, which accumulate. The way that this shows up is different to the other form of PTSD, in that the flashbacks they experience tend to be *emotional*, rather than visual. They are similarly sideswiped by them, and they can be debilitating. Complex PTSD can be triggered by all sorts of things, including memories, and most people don't even realize what they are experiencing.

Once triggered by an event, the sufferer's 'sympathetic nervous system' is thrown into overdrive, and the high levels of stress hormones (adrenaline and cortisol) cause feelings of panic, sweaty palms, a racing heart and breathlessness, and even pains or tightness in areas such as their throat or chest. Crucially, blood is diverted away from the thinking and logical areas of their brains to their muscles during these episodes (an evolutionary mechanism, designed to help them run away or fight). Of course, this leads to fuzzy thinking, and their 'inner critic' might make an appearance here too. So, what can you do if any of these types of experience are resonating with you?

Psychotherapy

Now you understand the seriousness of what you have experienced, you may want to consider finding a psychotherapist, as a means of building yourself up (whether you are planning to leave your relationship or not). But do bear in mind that not *everyone* needs therapy to heal from narcissistic abuse, and not all types of therapy are suitable for narcissistic abuse. For example, CBT (cognitive behavioral therapy), is a common type of therapy which does not address the emotional elements of healing that you might require, and so is unlikely to be effective on its own.

So many victims of narcissistic abuse have reported to me that they have had years of therapy, with no significant benefit, and this is likely to be because they were not able to find the right type of therapist. The problem is that a therapist who doesn't understand narcissistic abuse or trauma (and the majority don't) could actually make you feel *worse*, by focusing purely on how *you* need to change without validating, comprehending or taking account of what you have actually been through.

Things are getting better, however, and whilst most psychotherapists don't specifically understand narcissistic abuse, one that understands trauma should be able to help you. How well regulated the psychotherapy profession is varies from country to country, and charlatans abound, but at the very least you are looking for a therapist who is 'trauma informed' and accredited by an official body.

If you are suffering from complex PTSD, healing needs to occur on many emotional and cognitive levels, so your therapist will need to be well-versed in different techniques to be effective. The first step though, which everyone can achieve, is the cognitive step – which comes from a deep understanding of what you have been through, and how it has affected you – and I hope that this book has helped you here.

The following therapy types can be effective for treating complex PTSD, in combination with others.

- EMDR (Eye movement desensitization reprocessing)
- Somatic Experiencing
- Rosen Work
- Rolfing
- Rebirthing
- Reichian work
- Acceptance and Commitment therapy (ACT)
- Inner Child Work

Coaching and alternative therapies

Although these industries are often also poorly regulated, there are a growing number of narcissistic abuse coaches, who may be well suited to supporting you and who may work internationally. Some of these also use hypnotherapy, NLP (neurolinguistic programming), Logosynthesis, or EFT tapping in their work, which may be worth a try. I will include meditation and mindfulness in this section for completeness, as they are scientifically proven treatments for depression, anxiety and stress, but I will also go into their remarkable benefits for victims of narcissistic relationships a little later in this chapter.

Medication

It may also be that you would benefit from anti-anxiety medication, or antidepressants, and it's definitely worth discussing this with your doctor. If you are struggling with unexplained physical symptoms, which may actually be down to anxiety, they may well improve with medical treatments.

Dealing with addictions

If you've found yourself self-medicating with alcohol or other substances, to help you cope, you may want to consider the following: These *will* be used against you in your divorce or separation, if that is the route you are going to take. Getting a handle on them before the process begins will be really important. If you can't do this alone, specialist addictions psychotherapy can be helpful, and worldwide organizations such as Alcoholics Anonymous could be useful for you, although you may want to avoid advertising this to your narcissistic partner, if possible.

Building resilience

You will now be aware of the insidious ways in which your narcissist will have weakened you throughout your relationship, by devaluing you and gaslighting you. And you probably now appreciate that the point of them weakening you was to deplete you of the reserves you would need to leave them, so that you would remain in position as their best source of narcissistic supply. These reserves are made up of your

- self-confidence,
- self-esteem,
- self-worth,
- self-belief and
- healthy self-love

It stands to reason that you will need to build these reserves back up in order to escape, and you will also need to become absolutely sure of your own reality, so that you become immune to the increased devaluations and gaslighting that you will inevitably be subjected to during your separation or divorce.

One of the best ways to do this is by taking a good look at yourself, to remind yourself of who *you* are, so that you can be secure in that knowledge. Now I understand that, as a victim of narcissistic abuse, you might feel that it would be self-indulgent to spend time in this way, but if you do feel that type of resistance sneaking in, you probably need to try this all the more.

So, with pen and paper handy, in a place where you cannot be disturbed for an hour or so, try asking yourself the following questions:

- What have I achieved?
- What are my strengths?
- What are my core values?
- What sort of personality do I have?
- What do I want from my life?

It's perfectly possible that you are staring at this list with absolutely no idea how to even start to answer these questions, and this might be because you no longer have much idea of who you actually are. If this sounds like you, here are some powerful exercises and tips, to help you go deep.

What have I achieved?

Close your eyes and think back to your earliest memory. The aim is to replay your life from there onwards, *all the way to the present*, calling to mind all the things that have made you feel proud of yourself. Don't let your brain distract you from your task by pulling you down a chain of irrelevant or sad memories – if this happens, just notice it, and gently bring your mind back to the task in hand.

Every time you remember something, write it down quickly. Then go back to the memory, and take a few moments to really engage with the feeling of pride you had at that time. Remember what it was about the event that made you feel proud of yourself.

Bear in mind that I'm not just talking about huge events, like childbirth and getting your PhD here. I mean *everything* that you can think of that made you feel proud, no matter how seemingly small it might appear now. The time your painting was put up on the school art board when you were five-years-old. The tiny solo you played on the xylophone at the Christmas recital, when you were seven. The time you helped the old lady who had fallen in the street when you were 12, and how grateful she was.

You are likely to come out of this rather lovely exercise with a renewed sense of who you are, and what matters to you. You might remember a whole host of talents that you forgot you had, and you'll certainly be reminded of just how much you have actually achieved in your life so far.

Keep the list you have made, and refer to it whenever you need to top up your reserves and combat your narcissist's devaluations.

What are my strengths?

The VIA Institute on Character has a free ten-minute online test, which ranks your strengths in order. It can be found here: https://www.viacharacter.org/character-strengths. The 24 character strengths which they identify and explain are:

- Creativity
- Curiosity
- Judgment
- Love of learning
- Perspective
- Bravery
- Perseverance
- Honesty
- Zest (approaching life and situations with excitement and energy, rather than halfheartedly)
- Love
- Kindness
- Social intelligence (being aware of and understanding your own feelings and thoughts, as well as the feelings of those around you)
- Teamwork
- Fairness
- Leadership
- Forgiveness

- Humility
- Prudence (being careful about your choices, stopping and thinking before acting – a strength of restraint)
- Self-regulation
- Appreciation of beauty and excellence
- Gratitude
- Hope
- Humor
- Spirituality (feeling spiritual, believing in a sense of purpose or meaning in life, and seeing your place in the grand scheme of the universe)

It's highly likely that you came to believe many of your narcissistic partner's devaluations of you, and undermining your true strengths would have been an effective way for them to weaken you. Making you believe that you were 'less' than you actually are is a key part of narcissistic abuse, but luckily, a good honest look at this list, or better still, heading over to the website to take the official test, should help get you back on track.

What are my core values?

It's important to differentiate 'core values' from 'things you value'.

For example, you might value money, because it allows you to have a decent lifestyle, but it can't be a core value – if it can be taken away from you, then it can't be a value. Commonly, those who have been in narcissistic relationships take on the values of the narcissist, without even realizing it. This can undermine your whole sense of self, and even make you unsure of what is really important to you in life.

NARCISSISTS IN DIVORCE: FROM LOVE-LOCKED TO LEAVING

There is a lot of overlap between your strengths and your values, and you may want to take another look at the strengths list above to see which of those are also values by which you want to live. Other values that might be important for you to live in accordance with include:

- Loyalty
- Compassion
- Integrity
- Selflessness
- Generosity
- Tolerance
- Trustworthiness
- Equanimity (the ability to stay emotionally and mentally calm, even when under stress)
- Altruism
- Appreciation
- Empathy
- Toughness
- Self-reliance
- Attentiveness

What sort of personality do I have?

Not only can narcissists leave their victims not really *knowing* who they are, but they can also make them believe that they have personality traits that they *don't* really have. As you already know, they often project their own personality traits onto others – "You are so selfish", "You are so unreasonable" etc. This nonsense needs to be culled, if you are to manage the narcissist in your life without being diminished, or to build yourself up enough to be able to leave. There are a variety of great personality tests to research and try out, including:

- The Big Five
- Myers-Briggs
- Enneagram Personality Test
- DISC
- Color Code Personality Profile

What do I want from my life?

This exercise, 'the rocking chair test', is a powerful way of helping you to determine what you really want from life, which can be enormously helpful if you are dealing with a narcissist. Very often, people who have been orbiting a narcissist forget what *they* really want and need, because they have put the requirements of the narcissist first. They may even come to believe that the narcissist's desires are actually *their own,* and so find themselves striving to achieve things that they don't actually even want, which are not in line with their values (which hopefully by now, you have reacquainted yourself with).

You'll need a quiet, calm space for half an hour or so, and a pen and paper, to carry out this wonderfully life-affirming exercise.

Close your eyes, and focus for a few moments on your body. Notice the way your body makes contact with the chair or bed you are on. Notice the way your abdomen moves in and out as you breathe for a few moments. Notice any tension in your face – in the muscles of your forehead, in your cheeks, in your jaw and around your eyes, and allow that tension to soften, if you can.

And now imagine that you are 100 years old, and that you have lived the happiest, most fulfilled life imaginable. You are sitting in a rocking chair, perhaps on a verandah, perhaps on a warm summer evening. (Perhaps instead, you are sitting out on a cool evening, next to a fire or under a blanket – whatever works for you). Look around you for a moment. What do you see? Great-grandchildren playing in the garden? The sea? Your partner?

What do you hear? The birds singing? The sound of laughter? Silence? What sensations do you feel? The cool glass in your hand, or the hot mug? The fresh breeze on your face? The warm sun?

And now think back, as this wise old person, over the life that you have lived, with a smile. Think back to all the things that happened, for which you are grateful, and what made you happy. You may wish to think in categories, such as:

- Love
- Family
- Health
- Social life
- Finances
- Work
- Home

Once you have done this, you may wish to open your eyes and write a letter, perhaps to your grandchild or to a friend, explaining to them all the things that made you happy in your life – all the things that really mattered to you. Or perhaps you'd find it easier to list the points. However you do this, writing it down will be enormously helpful, as once you have finished, you really will have a clear idea of how *you* wish to live your life, unburdened by the demands or needs of other people or society.

Understanding this can really help to keep you focused during your separation or divorce, especially when the narcissist will try to goad you into reacting about things that actually don't matter to you. If they want your Uncle Frank's sofa, just because they know *you* loved it, or all the wedding china, your hundred-year-old self might be able to give a shrug, and just let them have their way. Picking your battles is going to be a big part of your separation process, as you will learn.

How to build healthy self-love

Now let's look at how you can boost your own positive feelings about yourself, because this is going to be fundamental in building up your intrinsic strength.

Firstly, know this: yes, you are lovable, no matter how much your narcissist has made you feel as though you are not – but the first person who needs to love you, unfailingly and unconditionally right now, is *you*.

Cringeworthy though this might seem, I'm going to ask you to do some daily 'mirror work' – but I promise you that it will be immensely powerful. So, a couple of times a day, perhaps just after you brush your teeth, I would like you to stare into your own eyes in the bathroom mirror, and say your name, followed by "I love you". As you do so, really try to engage with the feeling of love, and bask in it. This really does get a lot easier with practice. You may then wish to follow this up by saying the words "I am enough" to yourself. Try to do this every day for at least six weeks, and you might just be stunned by the results.

Another lovely exercise is to write a love letter to yourself – the sort of love letter that your perfect partner would write to you, in the future that one day will be yours. Explain, as if you are that person, what it is about you that they love, including your quirks and your talents, your character and strengths, and anything else that springs to mind. You may want to keep that letter, and refer to it when the chips are down, as you move through your separation. This is the love letter you *deserve*. And hopefully one day, it will be written to you, by someone else – someone who really sees and appreciates you, and who is actually worthy of your love.

Learning self-compassion

This is an essential part of getting over a narcissistic relationship, and an important thing to nurture. You are going to need to be very kind to yourself indeed through your break-up, because, as you know, there are tough times ahead. If you can consistently give yourself the kindness, understanding and empathy you need, this will go a long way to helping you get through. The first thing I'd like to tackle is how you can slay your 'inner critic'.

It might be that you've never recognized that little voice in your head that speaks to you so harshly. I call this voice 'the narcissist in your head', and the first step in slaying it, is to actually *hear* it, by bringing it into your awareness. It's probably been devaluing you and criticizing you for years – even calling you names. Even if you haven't been conscious of it, you will still have been emotionally reacting to its put-downs.

This inner critic is also a prominent feature of complex PTSD. Essentially, it's made up of reflex, negative thoughts that have become wired into your brain, through repetition, which are now ingrained as your default neural pathways.

So, every time you do become aware of it, instead of *believing* its assertions about you (which allows it to control your emotions), imagine what you would do if you caught someone speaking to your child or friend in such a way. Outraged, you would probably stomp up to them and tell them in no uncertain terms, to STOP, and to get the hell out. From now on, I want you to do exactly this, every single time the inner critic makes an appearance. You are going to have to stand up to it, just as your own best friend would, on your behalf, if they could hear it.

On the subject of self-compassion, when we talked about grief earlier, I mentioned the concept of 'healthy anger', and how it's perfectly justifiable to be angry with your narcissist, and all the people and circumstances that predisposed you to falling for their charms.

But what about the anger you may be directing at *yourself*, for inviting narcissism into your world, and failing to break free from it sooner? Is *that* justified? I think not. There is no way that *anyone* can understand something that they didn't know even existed, so how can you tell yourself that this was your fault? Of course you don't want to feel like a victim – what healthy person would? But this is what you were, and acceptance and self-compassion for your plight is the only way to move past victimhood.

If it helps, when emotions threaten to overwhelm you, imagine rocking yourself, as if you were a baby, and soothing yourself with a 'there there'. And try not to turn away from these powerful emotions, but succumb to them instead. That's how the brain processes them, and puts them away, for good. If you resist them, they will only keep popping up repeatedly later to hijack you – the last thing you need as you navigate your break-up.

Reducing negativity

The human brain has a natural 'negativity bias', which is one of its slightly outdated built-in protection mechanisms. Because of it, we are more likely to remember and dwell upon *negative* events than positive ones – and they will take up more of our mental space. Not only that, but negative events, thoughts and beliefs are more 'sticky' than positive ones – they are harder to shift, or change, than positive ones.

Studies have shown that it is actually easier for humans to change a positive belief into a negative belief, than it is to change a negative belief into a positive one, even when presented with compelling, corroborating facts. And the reason the brain does this, from an evolutionary perspective, is to try to keep us safe.

Have you ever had a perfectly good day at work, but then, say when driving home that evening, been cut up by another driver, or had to endure a bit of road rage? If that has happened to you, you would probably have got home in a foul mood, having replayed the event in your mind all the way home, and thinking of all the things you should have said and done in the moment. You'll likely be entertaining thoughts such as "I bet that man wouldn't have shouted at me like that if I was driving a truck/if I was male..." or "Why didn't I get his license plate number and report him to the police?"

You'll have completely forgotten about the thank-you card and flowers you received from a grateful client, the award you found out you were nominated for and the lucrative new contract you signed, all in that same day. This is the negativity bias, doing its thing. And as you can see, in today's modern world, it's not always particularly helpful.

There are going to be an awful lot of negative happenings once you kick off your divorce or separation, and it's not going to be easy to stay buoyant unless you rewire your brain to reduce your negativity bias. Thankfully, this is much easier than you might think, it's free, and it takes hardly any time at all. I'm talking here about the practice of 'gratitude' – another scientifically validated tool.

By far and away the simplest method is the 'ten finger gratitude exercise'. Last thing at night, every night, you count out on your fingers 10 things you are grateful for. This might not seem too difficult at present, but as your home life deteriorates, it can feel a lot harder, and if you are being dragged to court, and harassed and bullied by your narcissistic ex, it can seem almost impossible.

However, making this into a habit *before* you break-up can be really helpful. The way to practice this most effectively is to *actively* make a point of noticing all the little things that you are grateful for as you go about your day. As you notice them, deliberately make a mental note to add them to your nightly list of ten.

It's the tiniest of things that can be the most powerful – perhaps the unexpected feeling of the sun on your face as you open your blinds, or the wonderful smell of your new coffee. Maybe the funny anecdote you heard on the radio as you drove to work, or the warm fuzzy feeling you got when you stroked the new puppy your colleague brought into the office. Perhaps you will experience gratitude for the comforting warmth of the water you washed your hands in, for the impossible blueness of the afternoon sky or for the incredible light cast on your garden by the moon. Engaging all your senses – touch, smell, sight, taste and sound – as you search for your moments of daily gratitude makes this exercise even easier.

And when you run through them at the end of your day, if you could allow each one a brief moment whilst you re-engage with how you felt as you were actually experiencing it, this will be all the more powerful. This simple practice will have profound benefits when it comes to how you view your world and on your sense of perspective, and will be hugely effective in helping you to build your resilience, in preparation for what lies ahead.

Coping with being 'triggered'

It may be that you have not yet experienced being tipped into feelings of panic and fear, to the degree that they overwhelm your senses and cloud your thinking and judgment. Often a narcissist's behavior *within the relationship* is not overtly extreme enough to trigger these feelings in their partner, especially if they are dutifully complying with their role of 'primary supplier of narcissistic supply'.

But, regardless of what has gone before, you *will* experience these fear reactions during your separation, because your partner's narcissistic behaviors will escalate to levels you are likely to have never previously experienced, and your brain's instinctive protective mechanisms will reflexively kick in.

You will be thrown, within moments, into one of the four 'fear responses': flight, fight, freeze or fawn. The problem is that these triggering events will not be one-offs, and they will continue for as long as you have to have any contact with the narcissist.

An even greater problem is that the more of these triggering events you are subjected to, the lower your threshold seems to become for experiencing these fear responses, and this just seems to get worse over time. Even years after a divorce, people can experience feelings of dread from simply collecting letters from their mailbox, and many people continue to live in fear of receiving an email or message from their former partner.

What has happened here is that their biological reactions, to even *small* stressors related to their former partner, have become inflated way out of proportion to the actual stressor. Essentially, their brain's evolutionary protection system has started to react to anything to do with their ex, no matter how big or small, as if they are being chased by a lion.

This is actually one of the most difficult things to deal with during and after a narcissistic divorce or separation, and it's not something that happens in 'normal' divorces. It has absolutely nothing to do with how strong you are as a person, and although it can make you feel 'weak' and 'pathetic', you are not. Once again, this is example how a narcissist can effortlessly use your brain systems against you. This is pure biology, and it is something you are going to have to be prepared for.

There are two strands to managing this. One is to increase the threshold at which your brain becomes triggered by events, so that you are less susceptible to such triggers, and the other is to know how to terminate your unhelpful fear responses quickly, when they do kick in. To get to grips with these, we'll need to take a brief look at the biology.

When a narcissist triggers you, you might feel blind panic, fear and dread, or just tearfulness. Your inner critic, that berating voice in your own head, may kick in, and you will probably find yourself unable to think clearly. Perhaps physical symptoms will be more prominent for you (such as nausea, a racing heart, fast breathing, sweaty palms, or even chest pain). But whatever your symptoms, you are likely to be in one of the four 'self-protection' or 'fear' modes, known as the 'four F's'. Let's take a closer look at what each one feels like.

- Flight – wanting to, or actually running away from the problem
- Fight – feeling angry and verbally (or even physically) fighting back
- Freeze – clamming up and saying or doing nothing, paralyzed by fear or indecisiveness
- Fawn – trying to appease the narcissist, by agreeing to their demands or being extra nice to them

I commonly hear this last one, the 'fawn' response, described by partners of narcissists. Although they often *recognized* how they would react to the narcissist's bad behaviors by fawning over them and trying to appease them, they rarely linked this with being a stress response – and I wonder if this F response feels familiar to you. But regardless of which response you might find yourself in, all are completely normal, physiological reactions to stress.

Because the unconscious brain perceives the narcissist's actions as an *actual threat to your life*, the area in the brain called the 'amygdala' (which is involved with fear) is instantly triggered. It responds by sending signals to the adrenal glands (that sit on top of the kidneys), telling them to pour stress hormones (cortisol and adrenaline) into your bloodstream.

These stress hormones cause changes in your circulation, among other things. Your blood pressure rises, your heart beats faster and blood gets diverted away from your brain to your muscles, so that you can fight, or run away. These hormones also cause the other symptoms of anxiety I've mentioned, and all of these are signs that you have gone into one of the four F self-protection responses. This all happens reflexively, and within

> "The unconscious brain perceives the narcissist's actions as an actual threat to your life..."

moments, precisely because this is one of the body's inbuilt survival mechanisms. Because blood is being diverted away from your brain, you will lose the ability to think clearly during one of these attacks. Let's face it – this is hardly the cognitive state that you want to be in when you are trying to negotiate how to split your finances or your time with the children, let alone when you are being interviewed by the police, or social services. And it is definitely not going to help you if you end up feeling this way when on the witness stand in court, suffering the indignity of being cross examined as if you are some sort of criminal.

So, whether you have experienced these four F responses or not, you will need to learn some simple hacks to terminate them, because I'm afraid you *will* become familiar with them as you move through your break-up. Here are three easy methods:

1. **Engage your 'parasympathetic nervous system':** Your body has two systems which work in opposition to each other. When you are triggered by a narcissist into one of the four F responses, it is your *sympathetic* nervous system that has been activated. But very handily, you can deliberately engage your *parasympathetic* system to do the opposite, and calm you down. There are various ways of doing this, but one of the easiest is the 'physiological sigh' (Spiegel and Huberman, 2023). Firstly, you take a deep inhalation. You then follow that up with another short sharp inhalation, and

then you exhale in a deep slow sigh, through your mouth. Repeat this over 5 minutes to get the maximal effect. Even better, research has shown that if you do this every day for five minutes, even when you are not feeling stressed, your overall mood will be boosted, with greater feelings of joy, peacefulness and energy. Splashing cold water on your face, or immersing it in cold water briefly, touching your lips, and a breathing technique called 'box breathing' can also engage the parasympathetic system, and you may wish to get familiar with these too.

2. **Trick your brain:** Another surprising brain hack is to tell yourself, when your stress response kicks in, that you are *not* stressed, panicky or scared, but *excited*. It sounds crazy, but in fact the physiological feelings of fear and excitement are much the same – the butterflies, the racing pulse, the sweaty palms and the breathlessness. If you tell yourself that you are actually excited, *your brain will believe you* (even if *you* don't believe you), and will change the stress hormone ratios in your blood accordingly (decreasing cortisol and increasing a hormone known as DHEA), so that you actually *do* feel excited. This is called the 'excite and delight' response, and it has been scientifically shown that you can change the 'fight, flight, freeze or fawn' responses into it *just by believing it*. This is a great hack for nervous exam students and public speakers too, because it brings your logical brain back online by re-diverting the blood back to it.

3. **Awareness:** Just being *aware* of which of the four F responses you tend to react with can also be very helpful. So, when the narcissist triggers you, try to bring your rational

brain back online *in the moment*, by actively telling yourself which response you are in, and then ticking off what you notice happening physically (eg. I feel like running away, I want to appease the narcissist, my heart is beating fast, my palms are sweating, I am finding it difficult to think clearly). Just doing this can help re-divert blood to your brain and reduce these feelings. In the apt words of Fritz Perls, the founder of Gestalt therapy, "Awareness in itself is healing".

How to become less easily triggered

Even better than being able to quickly terminate an unwanted stress response is *raising the threshold* at which you (and your amygdala) can be triggered. As you now know, the problem is that your brain perceives the narcissist's behavior as an *actual threat* to your life, and so responds accordingly, when in fact its response is disproportionate and unhelpful.

You may be a little skeptical of what I am going to suggest at this point, so I do need to tell you that there have been numerous studies on this, and it really is scientifically validated. In fact, if there is only one thing you do, in preparation for your separation, then meditation should be it. There are numerous reasons why the vast majority of neuroscientists and psychologists have a personal practice of mindfulness and meditation, but one of its benefits is that it is one of the best ways to train your amygdala into becoming less trigger-happy.

But not only will meditating for 20 minutes a day make you less easily triggered by the narcissist, but it will teach you to learn how to examine your thoughts, and help you to differentiate the ones to believe from the ones that may be sabotaging you. In this way, it can give you a strong sense of perspective. It will also teach you how to observe your thoughts, so that you can make active decisions as to which ones you choose to engage with, rather than just being hijacked by them.

Remember that your narcissist will turn the volume up on their gaslighting and their

> *"If there is only one thing you do in preparation for your separation, then meditation should be it"*

devaluations of you throughout your separation, in an attempt to weaken and confuse you. Meditation is the secret weapon that can make you the master of your thoughts rather than a slave to them, and it is, without a doubt, one of the most powerful and effective ways to defend yourself from repeated narcissist attacks.

I recommend attending a mindfulness-based cognitive therapy (MBCT) course, or a mindfulness-based stress reduction (MBSR) course, to most easily develop the skills. Brain imaging studies conducted on these types of meditation show clear structural and functional changes in various areas of the brain, including significant increases in the density of the grey matter. These changes are present after just eight weeks, but you could start to notice a difference to how you actually *feel* in as little as three weeks. You may wish to start off with one of the many meditation apps available instead, such as Headspace or Calm, which offer free introductory sessions.

Some final thoughts

I do hope that this book has given you at least the beginnings of clarity about your relationship and your partner, and that over time, as the information sinks in, it will prove useful in helping you to decide upon your next steps.

If you've got this far in the book and have accepted, or are in the process of accepting, that your partner is high in narcissistic traits (something which I know no one actually *wants* to be true) then firstly, I am sorry that this happened to you. I know how difficult this is to take on board. But worse that that, I know how very unfair it is. You did not ask for this, and yet this is the card you were dealt.

I know how isolating this is, and how alone you might feel. I know how exhausting it is trying to explain this to disbelieving friends and family, who shoot pitying glances in your direction or just flatly refuse to accept what you are telling them. But they have been fooled, just as you once were, and if they are resistant to even trying to understand your point of view, then you may just have to keep them out of the loop for now. Your energy is going to have to be spent in more productive ways from now on, and you might find yourself with a completely new inner circle of supporters.

So many people, once they've seen narcissism for what it is, want to expose it to the world. They want to reveal the true nature of their narcissist to anyone who will listen, including the narcissist's friends and family. Understandably, they want justice, and retribution. A word of advice here: if you are planning on leaving your relationship, keep the information you have learnt from this book close, until you are several months or even a few years out of it, and have healed. Firstly, you will simply be re-traumatizing yourself as you try to explain it to others, and secondly, you are quite likely to see your own messages (even to third parties) and social media posts in legal correspondence or in court. This will not help your case at all.

NARCISSISTS IN DIVORCE: FROM LOVE-LOCKED TO LEAVING

But even more importantly, in understanding narcissism *you* actually hold the power that you need to move forwards in your life, especially if you have decided to leave your relationship. This book is like a manual to a narcissist's miswired brain, *and it's a manual that they themselves have not read*. If you are planning to leave your partner, you'll probably want to keep what you know under wraps, because this knowledge will be your biggest advantage when it comes to keeping you and your family safe and sane through the process.

The normal rules of divorce and separation simply do not apply, as you will, by now, have gleaned, and you will have a completely new rule book to get to grips with. Narcissists simply don't behave like non-narcissists, and you can't *expect them to*.

So, if you do make the unenviable decision to walk away from your relationship, and you feel you'd like a helping hand, then please do come and find me again, in the follow-up book to this, *Narcissists in Divorce: From Leaving to Liberty*.

Here I'll take you, step-by-step through everything you (and your lawyer) will need to know. I'll pre-empt your ex's behaviors, so that they can largely be prevented, teach you how to effectively communicate with them and show you what works and what doesn't. I'll give you coping strategies to get you through and boost your resilience, and I'll show you how to avoid the pitfalls that can lead to protracted post-separation narcissistic abuse. We'll discuss what you can do to protect your children, and how you can best parent alongside your ex. And we'll look at the realities and limitations of family legal systems (applicable wherever you live), so that you can make the most informed choices possible.

But for now, I will leave you here. I hope that you have found this guide to be a holistic source of knowledge, power and strength – and I also want you to know this: it is perfectly possible to find freedom, peace and joy after a narcissistic relationship. The path might not be the easiest one, but the benefits of undertaking the journey, should you so choose, can be immensely transformative. But whatever you decide to do, take care of yourself, and *believe in yourself.* And remember this – the narcissist needs *you*, more than you need them. You really do hold all the cards – and that I can promise you.

Glossary

Term	Definition
Altruistic Narcissist	Another name for Communal Narcissist
Blame-shifting	Narcissists cannot take the blame for their actions (except in the rare instances when doing so will give them narcissistic supply) and so pass the blame onto others with lightning speed, to avoid feeling shame.
Closet Narcissist	This type of narcissist (also called the 'Vulnerable', 'Introverted' or 'Covert' Narcissist) shies away from the limelight, and comes across as quiet, shy and self-effacing. They often try to feel special by association, by attaching themselves to a person, cause or object that they hold up as being special. They often play the hard done by victim.
Co-dependency	A type of relationship addiction characterized by preoccupation and extreme dependence – emotional, social and sometimes physical – on another person. Co-dependents feel responsible for the feelings and actions of their loved ones. The partners of narcissists, alcoholics, substance abusers and those with chronic illnesses are often co-dependents. They characteristically put the other's needs ahead of their own.

Term	Definition
Cognitive Dissonance	This occurs when a person is holding two or more contradictory thoughts or beliefs in their minds at the same time. This creates an uncomfortable sense of confusion, which the brain resolves by choosing just one of the beliefs to believe, discarding the other by denying it, minimizing it or justifying it.
Communal Narcissist	Also called the Altruistic Narcissist. These narcissists prop up their self-esteem and sense of specialness by giving to others. They obtain admiration, attention and a sense of specialness ('narcissistic supply') from good works and deeds. They need others to see them as being the most generous, the most caring, or the most kind person they know.
Covert Narcissist	Another name for a Closet, Vulnerable, or Introverted Narcissist.
Cycle of 'Idealize' and 'Devalue'	The initial stage of a relationship with a narcissist is the 'idealization' phase, also known as 'love bombing'. The next stage is the devaluation stage, where the narcissist puts down their victim. This cycle (nice narcissist/nasty narcissist) repeats, over and over, causing Trauma Bonding.
DARVO	Defend, Attack, Reverse Victim and Offender. This is a classic narcissistic strategy to shift the blame, by playing the victim, so the focus is shifted from their wrongdoing on to your alleged bad behavior.

Term	Definition
Deletions	Information that the brain filters out that is not in line with your beliefs, or your view of the world. You do not become consciously aware of this information, as a result.
Devaluations	Put-downs through being critical, ridiculing, or demeaning. The devaluations usually increase so slowly that the victim may not notice, so becoming the proverbial 'frog in boiling water', so staying in the relationship.
Devaluing Narcissist	Also called the 'Toxic' or 'Malignant' Narcissist. They exhibit many of the other more general narcissistic behaviors too, but what is more prominent in this type of narcissist is that they devalue, criticize, and demean others in order to inflate their own sense of self-worth.
Distortions	The brain distorts how we view reality, in line with our own personal prejudices resulting from former experiences. The brain magnifies or diminishes our perceptions of things, resulting in 'distortions'.
Drama Triangle	Karpman's drama triangle is a description of conflict in social interactions. There are three roles within the triangle – victim, rescuer and persecutor. In narcissistic relationships the narcissist moves themselves and others around the triangle, to take up different roles at different times. This perpetuates and continues the drama.

Term	Definition
Euphoric Recall	The tendency for the human brain to remember past events in a positive light, rather than in a negative light, by filtering out the bad bits. Seeing the world through rose-tinted spectacles in this way can lead to victims staying with their narcissistic abusers.
Exhibitionist Narcissist	Also known as 'Grandiose' or 'Overt' Narcissist. They are extroverted and superficially charming. They can appear haughty and arrogant, and give off an air of superiority. Many are financially successful in their chosen fields, but some are not, and prefer to exploit others financially instead.
False Self or False Persona	Narcissists outwardly project a 'false self', which they cannot maintain without attention from others (which comes in the form of drama, conflict and adoration). This false self is highly convincing and at odds with the underlying emptiness. Many refer to this outward image as a 'mask', which can temporarily drop when the narcissist feels threatened or abandoned.

Term	Definition
Fight, Flight, Freeze or Fawn Response	When a human brain sees a threat, which it perceives as a threat to life, the amygdala, a part of the brain, gets activated. Narcissists are good at triggering this response in their victims, so that without even thinking, the person is thrown into an instinctive fight, flight, freeze or fawn response. The release of various stress hormones, such as cortisol and adrenaline means that blood is diverted away from the cortex (the thinking part of the brain) to other areas of the body, such as muscles, so that they can fight harder or run away. Some victims may freeze and do nothing, and others may 'fawn', doing whatever their perpetrator wants, in order to stay safe.
Financial Abuse	A form of abuse commonly employed by narcissists. Other types include emotional, physical and legal abuse.
Flying Monkey	One of the narcissist's fan club. Named after the flying monkeys in *The Wizard of Oz*, who do the evil bidding of the wicked witch, they abuse the narcissist's victim on their behalf, spying on them and spreading lies about them.
Gaslighting	The act of undermining another person's reality by denying facts, their environment, or their feelings.

Term	Definition
Generalizations	Another way that the human brain filters out incoming information, by making automatic assumptions, based on the person's past experiences eg. 'all nurses are kind'. (See also deletions and distortions.)
No Contact	If at all possible, the victim of a narcissist should have no contact at all with the narcissist. However, if they share children, are still living under the same roof, or if they are involved in a joint business venture, this may not be possible. If it is possible, however, then they should block the narcissist from all methods of contact (including phone, email, social media, messaging apps and texts).
Golden Child	The child who is being idealized by the narcissist, who is treated differently to the other children in the household, as if they can do no wrong.
Grandiose Narcissist	Another name for an Exhibitionist or Overt Narcissist.
Hoovering	The term given to the narcissist's tactic of sucking the victim back into the relationship, so that they can continue to use them as a source of narcissistic supply. It occurs when they suspect that they are about to be abandoned.

Term	Definition
Idealization	Also called love bombing. Idealization occurs when the narcissist puts their victim on a pedestal, and treats them well. It is inevitably followed by 'devaluation'.
Intermittent Reinforcement	The technique used by narcissists to keep their victims hooked to them by giving them unpredictable, varying, wins and losses in the cycle of idealization and devaluation.
Introverted Narcissist	Same as a Closet Narcissist.
Love bombing	Also called 'idealization'. The initial stage of a relationship with a narcissist.
Malignant Narcissist	Another name for a Devaluing or Toxic Narcissist.
Mask	The mask is the outward projection of the narcissist's false self. But when the narcissist does not get enough narcissistic supply the mask can drop, to reveal their true nature. See also False Persona.
Narcissistic Abuse	Abuse carried out by someone with NPD. This is mostly covert emotional abuse, but physical abuse can also be a feature.
Narcissistic Collapse	The deep depression that some narcissists go into, when they suffer a narcissistic injury. Unlike true depression, they can quickly recover from it as soon as they get enough narcissistic supply.

Term	Definition
Narcissistic Injury	This occurs when the narcissist's outer bubble is punctured; when the protective suit of armour, the false persona, is penetrated by some external event. It could be a perceived personal slight which brings on the injury, or any situation in which things do not go the narcissist's way. It leads to a severe loss in narcissistic supply, which results in narcissistic rage, or a narcissistic collapse.
Narcissistic Personality Disorder	A diagnosable personality disorder, as defined in the Diagnostic and Statistical Manual of Mental Disorders (DSM-5).
Narcissistic Rage	Intense fury as a consequence of narcissistic injury.
Narcissistic Supply	Narcissists need 'feeding' attention, in some form or other, to maintain the fragile image that they present to the world. This external validation is 'Narcissistic Supply'. Without narcissistic supply those with NPD are forced to feel their own sense of unworthiness and shame. Almost everything a narcissist does is with the aim of securing narcissistic supply.
Object Constancy	The ability to believe that a relationship is stable and intact, despite the presence of setbacks, conflict, or disagreements. Narcissists have not developed this ability, so they cannot see you as somebody they love and someone who has angered them, at the same time.

Term	Definition
Overt Narcissist	Another name for an Exhibitionist or Grandiose Narcissist.
Passive Aggression	Examples are silent treatments, lateness, procrastinating on jobs, sabotaging another's work, name calling and insults re-framed as jokes.
Projection	A psychological defence mechanism unconsciously used by many people, but by all narcissists. Anyone who finds it difficult to accept their failures, weaknesses, poor behaviors and other less flattering traits, may unwittingly use projection as a way of feeling better about themselves, by accusing another person of exhibiting those traits or carrying out those behaviors. Essentially, they are assigning the imperfect or flawed parts of themselves to other people.
Projective Identification	If a victim has been gaslit for years, it is quite common for them to take on, believe and identify with whatever it is that the narcissist is projecting onto them. This is called 'projective identification'. They come to believe what the narcissist is telling them about themselves.
Pseudo-logic	A typical narcissist's communication style which includes contradictions, irrational conclusions, and false logic.

Term	Definition
Rescuers	Rescuers need to rescue others to feel needed and to matter. A narcissist will exploit this trait time and time again, in order to pull the target into the Narcissist Trap, by playing the victim.
Scapegoat	The child of a narcissist who is blamed, shamed and can do nothing right – the golden child's opposite number.
Shame-dumping	Giving away ('dumping') feelings of deep shame to others, so that a person does not have to feel the shame themselves – characteristic of narcissists.
Spectrum of Narcissism	Narcissism exists on a spectrum. Those at the lowest end of the spectrum are not narcissistic enough, and are attractive to narcissists. Those at the opposite end of the spectrum are the narcissists, who are blind to the needs and feelings of others, and concerned only with meeting their own needs to feel special. The middle part is the healthy zone.
Toxic Narcissist	Another name for a Devaluing or Malignant Narcissist.
Toxic Positivity	A form of invalidation, where only positive thoughts and attitudes are allowable. This means that any negative feelings are 'wrong' and therefore invalid.
Trauma Bonding	The neurochemical addiction of a victim to the narcissist, as a result of the cycle of idealization and devaluation.

Term	Definition
Triangulation	Where the narcissist brings a third person into the dynamic, to play one off against the other in the triangle.
Vulnerable Narcissist	Another name for a Closet, Covert, or Introverted Narcissist.
Whole Object Relations	The capacity to integrate the liked and disliked parts of a person into a single, realistic, stable picture, instead of alternating between seeing the person as either all-good or all-bad (as narcissists do).
Word Salad	The nonsensical style of communication from a narcissist after they have descended into a narcissistic rage – illogical and ranting in nature, with very loose associations between ideas.

About the author

Dr Supriya McKenna is one of the best-known names (and voices) in the field of narcissism. A former family doctor, the audiobook version of her 2020 book (*Divorcing a Narcissist: The Lure, the Loss and the Law*, with UK legal contributions from British family lawyer, Karin Walker) became an international bestseller.

Recognizing a huge need for education in UK family lawyers, also in 2020, Supriya conceived the groundbreaking guide, *Narcissism and Family Law: A Practitioner's Guide*, which she wrote in parallel with Karin, during the first Covid lockdown. Her third book, *The Narcissist Trap: The Mind-Bending Pull of the Great Pretenders,* explains narcissism to the general public, and *Narcissists in Divorce: From Leaving to Liberty* is the follow-up book to this book (*Narcissists in Divorce: From Love-Locked to Leaving*), which provide in-depth practical advice and support for anyone leaving a narcissistic partnership.

Supriya has trained thousands of family law professionals in narcissistic personality disorder. She works directly with those who have fallen victim to narcissistic abuse, and produces and hosts the top 5% podcast *Narcissists in Divorce: The Narcissist Trap.*

Her resources can be found on her websites, thelifedoctor.org and doctorsupriya.com, and she regularly posts insights on Twitter, Instagram and LinkedIn.

A speaker and media commentator, Supriya started her writing career whilst working as a young doctor, when she regularly contributed health features to magazines such as Cosmopolitan and Marie Claire. She continues to write features and articles for various well-known publications to raise awareness of this personality disorder.

Printed in Great Britain
by Amazon